A Separate Civil War

A NATION DIVIDED: NEW STUDIES IN CIVIL WAR HISTORY
James I. Robertson Jr., Editor

A Separate Civil War

Communities in Conflict in the Mountain South

JONATHAN DEAN SARRIS

University of Virginia Press
Charlottesville and London

University of Virginia Press

© 2006 by the Rector and Visitors of the University of Virginia

All rights reserved

Printed in the United States of America on acid-free paper

First published 2006

9 8 7 6 5 4 3 2 1

LIBRARY OF CONGRESS CATALOGING-IN-PUBLICATION DATA

Sarris, Jonathan Dean, 1967–

  A separate Civil War : communities in conflict in the mountain South /
Jonathan Dean Sarris.

    p.   cm. — (A nation divided)

  Includes bibliographical references and index.

  ISBN 0-8139-2549-5 (cloth : alk. paper) — ISBN 0-8139-2555-X (pbk. : alk. paper)

  1. Fannin County (Ga.)—History, Military—19th century.   2. Lumpkin
County (Ga.)—History, Military—19th century.   3. Georgia—History—Civil
War, 1861–1865—Social aspects.   4. Mountain people—Georgia—Fannin
County—History—19th century.   5. Mountain people—Georgia—Lumpkin
County—History—19th century.   6. Community life—Georgia—History—
19th century.   7. Allegiance—Georgia—History—19th century.   8. Violence—
Georgia—History—19th century.   9. Fannin County (Ga.)—Social condi-
tions—19th century.   10. Lumpkin County (Ga.)—Social conditions—19th
century.   I. Title.   II. Series.

F292.F2S27   2006

973.7'458293—dc22

                                                        2005034428

For Karin,
and for my parents

CONTENTS

ILLUSTRATIONS

ACKNOWLEDGMENTS

I owe many debts to many people for helping me complete this book. I was extremely fortunate to attend graduate school at the University of Georgia in the 1990s, a time when the institution boasted some of the best and most influential minds in the fields of Southern history and Civil War history. During my eight years in Athens, many of these faculty members did their best to turn me into a serious scholar, despite my best efforts to confound their plans. I am especially grateful to professors Thomas Dyer, Peter Hoffer, William Holmes, William Leary, William McFeely, and David Roberts. This book began as a master's thesis under the direction of John Inscoe, who, in addition to being one of the leading scholars of Appalachia and the Civil War, is also a thorough editor, constructive critic, and friendly mentor. Emory Thomas, who supervised my expansion of this topic into a doctoral dissertation, was also a wonderfully supportive counselor and guide. Besieged by legions of other students at the University of Georgia, Dr. Thomas nonetheless found time for me, challenged me, and supported me in my scholarship and my career path. He also saved my dog's life (if I had had one).

I am also thankful to have been part of a talented and close-knit cadre of graduate students at Georgia. Among those who offered me invaluable friendship and intellectual sustenance were Rod Andrew, Keith Bohannon, Patrick Breen, Frank Byrne, Lesley Gordon, Elisabeth Hughes, David McGee, Leslie Miller, and Jennifer Lund Smith. I am particularly grateful to Chuck Wineholt and Chris Schutz for graciously welcoming me into their homes and families, and for sharing with me all the rigors and reversals of graduate school.

Several prominent scholars assisted me in my research by reading drafts, offering advice, serving with me on conference panels, and helping with grant proposals. These include Victoria Bynum, Michael Fellman, Kenneth Noe, Daniel Sutherland, and Altina Waller. I am thankful for their generosity, graciousness, and guidance.

Some key institutions, archives, and libraries provided critical support during the research of this book. I am especially grateful to the staff at the following institutions: the Georgia Division of Archives and History; the Southern Historical Collection, Wilson Library, University of North Carolina at Chapel Hill; the Rare Book, Manuscript, and Special Collections Library, Duke University; the Hargrett Rare Book and Manuscript Library, University of Georgia; the Calvin McClung Historical Collection, Knox County Public Libraries, Knoxville, Tennessee; the R. G. Dun and Company Collection, Baker Library, Harvard Business School; the National Archives, Washington, D.C. In addition, I thank the Cratis D. Williams Graduate School at Appalachian State University for providing research support funding and the United States Military Academy at West Point for sponsoring me for a summer seminar in military history in 2002.

Many colleagues offered me support, guidance, and comradeship as I embarked on my academic career at Appalachian State University in Boone, North Carolina. For this, I am grateful to Karl Campbell, Michael Krenn, Sheila Phipps, Shirley Baber, John Alexander Williams, Tim Silver, and Mary Valante. I offer special thanks to Craig Fischer and Kathy Parham, who helped make my years in Boone memorable ones.

My parents, Louis and Lulu Sarris, inspired me by living the American Dream. The children of immigrants, they endured some of the most difficult times in our nation's history. They went on to build a home and family within which their five children always felt loved, secure, and successful. They taught me the value of my own personal history and urged me on when I became interested in studying history as a career. They were and remain the best teachers I have ever known.

Karin Zipf is the person most responsible for helping me bring this book into being. She is a masterful scholar, a fearless intellect, and an indefatigable personality. As I wrote this book, she selflessly offered her constructive criticism, unconditional optimism, and unflagging spirit. She also did me the great favor of marrying me in 1995. That we have managed to make a life and a family together, despite long separations and career crises, is almost entirely due to her perseverance. I love, respect, and am thankful for her.

A Separate Civil War

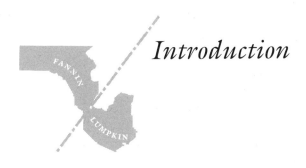

Introduction

The meteoric success of Charles Frazier's 1997 novel *Cold Mountain* surprised many people. And well it should have. The novel does not offer the romantic portrayal of the Civil War found in much of the traditional fiction. In *Cold Mountain*, there are no grand battles, no victories, and no glory. Instead, Frazier tells a story of a broken, disillusioned ex-soldier and a civilian population numbed and brutalized by conflict. The novel awakened the American public to a version of the Civil War very different from the celebratory, heroic one found in many previous popular treatments. Frazier gave Americans a new myth to ponder, one that called into question all we thought we knew about the motivations and experiences of the Americans who fought our greatest war. In this new story, the common men and women of the Southern Appalachians strive to deal with the war's destructive impact upon their homes, their families, and their very landscape. Combatants are driven to fight by local, familial, and individual concerns, not abstract ideological commitments. And in defense of these narrow goals, the highlanders of *Cold Mountain* fight a merciless, savage conflict that is far from the glorious battlefields of Civil War myth but that bears a rather close resemblance to the killing fields of the twenty-first-century Balkans. This is a war that escaped Ken Burns's sepia-tinted camera lens.

Scholars are only a little ahead of the novelists in discovering this facet of the Civil War. Historians are only now beginning to analyze the war's unique impact upon Appalachia, and in doing so we are discovering new truths about the conflict as a whole. This book examines the Civil War's

impact on two communities in the mountains of north Georgia. I analyze the wartime experiences of Fannin and Lumpkin counties, located
in the southern spur of the Blue Ridge Mountains. Here, Unionist and
Confederate factions fought a brutal internal conflict between 1861 and
1865, a conflict that paralleled the broader war but responded to local
concerns and motivations. By unpacking the multifaceted allegiances of
these mountaineers, I explore the complex web of local, regional, and national loyalties that connected pre-industrial mountain societies. Under
the stress of war, these competing loyalties produced extreme social anxiety, setting the stage for the bloody atrocities that characterized north
Georgia's Civil War. Soldiers on both sides victimized civilians, destroyed
private property, and murdered prisoners and noncombatants.

At first, studying two obscure counties may seem a puzzling choice.
The Civil War never touched this region directly—rather, the conflict
lapped around the edges of the Georgia mountains. The region held little importance for the Union or the Confederacy. There were no major
battles fought there—indeed, to this day north Georgia is notably barren
of the monuments and national battlefield parks that dot much of the
South. But what happened in these communities between 1861 and 1865
helps us answer broader questions about the interaction of localism and
nationalism, the nature of Southern regional identity, and the American way of war. This book addresses some important historical questions
about the Civil War and about Appalachian society that scholars have
been debating for many years. Why did Civil War soldiers fight? What
caused the Confederacy to collapse? What role did the people of the Appalachian region play in the war? All these issues are illuminated in a study
of a relatively small area in the Georgia mountains.

Over 130 years after the conflict, historians still debate what would
seem to be the most basic of questions—the motivations of Civil War
soldiers. Though Civil War combatants left no shortage of manuscripts,
letters, and diaries, a clear understanding of what motivated soldiers to
fight in that conflict is still elusive. In several recent books and articles,
the preeminent scholar of the period, James M. McPherson, argues that
Civil War soldiers were motivated primarily by ideological concerns and,
therefore, that the war represented a philosophical struggle between two
competing national visions.[1] When dissecting the war at the community level, I see far more complex motivating forces at play. The warriors
in north Georgia's Civil War fought primarily for local goals having to
do with the safety and security of their mountain communities. These

soldiers were fundamentally different from the educated, politically sophisticated individuals whose letters and diaries informed McPherson's research. The mountain guerrillas described in this book were largely illiterate, pragmatic, ruthless people who fought not for "cause and comrades" but for local power and influence. Although McPherson has revolutionized military history by placing deserved focus on the motivations, ideas, and behavior of the common fighting man, his analysis leaves room for additional sophistication. If we are to gain a full understanding of this period in American history, I argue that we must add complexity to our perspective of the Civil War and the people who fought it.

Students of the Confederacy have striven to answer this question of motivation in order to discern the reasons for the Southern defeat. Some scholars, such as Paul Escott, Drew Gilpin Faust, Herman Hattaway, and others, have argued that Confederate nationalism was a weak motivator, and that Union victory resulted largely from a failure of Southern will. Other historians, such as Emory M. Thomas and Garry Gallagher, see events upon the battlefield determining Southern morale, not vice versa.[2]

One method of exploring these issues of loyalty and motivation is to analyze individual Southern communities and map out the dynamics of loyalty within them. Historians have in recent years written a growing number of community studies, which seek to explain the war's impact upon local social structures. Breaking down the war into its constituent parts, these scholars have made some revealing if tentative discoveries. One of the most salient of these is the extent of the divisions within the Confederacy. Although historians have long known about pro-Union minorities in regions like East Tennessee, current scholarship has uncovered divided loyalties in communities from the beaches and sounds of North Carolina to the plains of Missouri. In many Southern communities, these divisions led to miniature civil wars, conflicts involving family solidarity, local identity, and the meanings of loyalty. These revelations have added complexity to our understanding of the Civil War by showing how not one but many souths existed within the bounds of the Confederate States of America.[3]

By focusing on Fannin and Lumpkin counties, this book reveals the way in which local, regional, and national issues combined to influence the allegiances of people in the region. Thus, loyalty to the Confederacy depended in most cases upon local conceptions of allegiance, manhood, duty, kinship, and economics. In Fannin and Lumpkin counties, where

"Unionists" and "Confederates" were divided largely along community lines. In north Georgia, between 1861 and 1865, citizens had to choose between Union or secession, or more accurately, between supporting or opposing the Confederacy. Their loyalties depended upon a number of factors—ideological, economic, familial, and situational—and this study attempts to weigh the effect of each of these components.

The role of class seems an obvious place to start. The traditional analysis of Southern loyalty holds that slaveholders had the most invested in the Confederacy, while the plain white folk were less likely to identify with or defend the planter class. To a degree, this analysis holds up in Fannin and Lumpkin. A cursory examination of the documents of Unionists, anti-Confederate guerrillas, and refugees who fled Georgia for Union lines shows that many were tenant farmers or mine laborers who voiced their disgust with the plantation elite and their Confederacy. However, class was not an ironclad determinant of loyalty in the region. In Fannin County, some of the most prominent "Unionists" were relatively wealthy town-dwellers, attorneys, and slaveholders. The Lumpkin County elite, by contrast, were in general more supportive of the Confederacy.[4] How did class influence loyalty differently in the two counties?

A dichotomy between town/country also affected loyalty. Both counties witnessed significant anti-Confederate dissent, but disaffection seemed to be more rampant in isolated Fannin County, where allegiance to any outside power was tenuous, and economic ties to the greater South were limited. Lumpkin's mountaineers were more involved in markets and broader political events, linked to the outside world through the extensive mining industry centered in the important town of Dahlonega.

The simple dynamics of war—the progress of events and the manner in which people reacted to them—also determined loyalty in the mountains. By the war's second year, higher taxes, state impressment of livestock and foodstuffs, and above all the military draft had made inroads into the mountain counties. Conscription created a class of deserters from all over the state who sought refuge from Confederate officials and turned the region into a guerrilla battleground, with civilians caught in the middle. The "invasion" of the mountains by outsiders caused many north Georgians to choose sides on a predominantly local basis, and whether one helped or hindered the Confederacy depended on how one perceived the threat to home and personal security. Thus, warfare, like politics, is local. Whether they joined the Union or Confederate armies, soldiers from north Georgia often deserted if their military duties took them far from home.

In addition, this book helps to reconfigure the history of the mountain South and to close significant gaps in our understanding of Appalachian society. Although perhaps more is written about the Civil War than any other subject in American history, the effect of the war upon the people living in the Southern Appalachians has been largely ignored. From the end of the Civil War through the early twentieth century, historians either ignored the war in the mountains or explained it simplistically as a struggle between loyal Unionist mountaineers and oppressive Confederate authorities. These early studies usually idealized mountain people as sentimental, patriotic, freedom-loving folk, or instead demonized them as savage, violent, clannish semi-barbarians who resisted all "outsiders." These stereotypes persisted for decades. Only in recent years have serious historians begun to dissect these perceptions and explore the war's true impact on Appalachia. Scholars are now shedding new light on the war in the mountains of Virginia, North Carolina, and Tennessee. By focusing on north Georgia, my research adds to this new trend in the scholarship as well as contributing something original.[5] I show that the "war crimes" and terrorism that characterized Appalachia's Civil War sprang from identifiable, specific social crises, not some natural cultural predisposition toward violence, as early analysis of the region often claimed.

This work, therefore, attempts to analyze a region of the Confederacy that has not been extensively studied and to offer some important conclusions about the nature of loyalty, the role of the Southern community during the Civil War, the dynamics of violence, and the validity of Appalachian exceptionalism. I hope this research will also fill some important gaps in Civil War scholarship and introduce readers to a part of the nineteenth-century South too long obscured by myth and indifference.

I / *Mountain Neighbors*

TWO COMMUNITIES ON THE
FRONTIER OF THE ANTEBELLUM
SOUTH

Perhaps no region of the United States has been so misunderstood and misrepresented as the Southern mountain lands known collectively as *Appalachia*. When Americans think of Appalachia, they often believe it to be a distinct region with identifiable characteristics. Fed by media depictions and the writings of some "experts," our society has constructed a cultural stereotype of a people and a region. The characteristics of this stereotype are obvious to most readers: Appalachia is poor, backward, isolated, wild, rugged, mysterious, unique. And, above all, Appalachia is basically the same all over. Scholars have made some similar assumptions and have argued over the years that Appalachia possessed a kind of regional integrity, a series of social, economic, and political features that permeated the entire mountain area of Virginia, West Virginia, Kentucky, Tennessee, North Carolina, and Georgia. In the last twenty years, however, newer scholarship has applied the deconstructing techniques of community study to Appalachia. The resulting portrait is a variegated, locally unique Appalachia, a mosaic that explains rather than ignores local differences.

Lumpkin County and Fannin County are two north Georgia counties that lie astride the Blue Ridge Mountains. Both were founded in the three decades before the Civil War. They share a common border and a common geography. During the Civil War, the residents of both counties endured divided loyalties and internal strife. But despite these similarities, the two counties responded differently to the war because of different histories, economic foundations, and demographic realities. Their story illustrates how complex differences exist even within this supposedly monolithic region of America.

The images are familiarly American—crude, lawless boomtowns; a spectacular and dangerous wilderness; Native American tribespeople; hardscrabble prospectors and settlers. But although these descriptions might seem conjured from America's mythic Wild West, they also depict a vital period in antebellum Southern history, a period in which the nascent forces of development began their assault on one of the last of the South's frontiers. Beginning in the late 1820s, the state of Georgia extended full sovereignty over its mountainous northern section, previously linked only tenuously with the rest of the state. Pursuing mineral wealth, land, and independence, white Georgians swarmed into the Blue Ridge country, ultimately expelling the indigenous Cherokee peoples and starting the integration of this peripheral section into the regional and national mainstream. The catalyst for this invasion was the first genuine gold rush in American history, resulting in a rapid and uncontrolled demographic explosion that had profound consequences for the future of the region.

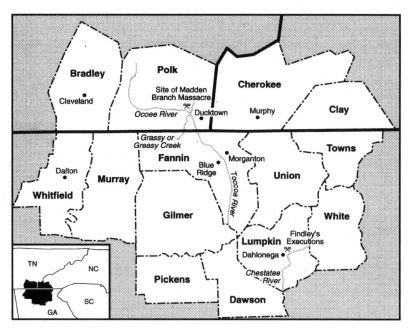

Map of the north Georgia border counties. (Courtesy Georgia Historical Society)

Although most of the "twenty-niners" in this initial wave of settlement abandoned north Georgia after the gold ran out in the 1840s, those who remained lived with the legacy of this frontier period for decades to come. The antebellum history of the region saw the development of rival visions of society, one developed, ordered, commercial, the other chaotic, lawless, and violent. This dual heritage had profound consequences for north Georgia's experience during the Civil War.

Prospectors may have discovered gold in what would become Lumpkin County as early as 1828. By the summer of the following year, newspapers were proclaiming that the region still known as *Cherokee Georgia* was full of "the hidden treasures of the earth."[1] Over the next several months, thousands of miners infiltrated what was still legally Indian territory, leaving the state of Georgia, the president of the United States, and John Marshall's Supreme Court to debate the constitutional ramifica-

Gold miners scouring a stream in Lumpkin County. The gold boom of the 1830s put Lumpkin County on the map and would later lead to the founding of a branch U.S. mint in Dahlonega. (*Harper's New Monthly Magazine,* September 1879, p. 519, courtesy of Cornell University Library, Making of America Digital Collection)

tions. In 1830, the Georgia legislature ratified the miners' trespass by formally extending the state's jurisdiction over the disputed northern territory. When, in 1832, Andrew Jackson refused to enforce the U.S. Supreme Court's decree of Cherokee autonomy, the fate of the region's Native people was sealed. Within five years, the federal government completed the expulsion of Georgia's Indians.[2]

Gold fever spread throughout north Georgia, from the Etowah River in the west to the Chattahoochee River in the east. The heart of the mining region lay along the banks of the Chestatee River, between Gainesville and the southern slopes of the Blue Ridge Mountains, in what became Lumpkin County. Some of the region's most productive mines were here, including one owned by states' rights advocate John C. Calhoun. Auraria, a village lying between the Etowah and Chestatee, became a locus of the mining industry in the spring of 1832. Within a year of its founding, Auraria grew from a single trading post to a thriving town of a thousand people, "100 dwellings, 18 or 20 stores, 12 or 15 law offices, and 4 or 5 taverns." An astonished observer wrote that "an election was held in a county where a year before there was none but the Indian population. Now, 'Intruders,' as the Indians called us, cast 1,800 votes for county offices." When the Georgia Legislature formally created Lumpkin County in December 1832, they named Auraria its seat. The new county, one of the smallest in area in Georgia, bustled with 10,000 people by 1833.[3]

This was the formative event of Lumpkin County history. The Cherokee presence and the gold rush experience profoundly shaped the development of north Georgia society, politics, and culture. The influx of miners began an exuberant, if attenuated, drive toward economic development and integration. The resulting chaos of the frontier period would also generate a negative historical stereotype for future residents to overcome. And the interaction with the Cherokee taught north Georgians to treat enemies with ruthlessness and even savagery. The experience gained in "othering" the Native peoples would resurface later during another period of social flux—the Civil War.

Lumpkin County in the 1830s was a frontier in every sense of the word. Rugged terrain, crossed only at intervals by muddy roads, isolated the mining communities from each other and from the rest of the state. One of the original miners recalled that "living was precarious. All the supplies had to be carried by wagon . . . across the mountains, and the necessities of life were expensive, while the luxuries were unknown." On the periphery of civilization, some of the new immigrants paid little heed to the rules and conventions of respectable society. "The miners were a rough and ready set," admitted one observer, who lived in "bark shanties which were regarded as common property and might be appropriated by any miner who might be temporarily located in any portion of the country."[4] Indeed, to some outsiders it appeared that the miners reveled in their defiance of societal norms and institutions. Garrett Andrews, a visiting attorney, recounted with amusement that established religion seemed an especially unwelcome trapping of civilization in the mountains. Andrews noted that the miners spent their leisure hours gathered in their hovels, "drinking and gambling," ignoring the imputations of a certain "preacher from the interior of Georgia . . . [who] went to one of these sinks of iniquity for the purpose of rebuking the sins of that place." As Andrews recollected, the miners promptly laughed their would-be deliverer out of camp. Other missionaries were not as devoted, and several who came to rescue the miners from "the drunken hells and gambling holes" abandoned their charges and were "found in the gold pits rather than in the work of reformation."[5]

The boisterous lifestyle often offended established sexual norms and gender roles, as women took on "masculine" characteristics in the rough-and-tumble mining camps. To be sure, elite women served in conventional semipublic roles. Agnes Paschal managed an Auraria hotel and also helped nurse the residents of the town through an outbreak of fever in the summer of 1833. She earned a local reputation as a "ministering angel" for her efforts. But other mountain women clearly lived outside the bounds of conventional society. Women were "as vile and wicked" as men, wrote one middle-class resident of Lumpkin County, and "gambling houses, dancing houses, drinking saloons, houses of ill-fame, billiard saloons, and tenpin alleys were open day and night." Miner Edward Isham had paramours and common-law wives of both races who seemed to drift in and out of sexual relationships as easily as he did. One miner recalled that "sometimes both sexes engaged in . . . fisticuff fights by the hundreds" that often raged in the mining camps. Other women worked in the mines and taverns, despite the derision of male miners. A lawyer from lower Georgia, riding the mountain circuit in the 1830s, noted the unrestrained and decidedly unfeminine behavior of local females brought before the bar on such charges as assault and battery. During one trial, a woman defendant, a "wiry and sinewy girl in her twenties," admitted to beating another woman with a piece of wood, exclaiming "that she was little in body, but mighty big in spirit, that she was as supple as a lumberjack, strong as a jack-screw, and savage as a wild-cat!"[6] Qualities attributed to frontier men thus applied to some women as well.

Lumpkin County was born in violence and lawlessness, and these characteristics were elemental components of north Georgia's frontier culture. The invasion of north Georgia that followed the discovery of gold was in effect a gigantic violation of the federal law protecting these lands for the Cherokee. From the outset, miners diligently evaded restrictions on their activities, ignoring federal decrees and hiding from U.S. troops sent to expel trespassers in 1830. Miners showed few compunctions about using violence to defend their interests, something that Colonel John W. A. Sanders discovered when his troops arrested several white intruders in Lumpkin County in the winter of 1831. As the troops led their prisoners out of the mountains, dozens of miners gathered in ambush, felling trees in the troops' path and attacking the rear guard as they attempted to cross the Chestatee River at Leather's Ford. The commanding officer reported that the miners "continued the assault with great fury, until checked with the bayonet."[7]

If miners were eager to fight the authorities to defend their gold claims, they were often equally content to fight each other. Though murder was rare even in the early days, assault, mayhem, and other violent crimes were rife. The autobiography of Edward Isham, who mined in north Georgia in 1840 and 1850s, is largely a litany of scuffles with other mountaineers, in which the quick-tempered miner boasted of committing numerous stabbings, shootings, and beatings. In addition to the commonplace individual battles, scores of miners sometimes filled the streets of Auraria and Dahlonega in massive brawls, "swearing, striking, and gouging, as frontier men only can do these things," as one observer complained. One miner recollected cavalierly "that only a dozen or so . . . battles occurred, in which clubs, rocks, picks and knives were freely used and a few dozen heads broken and several men's bread sacks cut out." Auraria's public officials decried the lack of a regular police force to quell such violence, but police could have done little to stop such huge scuffles, some of which involved almost a hundred men. As in other frontier communities from Texas to California, north Georgians sometimes resorted to vigilante justice to restore order. Men who broke the miner's code were whipped, branded, or ridden on a rail. Later, after county government became more established, Lumpkin residents were content to give the regular justice system a reasonable chance to keep order before resorting to extralegal means.[8]

Much of the violence in the gold region involved the Cherokee directly or indirectly. The Cherokee had ceased organized warfare against whites by time of the gold rush. Intermarriage with whites was common, and a Cherokee elite pursued a lifestyle virtually indistinguishable from Southern middle-class planters. Despite this, white Georgians who flocked into the mountains brought with them the stereotype of the demonic red savage, eager to shed the blood of white men, women, and children. Local papers carried frequent alarms of real or rumored Indian atrocities, reports that frightened those ready to believe in the inherent ruthlessness of Native Americans. In the spring of 1833, the *Auraria Western Herald* used barbaric imagery to report a harrowing battle between Indians and whites in which "25 or 30 Indians, all painted and undressed, rushed out and attacked" a group of white miners "with sticks, clubs and rocks." Hand-to-hand combat raged for hours, with the miners fighting back with picks, shovels, and mining tools.[9]

In fact, although such clashes did occur, whites were more often the aggressors. Miners showed little regard for Indians' claims of ancestral rights and from the beginning of the gold rush violated them with impunity. Groups of white outlaws calling themselves "pony clubs" roamed north Georgia during the early 1830s, terrorizing Indian families, stealing livestock, and occasionally murdering those who resisted. Cherokee leaders protested. "Our neighbors who regard no law and pay no respects to the laws of humanity are now reaping a plentiful harvest," the editors of the *Cherokee Phoenix* charged in 1829. "These neighbors . . . take the cattle belonging to the Cherokees. The Cherokees go in pursuit of their property, but all they can effect is to see their cattle snugly kept in the lots of the robbers" (Georgia law forbade Indians from pursuing such claims in state courts). This violence culminated in 1838, when President Martin Van Buren ordered U.S. troops to north Georgia to expel the Cherokee from their property. North Georgia militia and civilians joined in the exercise, often looting and burning Indian homes in the wake of the evictions. When some Indians resisted by force, mountaineers called for brutal retaliation, demanding that any white casualties be repaid with three times as many Cherokee deaths. Local whites who did not participate in the removal nevertheless took satisfaction in the event. While thousands of Indians were dying on the Trail of Tears, the Lumpkin County Grand Jury expressed "unmixed pride and pleasure" at the swift progress of the expulsion.[10]

In Lumpkin County, therefore, geographical isolation and a lack of strong institutions created a relatively unstructured society. For many twenty-niners, life in the Georgia mountains was chaotic, violent, unrestricted, and individualistic. Indeed, these are the qualities that chroniclers of Appalachia have long attributed to the region as a whole. Beginning in the 1870s, local color writers, missionaries, politicians, and sociologists portrayed Appalachia as a primitive and unchanging land of clannish, unenlightened, and anachronistic communities. Outsiders either castigated or pitied mountaineers as backward barbarians who were beyond the reach of broader societal values or morals—people whom time forgot. It is important to note that historians of Appalachia have sought to debunk this interpretation since the 1970s. Recent scholars who seek to dispel these stereotypes find support in the case of north Georgia. For although some elements of the Appalachian stereotype undoubtedly applied to north Georgia society in the 1830s, countervailing cultural trends developed. The frontier culture of early Lumpkin County always coexisted with a different set of values, values devoted to development, a market economy, institutions, and social order.[11]

Even at the height of the gold rush, when thousands of transients flooded the mountains seeking only to get rich, some in Lumpkin County had their eye on the long term. These people focused their energies on transforming the wilderness into solid communities with ties to the rest of the state, region, and nation. Agnes Paschal, who immigrated to Auraria from lower Georgia with her son in 1833, was an example of this spirit. Offended by the lack of organized religion in the mining camps, Paschal led an effort to build the first Baptist church in Lumpkin County. Others followed her lead, and by the end of the decade Baptist, Methodist, and Presbyterian churches had sprung up throughout the county. The new churches enforced middle-class, Christian values upon the frontier. Congregations tried members for moral offenses such as drunkenness, whipped up mobs of men and boys to remove "vile, lewd women," and took the lead in forming temperance societies, which were quite numerous by the 1840s. When one enterprising miner tried to open a saloon on the grounds of the county court house, a polite mob of temperance men told the proprietors that "if the groggery was put up they would tear it down." The bar never opened.[12]

As the county grew more established, it attracted an increasing number of persons seeking long-term settlement. During the early to mid-1830s, Lumpkin's "founding families" arrived and began the process of "civilizing" the region that would characterize the post–gold rush decades. Archibald G. Wimpy arrived in Dahlonega in 1837 and established a small dry-goods store. Success followed, and Wimpy soon expanded into mill operations and plantation agriculture. He became the largest slaveholder in the county and was one of the wealthiest and best-known residents of the county by the time of the Civil War. Weir Boyd emigrated to Lumpkin as a teenager with his parents in 1835. When Boyd grew to manhood he became a successful attorney and local politician, served several terms in the state legislature, and was a leader in the local temperance society. He also become a key figure on the home front during the Civil War. Harrison W. Riley was one of the most colorful of these early settlers, a man who combined the frontier traits of violence and rugged individualism with more conventional entrepreneurship. An ambitious liquor merchant, the quick-tempered Riley frequently engaged in fistfights and gun battles but also built some of Lumpkin's first stores, taverns, and hotels. His credit report noted that the Rileys were of "notoriously bad character," and the auditor warned that "on account of their anxiety to accumulate wealth and their utter disregard as to the means I can't recommend them." Despite these negative perceptions, Harrison Riley made an impressive fortune in the decades before the war and became a decisive local political force as well. When he died in the 1870s, Riley's epitaph read in part, "let his faults be buried with his bones."[13]

The Boyd, Wimpy, and Riley families formed the core of Lumpkin County's antebellum leadership. These and other founding families recalled their frontier heritage with pride—many clan memoirs made special note of an original ancestor who came to Lumpkin "before a stick of timber was cut" or "when the red man was still in our midst." But to people like these, the frontier was a place to be transformed, not simply exploited—a place to call home. The Georgia land lottery of 1832 reinforced this impulse; over 18,000 Georgia residents won 160-acre parcels of farmland in the newly acquired Cherokee lands. This relatively democratic process of distributing land ensured that thousands of settlers would flock to Lumpkin County, not only to pan for gold, but to live permanently. By the eve of the Civil War, approximately half of all Lumpkin heads of household owned their own land.[14]

The settler's ultimate symbol of modernizing spirit was the town they built, Dahlonega. Dahlonega was founded in 1833 five miles north of Auraria, and like the latter town, Dahlonega served initially as a collection point for miners. But Dahlonega soon outshone its neighbor to the south, earning designation as the county seat in the spring of 1833.

Almost immediately, the erstwhile mining village flooded with almost a thousand people, many of whom gathered frequently in the public square to do business in the burgeoning stores or in the imposing brick courthouse built in 1836. Dahlonegans experienced their share of anarchy and frontier violence, but by the time of the Cherokee removal, the town "was all life and animation . . . its hotels were large and commodious . . . her merchants were numerous and kept their stocks well-supplied . . . [and] her streets and public square presented a degree of neatness and cleanliness while peace and good order were maintained." [15]

Dahlonegan's central claim to legitimacy was the branch federal mint established there in 1838. Due in part to the discovery of Southern mineral deposits, the U.S. Congress decided to create three mints in the South to supplement the main coining plant in Philadelphia. New Orleans and Charlotte, North Carolina, became sites for the new mints. In Dahlonega, a coalition of hard-money Democrats and capitalists agitated for creation of a third mint there. John C. Calhoun, who owned a mine in the region, helped to sponsor the campaign for a third branch mint in Dahlonega. Three years later, after machinery had been painstakingly hauled overland from Savannah and thousands had been spent in construction, an imposing edifice was dedicated north of the town square. Soon flooded with gold deposits from throughout the region, the mint

Dahlonega as it appeared in the nineteenth century. In the foreground is the Lumpkin County Courthouse, where Colonel James Jefferson Findley imprisoned anti-Confederate guerrillas in 1864. (*Harper's New Monthly Magazine,* September 1879, p. 508, courtesy of Cornell University Library, Making of America Digital Collection)

coined over $100,000 in bullion during its first year in operation. The mint made Dahlonega a nationally known locale and connected the town to the patronage of the federal government. It also lent a gilded layer of sophistication to the town and represented an important victory for those who wanted to develop Lumpkin County as an important center of trade.

Although Dahlonega and Lumpkin County remained somewhat remote and isolated during the 1830s, a number of factors brought the residents increasingly into the orbit of state, regional, and national trends. One of the most important of these factors was the growing market economy. Antebellum north Georgia was certainly not industrialized. Though mining was the preeminent economic activity during those years, it was nowhere near the scale of the coal-mining boom of the late nineteenth century, which denuded Southern Appalachia's wilderness and transformed many of its inhabitants into wage laborers. By contrast, mining in north Georgia's gold-rush period was an individualized, haphazard affair. But this does not mean that north Georgians were totally resistant to market values or isolated from the trends of national or world capital. Indeed, the early history of Lumpkin County demonstrates the opposite case.

Contrary to the image of the rugged individual miner panning in streams and creek beds, larger companies with organized production methods were the most productive agents in the gold fields. Within a very short time after the first discovery of gold, firms such as the Pigeon Roost Mining Company dominated the area. Pigeon Roost, backed by wealthy Southern and Northern capital, owned several of the most productive lots in Lumpkin and offered hundreds of thousands of dollars in public stock. Some rich individuals, most notably John C. Calhoun, also ran highly rationalized mining operations in the area, using slave labor to extract thousands of dollars in gold. By the 1850s, when Lumpkin County experienced a second gold boom, even larger firms operated in the region. With the help of outside investors and imported state-of-the-art technology, mining operations in Lumpkin became organized, sophisticated, and destructive. The Yahoola and Cane Creek Hydraulic Company, a Boston-owned firm, employed hundreds of slave and free laborers and invested one million dollars in an attempt to build a thirty-three-mile-long system of trenches and flumes in Lumpkin County. The canals and aqueducts provided waterpower for an ambitious high-pressure hydraulic mining process that became known as the *Dahlonega method*. This early form of strip-mining ripped the forests and topsoil from the mountains surrounding the town in huge swaths. When taken together with the branch mint in Dahlonega, which produced over $6 million in gold coins before the Civil War, these activities are evidence of a rather advanced commercial system connecting the extractive industries of Lumpkin County to a global market.[16]

Many Lumpkin County residents embraced the market economy. Even in rural areas, commerce and cash exchange thrived. During the height of the gold rush, merchants from all over the South and North entered the mountains, providing needed services to the miners. Not only was Dahlonega "the trading post for everybody in North Georgia," but it also became a locus of regional and even national commerce. Corn was imported from Knoxville. Hog drovers from Tennessee herded thousands of swine into north Georgia, penned them in huge slaughterhouses outside Auraria, and sold pork to miners at 2.5 cents per pound. Lumpkin women often contracted with these drivers to render the lard. Dozens of businesses opened, thrived, went bankrupt, and revived in the decades preceding the war. Many borrowed money from large Northern financial houses to jumpstart their operations, and their names turned up in the records of the largest credit-reporting agency in the nation, the New York–based R. G. Dun and Company. Some of these men were sober and industrious—good credit risks—whereas others were reportedly "worthless," "drank too much," or "[had] but little honor among them." But whatever their character strengths or flaws, the fact remains that grocers, miners, mill owners, merchants, hoteliers, and land speculators all made Dahlonega the center of their operations, bringing an ethic of entrepreneurship to the region. Store owners such as A. G. Wimpy stocked their shelves with goods imported from New Orleans, New England, and New York. In Auraria, miners could buy Spanish cigars, peach brandy from the Netherlands, and soap from London. And although a barter economy probably existed in north Georgia, most people purchased these goods with cash or gold dust. Local newspapers listed prices of everyday items daily, prices that fluctuated in accordance with the regional, national, and global markets.[17]

As early as 1833, prominent Lumpkin residents agitated for banking institutions. Miners tired of having to travel to Augusta to make a bank deposit, and so the Pigeon Roost Mining Company established its own bank that year and issued its own notes. In 1835, a branch of the Bank of Darien opened in Dahlonega and did a brisk business during the height of the gold rush. It was one of the few financial institutions available to mountain residents north of Athens, Georgia, facilitating commerce and building connections with the regional and national economy.[18]

Thus, Lumpkin County's people were not, as one chief architect of the Appalachian stereotype put it, "a sequestered folk" who lived in "amazing isolation from all that lies beyond the hazy blue skyline of their mountains." They traveled on regional and national paths of commerce. And there were always community leaders who sought to make those connections firmer still. The editor of the county's first newspaper, the *Auraria Western Herald,* was an early and tireless booster for local development. Other local leaders wrote of "Lumpkin County, a land of enterprise, well deserving the attention of the most permanent capitalist." By the early 1850s, Dahlonegans had created a committee of almost one hundred men to agitate for extending the rail line from Marietta to their town. Led by rising elites such as Weir Boyd, A. G. Wimpy, and Harrison Riley, the committee pressed the legislature to approve the project, which they claimed would "add to the wealth of the section, [and] open up one of the most important routes for trade and travel." The committee asserted further that "all the upper parts of Georgia and North Carolina could obtain their groceries on a very nearly direct route from New Orleans, while they could send their produce to the numerous markets on the sea coast from Charleston to Texas." The rhetoric of commerce and development echoed from the mountains of north Georgia.[19]

The institution of slavery was another force binding Lumpkin to the rest of Georgia, and indeed to the South as a whole. Part of the myth of Appalachia has always been that mountaineers were white non-slaveholders. As one of the early mythmakers put it: "There were but few slaves in that region, and the people knew but little from any actual experience, of the dominating character and purpose of the slave power, except that they were not the objects of its solicitude; were not its beneficiaries, and were practically excluded from all participation in the conduct of public affairs."[20]

In fact, some of the earliest local color writers extolled the region's people as the purest example of the Anglo-Saxon racial stock, whose geographic isolation had protected them from diluting their breed with other ethnic groups. But recent scholars have deconstructed this aspect of the Appalachian stereotype and found it distorted and inaccurate. Lumpkin residents were very familiar with slavery. From the beginning of the gold rush, black labor had been a visible and vital aspect of the mining economy. John C. Calhoun brought dozens of slaves to work

Archibald Wimpy's family posing outside their home sometime between 1860 and 1880. Wimpy was a successful merchant, a slave owner, and one of the wealthiest men in Lumpkin County. (*Vanishing Georgia*, lum136, Georgia Division of Archives and History, Office of Secretary of State)

his mine on the Chestatee, and other part-time miners did the same. It was a common sight in the 1830s to see part-time miners from lower Georgia bringing coffles of black men up to the mountains to engage in the hard, dangerous work of extracting gold from the streambeds and hillsides. Slaves made up approximately half of the mining workforce in north Georgia by 1830.[21]

But blacks were not merely transient sojourners in Lumpkin. They were an integral part of life of the county and the region as a whole. African American men and women were bought and sold from the steps of the Dahlonega courthouse. Lumpkin newspapers carried frequent advertisements regarding runway slaves, and one of the first tasks of the county government was establishing a militia system to patrol the countryside for fleeing black servants. When the owners of the Yahoola and Cane Creek Hydraulic Company came to Dahlonega in the 1850s, they rented scores of slaves to work on building miles of flumes and canals necessary to provide waterpower. Although slaves were never a large presence in Lumpkin, their numbers remained constant at about 10 percent of the total population—numbers that rose higher during the height of the gold rush, when many slaves came as seasonal workers. Even after the gold ran out and the necessity for mining labor declined, blacks remained a small but significant minority in the county. Slaves lived in virtually every settled part of the county, although by 1860 they were concentrated around the Dahlonega area. Most were engaged in farming, in mining, or as personal servants to members of the town's commercial/professional class. Dahlonega also had a small free black community. A free black man was one of the first members of the Dahlonega Baptist Church, and several free black families lived in Lumpkin in 1860. Indeed, one of the most successful early businessmen in the county was a free black man named James Bosclair. In the 1830s, "Free Jim" parleyed a lucrative gold strike into ownership of a large dry-goods store, an icehouse, and a saloon. Unlike his white competitors, Bosclair had to have an outside guardian sponsor all his business dealings and purchases, but still his business thrived.[22]

The African American witnesses who recounted their stories to the Federal Writer's Project investigators in the 1930s left a vivid portrait of what it was like to live as a slave in the mountain counties along the border of Georgia, North Carolina, and Tennessee. These and other sources show that enslaved people were a strong, vibrant presence in the mountains. And although these black mountaineers had many variable experiences that were unique to Appalachia, their lives were not very different from those of slaves in the plantation South.[23]

Some highland slaves worked on sprawling plantations with scores of other human chattel. Jordan Smith's master owned hundreds of slaves working a two-thousand-acre spread in Union County, Georgia. But this was rare. Most black laborers in the region lived in groups of fifteen to twenty on farms of a few hundred acres. Although cotton was not cultivated in the high country, the slaves who lived there did devote most of their labor to commercial agriculture. Mountain planters and their slaves cultivated corn, wheat, and pork for export, in addition to producing foodstuffs for the farm. Whatever crop they tended for their owner, black north Georgians worked with the same back-breaking intensity as other enslaved persons in the antebellum South, relieved only by periodic respites on Sundays or holidays. When Tom Singleton recalled his slave days on a Lumpkin County plantation, he stated: "I don't recollect nothin' t'all about my grandma and grandpa, cause us wuz so whupped out from hard wuk us jus went off to sleep early and never talked much at no time." Jordan Smith commented, "the first work I done was hoeing, and we worked as long as we could see . . . a hill of corn." Another north Georgia ex-slave concurred: "When slaves got in from de fields dey et deir somptin t' eat and went to bed. Dey didn't have to wuk on Saddays after dinnertime. When our old master turned us loose, he turned us loose; and when he wuked us, us sho' was wuked."[24]

For some, their age or gender insulated them from the harshest field labor. African American children under the age of twelve often had a relatively carefree period before they were put to work. They would "fight and frolic like youngsters will do when they get together," or else spend the days playing with whatever toys their imagination and labor could devise—dried-mud marbles, balls made of tightly bundled rags, or miniature pistols carved out of soapstone. It was generally a time to "kick up their heels till they was grown." And for some black women, labor was restricted to the household. Young Sally Hillyer was solely responsible for the care of other slave children on her north Georgia farm. Another Lumpkin County slave reported proudly that "My mother never was no field hand. She was cook in de big house, her and gran'mah." But these protections were rare and usually temporary. Even as children, most upcountry slaves had labor assigned them—hauling wood and water, feeding livestock, or helping their parents in the field during planting time. One north Georgia slave, assuming these duties were the master's punishment for his childhood antics, allowed that the chores "kept us purty busy and we wasn't so bad after that." For many black women, too, Appalachian farm life was full of hard outdoor toil. "Master Ab had hundreds of acres of wheat and made the wimmen stack hay in the fiel'," a Union County slave reported. "Sometime one of them got sick and wanted to go in the house, but he made them lay down on a straw-pile in the fiel'. Lots of chil'ren was born on a straw-pile in the fiel'."[25]

African Americans working the region's large mining industry faced even more arduous work schedules. Few were full-time miners. Mountain masters who were involved in extractive industries usually put their workforce to dual use—their slaves worked the mines in addition to their agricultural duties. Tom Singleton's master had a large plantation in Lumpkin County but "owned a gold mine and a copper mine too." Abner Griffin plowed the fields as a child but later went to labor in Lumpkin County's gold mines. "I worked in water and mud up to my waist," he remembered, "[I] drilled many a hole and shot it out . . . Worked at mining 14 years, shake it and wash it and it shine dus' as pretty! Flux it and retort it and den dey ship it to North Carolina and make bars." Besides the innumerable dangers of mine work—rockslides, explosives mishaps, and tunnel cave-ins—slaves in extractive industries also faced extra scrutiny from their masters. Black mine laborers were often subjected to intrusive body searches when they left work, as masters sought to discover any valuable ore that slaves might try to smuggle out in their clothing. One master in Gilmer County, Georgia, forcibly shaved his black laborers to prevent their hiding gold dust in their hair. Punishments for smuggling were severe.[26]

It is impossible to believe, as some early Appalachian mythmakers asserted, that white mountaineers had no contact with slaves or slavery. On the small farms, mines, and towns in which they worked, north Georgia blacks came into frequent and intimate contact with whites. Of course, most blacks worshipped on Sundays with their masters. "Slaves went to de white folks' church," one upcountry ex-slave recalled, "and white folks and slaves wuz ducked in de same pool of water. White folks went in fust and den de Niggers." This common worship was in addition to whatever independent services the slaves might conduct later in the day. The racial boundaries were no less porous on the plantation. When young Steve Connally's mother took ill on their Murray County farm, the slave boy was taken in by his mistress. He ran errands with the white lady, accompanied her to the doctor's office, and even slept in her room. Other black children were taken in by their masters and mistresses when their parents died. They worked, dined, and slept in the same physical space with their white owners. Morris Hillyer was owned by a prominent local judge and politician in north Georgia. Morris hunted rabbits with his master, often accompanied him into town, and was allowed to watch and listen as the judge "lounge[d] with his cronies" and talked politics. Indeed, some outside observers feared that mountain blacks mixed all too freely with whites, threatening to destabilize the racial caste system. Emily Burke recalled disdainfully that, in the Georgia mountains, "they all work in the fields together, white and black. When work is done, they all repair to the house . . . and help themselves out of the same dish." The frontier culture of the gold rush days facilitated the blurring of racial boundaries. In the rough mining camps around Dahlonega and Auraria, free and enslaved blacks drank, fought, and performed in saloons with whites. In 1835, the Lumpkin County grand jury expressed official opprobrium at the multicultural clientele of a local tavern, noting that "whites and negroes loiter about these places, particularly on the Sabbath." Georgia newspapers printed a doggerel that depicted Cherokee Georgia as a place "where everyone is conscience free . . . where gin by the barrel-full is drank, and *whites and blacks are all the same*." Edward Isham, a poor white miner who worked throughout the region in the 1840s and 1850s, epitomized the looser racial strictures in the mountains. At various times in his short and violent life, Isham had black enemies, rivals, lovers, and comrades. After one particularly vicious hand-to-hand struggle with a black man named Wash Smith, Isham recalled that "afterwards we made friends." Remarkably, there appeared to be no social or personal recriminations for this particular black man who had tried to choke a white man to death.[27]

Regardless of physical proximity or social connection, however, mountain slaves lived in constant terror of brutal punishment. Whether they worked on farms or in households, in town or in the countryside, most black highlanders suffered the harshest aspects of bondage at one time or another. "Old Marster . . . was all time knockin' on his Niggers 'bout somepin," Anderson Furr recalled, "He 'lowed dey didn't do dis, or dat, or somepin else right—he allus had to have some 'scuse to knock 'em round." Although some masters reserved whippings for certain identifiable infractions (stealing, running away), arbitrary punishments were not uncommon. "They were whipped for mighty small offenses," recalled one ex-slave, and another remembered his master as a cruel man who, "if you crossed him or Mistress . . . it was 'double trouble' and a cow-hiding most anything they do." Of the punishments themselves, enslaved mountaineers later spoke in horrifying detail. "Marse George would have them tied hand and foot over a barrel and would beat them with a cow-hide or cat-o-nine tails lash," one black mountaineer reported. And on another north Georgia plantation, female slaves were tied to the kitchen wall and whipped by their master's wife until "she cut their back most to pieces." Afterward, the mistress gave the women long dresses to wear to church, so as "to hide the stripes where she had beat them." Yet another bondsman watched in terror one day as a driver laid 250 lashes on a run-away slave, until "it didn't look like there was anyplace left to hit." The whole time, the master sat nearby calmly smoking cigars and drinking whisky.[28]

For other high country slaves, even brutality of the lash was still less onerous than another symbol of their oppression—the auction block. The uncertainty of being sold to a new master, the indignity of being publicly hawked like livestock, and above all the separation of families left permanent psychic scars on the enslaved people of north Georgia. When Tom Singleton's master died in Lumpkin County, his life was thrown into turmoil. The mistress was too old to run the plantation herself, so she sold her plantation and its human property at a sheriff's auction. "My pa, my sister, an' me wuz sold on the block," Tom remembered. "Durin' the sale my sister cried all the time, and Pa rubbed his han' over her head and face, an' he said 'Don't cry, you is gwine live wid young Miss Mattie.' I didn't cry none, cause I didn't care." Even slaves who never endured the block themselves were always haunted by the fear of sale, a fear that in-tensified whenever they witnessed the public auction of other blacks. The dehumanization of the process burned itself into the memories of these witnesses, so that even decades later they could recall in detail how whites "would stand de slaves up on the block and talk about what a fine look-ing specimen of black manhood or womanhood dey was, tell how healthy dey was, look in their mouth and examine their teeth just like they was a horse." Other slaves recalled with bitterness how sexuality and economics converged on the block. One reported: "A buyer would walk up between the two rows and grab a woman and try to throw her down, and feel of her to see how she was put up. If she was pretty strong, he would say to the trader, 'Is she a good breeder? How much is she worth?'" For the rest of his life, Jordan Smith remembered hearing the cries of husbands and wives being separated on the block, begging fruitlessly to be sold together. Morris Hillyer only withstood the shock of such a scene by convincing himself that he was too valuable for his master to sell. "It never entered my mind to be afraid for I knowed the old Judge wasn't going to sell me. I thought I was an important member of his family," Hillyer insisted.[29]

Like enslaved persons throughout the American South, Appalachian slaves resisted their bondage in countless direct and indirect ways. Slaves broke tools, killed livestock, feigned illness, slowed down the pace of work, deliberately misunderstood orders, and mocked the master behind his back—all part of an effort to assert their individuality and loosen the shackles that bound their daily lives. Sometimes this resistance had an economic objective, as when slaves on one north Georgia farm stole the master's whisky and secretly sold it for cash. At other times, slaves violated the master's rules in order to feel in control of their own lives, if only briefly. Morris Hillyer frequently left his Floyd County farm without permission, even though he knew the inevitable punishments that would follow (stringing transgressors up by their thumbs was his master's favored method). But for Hillyer, having some leisure time to see the circus in town or wager on dogfights was worth the price he paid when he returned to his master. On other north Georgia plantations, slaves stole away from the quarters at night to attend parties or dances, braving the lashes and dogs of the slave patrols for the opportunity to mix and mingle with the African American community.[30]

Many other mountain slaves fled the plantation altogether, although their goal was less often permanent freedom in the North than it was a temporary respite from forced labor. These escapees fled to the wooded coves or high ridges near their homes, living off the country and hiding from patrollers for weeks or months at a time. Groups of these refugees formed small maroon communities to avoid or at least delay recapture, aided by a network of spies and collaborators within the enslaved community. They sometimes resorted to violence to keep their freedom for even a few more days. One runaway overturned a pot of boiling lard on a group of white pursuers. Others "stretched ropes or grapevines across the road where they knew the paterollers would be riding," disabling horses and riders. Eventually, almost all these escapees were swept up by patrollers, or else they returned voluntarily due to hunger or hopelessness. But despite harsh punishments, many of these slaves ran away again and again. Some of them, local blacks insisted, "stayed in the woods until the surrender" at Appomattox in 1865. Whether these stories were real or fantasy, they served a potent mythological purpose among the enslaved people of north Georgia. They represented heroic resistance against the white power structure, which gave African Americans in the mountains a sense of identity and self-worth. As one recalled:

> De timber was awful heavy in de river bottoms, and dey was one nigger dat run off from his master and lived for years in these bottoms. He was there all during de War and come out after de surrender. Every man in that county owned him at some time or another. His owner sold him to a man who was sure he could catch him—he never did, so he sold him to another slave owner and so on 'till nearly everybody had him. They would come in droves with blood hounds and hunt for him but dey couldn't catch him for he knowed the woods too well. He'd feed the dogs and make friends with 'em and they wouldn't bother him. He lived on nuts, fruit, and wild game, and niggers would slip food to him. He'd slip into town and get whisky and trade it to de niggers for food.[31]

Of course, most Appalachian slaves did not run away, attack slave patrols, or plan organized rebellions. Most resisted slavery by building a rich and autonomous cultural system that insulated them from the soul-crushing system of human bondage. They forged a collective spiritual consciousness in church services, wedding ceremonies, and funeral rites. They built resilient family structures that endured through sale, separation, and punishment. They established their own folkways, borrowing from remembered African traditions of storytelling, language, and music. They constructed a strong set of social networks that found full expression during their leisure time—holidays, evening dances, hunting and fishing expeditions, and corn-shuckings. And they also created a quasi-independent slave economy that gave a measure of power over their own lives. Even though he worked long, exhausting hours in the fields, Tom Singleton often hired himself out to white yeoman farmers near his Lumpkin County home. He worked through "bright moonshiney nights," cutting wood and mending fences, to make the extra cash his master allowed him. "Wid de money dey paid me," Tom recalled, "I bought Sunday shoes and a Sunday coat and suck lak, cause I . . . always did lak to look good on Sunday." Some children managed to collect small wages for performing extra household duties. Anderson Furr "jus turned it over to my Ma," but Morris Hillyer took his hard earned cash to town, spending it all on "lemon stock candy, ginger cakes, peanuts, and firecrackers." Hillyer relished the experience for the feeling of self-worth it offered: "I spent it [the money] for it was mine to do with just as I pleased." Many other black Appalachians tended their own gardens, hunted, or fished to supplement their rations. In all these things, they built a physical and psychological space within which they could withstand their oppression.[32]

White mountaineers were often oblivious to the realities of the black experience. Some contemporary white observers concluded that the close interaction between whites and blacks indicated a comparatively benign slave system in the mountains. They contended that mountain slavery allowed blacks more autonomy and equality than was possible on the plantations of the Black Belt. Charles Lanman noted on his trip through Lumpkin County in the 1840s that north Georgians "are in the habit of treating [their slaves] as intelligent beings and in the most kindly manner." To Lanman, local slaves seemed "the happiest and most independent portion of the population, and I have had many a one pilot me over the mountains who would not have exchanged places even with his master."[33] For decades, one of the myths of Appalachia portrayed white highlanders as racially enlightened despisers of black bondage and proponents of a rough sort of frontier racial equality. Frederick Law Olmsted, the early chronicler of Southern society who traveled though the mountains in 1854, painted a more complicated picture. Olmsted spent only a little time in north Georgia, but if his observations of other Appalachian regions are any indication, then whites in Lumpkin probably felt ambivalence about slavery. Although Olmsted found a general disaffection with the slave system in the Southern mountains, true abolitionist sentiment was rare, perhaps nonexistent. In East Tennessee and western North Carolina, the Northern writer found that many whites there held the slave system and black people in equally low regard. Another Yankee observer who toured north Georgia in the 1840s concurred with this view, reporting that mountain Georgians "would be glad to see the institution of slavery abolished . . . but they hate a political abolitionist as they do the very Father of Lies." When Garrett Andrews brought his black body servant to Auraria in the 1830s, he observed firsthand the racism of which mountaineers were so capable, and found that the yeoman and poor whites of Lumpkin County could be quite hostile to the blacks in their midst. One boisterous miner confronted Andrew's slave Lewie in the streets of town: "This blurting young mountaineer . . . stood in his shirt sleeves . . . his wool hat jauntily to one side, his suspenders . . .

bringing up his striped pants several inches above his bare feet . . . admiring as well as envying the well dressed and proud looking fiddler before him [and said,] 'I G_____d, I believe you low-country niggers think you are as good as white folks!' "[34]

Whatever their feelings about slaves or slavery, Lumpkin whites could not help being aware of the system. Most of Dahlonega's elite families—the Boyds, Wimpys, and Rileys—owned slaves, and as a system of labor slavery was a vital component of Lumpkin's economy. Residents had to pay attention when regional and national spokesmen discussed slavery and its place within the republic. It was one more tie binding the county to the broader world. And during the Civil War, the literal and metaphoric presence of the slave would play a vital role in the region.[35]

If Lumpkin was forging economic links to the outside world during the antebellum period, it was also developing political ties to the state, region, and nation. The advent of the Jacksonian party system brought Georgia into the national political mainstream by mobilizing localities to participate in broad partisan organizations that evolved during the 1830s. In Lumpkin County, local newspapers bristled with commentary on issues such as the tariff, the national banking system, and the increasing power of the U.S. presidency. Most significantly, the controversy over nullification of federal authority dominated local news during much of 1833. The presence of states' rights spokesman John C. Calhoun in Auraria during the gold rush lent an air of urgency to national events as perceived in Lumpkin. The local press, stubbornly pro-nullification, lionized Calhoun as "the distinguished statesman . . . [who] is opposed to the usurpations of power upon the part of the general government, which are unjust in their nature, unconstitutional in their bearings, and sorely oppressive [to] the southern people." Union and States Rights parties both organized in Lumpkin in the spring of 1833 during the crisis over the Force Bill, which gave the president the right to use the military to enforce federal tariffs, as residents debated national political issues in the streets of their small towns.[36]

Throughout most of the antebellum period Lumpkin County was solidly Democratic. Like many frontier residents, north Georgians embraced Andrew Jackson's rough-hewn, aggressively masculine, populist image. Further, mountain Georgia felt a debt to Jackson for his steadfast opposition to Cherokee rights and his endorsement of removal. Lumpkin voted Democratic in every presidential election between 1832 and 1860 and usually awarded its ballots to Democratic gubernatorial and state legislative candidates. However, pro-development Whigs also had influence in Lumpkin. During the Nullification Crisis, pro-Calhoun residents rallied under the leadership of *Auraria Western Herald* editor A. G. Fambrough to assert "southern rights" in defiance of "the military chieftain" Jackson. In state and national elections throughout the 1840s and 1850s, between 30 and 40 percent of Lumpkin's residents consistently voted for the Whig or anti-Democratic candidates.[37]

While numerous local, familial, and traditional alignments influenced voting behavior in antebellum Georgia, economic concerns were also significant. In Lumpkin County, it seems probable that residents shaped their political sympathies in accordance with their relationship to and opinion of the market revolution engulfing the nation in the four decades preceding the Civil War. The relatively urban, commercial environment of Dahlonega provided fertile ground for the market-oriented Whig ideology. On the other hand, the miners, laborers, and farmers who feared banks and a cohesive national economic system were attracted to the Democratic Party. These elements were also hostile to the slave-owning elites of the low country, who benefited from the disproportionate electoral power accorded to them by the three-fifth's clauses of the U.S. and Georgia constitutions. As one mountain Democrat stated boldly during the constitutional referendum of 1833, "fellow citizens, I am a Union man and a friend of General Jackson, and I always said if I ever got a chance at that infernal nigger basis in the constitution I would tear it out." The class-based politics of Lumpkin County was most evident at the polling places. One early Auraria settler recalled that on one election day in the 1830s "the wisest and most distinguished persons in the locality" gathered around John C. Calhoun's headquarters at the Paschal Hotel to "absorb his words of wisdom." Meanwhile, the "pick and shovel boys" attended political barbecues and marched through the streets waving hickory bushes and wearing coonskin caps. Thus, "the great mass of gold-diggers . . . defeat[ed] the best laid plans of the nullification party."[38]

As the issues of Union, secession, and the territorial expansion of slavery dominated national political rhetoric during the 1840s and 1850s, Lumpkin County residents actively participated in these national debates. When the crisis of 1850 threatened the Union, most north Georgians took a cautiously anti-secession stance. Lumpkin residents supported the gubernatorial campaign of Howell Cobb, who professed loyalty to the Union and supported Henry Clay's compromise for holding the nation together. When anti-compromise Southerners convened a convention in

Nashville in the spring of 1850 to discuss secession, residents of Lumpkin County remained aloof from the proceedings. Only twenty-seven residents cast votes in the election for convention delegates, and the candidate elected from Lumpkin refused to attend the convention on the grounds that his constituents "have no sympathy with the contemplated movement of the Southern states on the subject of slavery."[39]

Residents of Lumpkin County were seriously engaged in the political events shaping the South and the Union. And north Georgians took their elections seriously. The vitality and passion of mass politics engaged both men and women and could create bitter, even violent, community divisions. Whigs and Democrats tenaciously defended their positions and mercilessly attacked opponents. At the height of the nullification controversy, the *Auraria Western Herald* printed an incendiary letter written by one Mary Johnstone, who vigorously defended Calhoun and states' rights with an appeal to the spirit of the American Revolution. In the process she denounced a neighbor who opposed nullification, comparing the Jacksonite to the Tories who betrayed the colonists during the war for independence. Indeed, Johnstone recalled, the neighbor's ancestors had served most dishonorably in the late conflict, helping pro-British Cherokees to rape, murder, and plunder patriot homes. "I ask you," she concluded, "do you think that the old Tories instilled their principles into their children? . . . I have a right to hate them." Sometimes north Georgians resorted to more than hostile rhetoric. During the tumultuous gubernatorial election of 1850, a witness in north Georgia reported that "I can't say how many lives were lost in this contest. Two were killed in Cartersville, one in my neighborhood, two or three in Rome, and this is but a small account." The tendency to identify political enemies with treason and to strike at them with violence would recur during Lumpkin's Civil War experience.[40]

Therefore, by the 1850s, Lumpkin County was connected firmly to the economic and political trends in the state, region, and nation. To be sure, frontier conditions still applied. It still took almost a week to travel from Dahlonega to Atlanta, and the occasional gunfight still broke the silence of the hills. But Lumpkin was far from the isolated, lawless place it had once been in the public imagination. A second gold rush in the 1850s brought an infusion of Northern capital and invigorated the developmental spirit. Churches, stores, and schools replaced tents, trading posts, and saloons (although plenty of the latter still existed). The vast majority of Lumpkin residents in the 1850s were farmers with families, not unattached miners. Dahlonega was arguably the largest and most important town in northeast Georgia. Many mountaineers saw an even brighter future ahead. But Lumpkin residents still felt weighed down by the dead hand of the past. The image of Cherokee Georgia as a wild, violent back-water prevailed in the popular imagination, and Dahlonegans constantly wrestled with this frontier image. The struggle to deal with the image of the primitive would be a central aspect of nineteenth-century north Georgia history.[41]

Lumpkin residents felt embattled from the beginning over their county's image, partially because the frontier myth of the gold rush days contained a large kernel of truth. But this did not prevent elites from taking exception to negative portrayals of their home. Correspondents to Lumpkin newspapers constantly rebutted charges that the mountain society was less than virtuous. At the height of the first gold rush, one Aurarian objected to a critical press portrait as having "willfully slandered our town." The writer continued: "we defy the world . . . to produce a [similar] precedent for good order and respectability. . . . It is true that many people visit here . . . who's moral example is neither seen nor heard . . . but we hear of no midnight assassinations, no pickpockets, no robberies, no stealing . . . we have good taverns here, kept by respect-able men."[42]

M. H. Gathwright, a Dahlonega lawyer of the 1830s, complained that the lower Georgia press depicted his town as an uncivilized place un-fit for respectable women, where "forty old bachelors [chase] after one lady." Residents were especially sensitive to charges of irreligion. In the winter of 1833, an anonymous letter appeared in the *Atlanta Christian Index* charging that "the circulation of some moral precepts in [Lump-kin] is absolutely necessary . . . the enterprising settlers of this country are almost as destitute as the savage. . . . The wicked one increases his ranks and public morals suffer much." An angry Aurarian responded that "our town and country suffer much from the misrepresentations of the malicious man." Suffer, indeed. Those who sought to develop Cherokee Georgia into a middle-class, commercial region feared the perception of an untamed region filled with Indians and "white savages" that would dissuade investment and condemn them to isolation.[43]

Antebellum Georgia politicians were aware of the sensitivity of the issue and played upon it at election time. When Know-Nothing politi-cian Benjamin Hill visited Dahlonega to campaign for governor in 1857, he made the mistake of condescending to his audience by claiming they were "remote . . . and had not the means of making money like others," and that "there were among them many people who were wholly unable to send their children to school." The Democratic Party sought to build upon their solid mountain base by making the most of such comments. During one 1853 campaign, Jacksonians derided Whig attempts to curry favor in the mountains, reminding upcountry voters that certain Whig leaders "have more than once hinted . . . that Cherokee was half a century behind the age . . . they have hooted and ridiculed the mountain boys as a set of outside barbarians."[44]

The "otherness" of mountain society was reinforced by the accounts of Northern visitors to the region. In the 1840s, a New England schoolteacher named Emily Burke described a Cherokee Georgia that lacked the industry of character so vital to free labor ideology. The inhabitants, she wrote, "have no idea of style and refinement in living . . . when compared to New England its inhabitants are all 100 years behind the times in education . . . many cannot read a word or write their own names." Another Yankee traveler spun tales for his readers of a grizzled, north Georgia backwoodsman named Vandiver, who was the essence of the violent, irresponsible, primitive mountain man. Vandiver lived with an Indian women, reputedly "claimed to be the father of thirty children," lived all year round in a lean-to open to the elements, and fought wolf, bear, and mountain cat with his bare hands. The supermasculine, Davy Crockett–like figure provided many with a believable image of the typical Appalachian man. Even Northerners who tried to be less critical and more understanding of their subjects ultimately perpetuated the same stereotypes of the isolated, backward highlander. When Charles Lanman of New York traveled through Lumpkin County in the 1840s, he found the locals "distinguished for their hospitality . . . and sobriety," people who gladly offered the stranger from the North the best food and forage they could offer. But Lanman but also labeled north Georgians "deplorably ignoran[t] . . . isolated, and uncultivated," and he lamented their illiteracy, irreligion, and parochialism.[45]

In subtler ways, mountaineers themselves often reinforced these stereotypes. Middle-class town dwellers were often quick to shift the negative qualities popularly associated with their region to more rural, less "civilized" Georgians. Congregants of Dahlonega's established Baptist and Methodist churches often looked down upon the "country churches" of the hinterland for resisting townspeople's "advanced views on missions, temperance, Sunday schools, and secret societies." Pro-development

Dahlonegans described the outlying area around town as "terra incognita" waiting to be filled up with "an industrious and intelligent population." In 1834, Dahlonega physician and amateur geologist Matthew Stephenson wrote a profile of the country north of Lumpkin that rivaled some of the most outrageous local color authors of later years in its depiction of an untamed and mysterious Georgia wilderness. On a visit to Enchanted Mountain, Stephenson described a barren, beautiful landscape, populated by none but Indian ghosts and wild animals. The capstone of the trip was the discovery of ancient Cherokee footprints left in the stone, some of which, Stephenson claimed, measured over seventeen inches and contained six toes ("a descendant of Titan," the good doctor asserted). The mixture of amazement and horror, embodied in physical deformity, prefigured author James Dickey's later characterization of Appalachian Georgia as an unnatural "country of nine-fingered people."[46]

Thus, during the decade before the Civil War, Lumpkin County residents, and especially Dahlonegans, had achieved a degree of commercial development and gentrification quite at odds with their frontier roots. They were linked to the economic and political mainstream of the state. However, the perceptions of the rest of Georgia had not kept pace with this evolution. To many inhabitants of the agricultural Black Belt and the urban centers of Georgia, the mountains were still a benighted region. Many north Georgians combated this perception fiercely, asserting their sophistication and seeking further development. Others reacted to the affront by transferring the wilderness image to the less advanced subregions further up in the mountains. The newer Appalachian frontier was represented by Fannin County, Georgia, Lumpkin's neighbor to the northwest.

Just north of Dahlonega, the Blue Ridge rises like a wall. Between that point and the state line, the terrain is rugged. Hills and mountains are broken intermittently by valleys, running streams, and wild river gorges. Much of this area is wilderness still, part of the Cohutta Wilderness Area and the Chattahoochee National Forest. This was the land that would become Fannin County, Georgia, in the 1850s.[47] Whites may have started settling in the extreme north of Georgia in the early 1820s, but as had been the case in Lumpkin County, the gold rush and the termination of Cherokee sovereignty truly began the transformation of this region. When the state divided up the Cherokee lands, this territory was organized into Union and Gilmer Counties, lying just south of Georgia's borders with Tennessee and North Carolina and bestriding some of the

highest elevations in Georgia's Blue Ridge country. Soon thereafter, settlers began to seep into the region. Hundreds of Georgians won land
lots in Union and Gilmer during the lottery of 1832; many settled along
the Toccoa River and its feeder streams, which crisscrossed the landscape
back and forth between Tennessee, North Carolina, and Georgia. Cabins, post offices, and small towns dotted the area by 1840. By that time,
Gilmer and Union contained over five thousand people.[48]

Like the waters, settlers came from all points of the compass. Many
pushed north from the lowlands; others came west from Habersham
County. Many others did not come from Georgia at all. One of the first
to settle permanently in the region was Lewis Vanzant, who moved there
from western North Carolina in 1834. Settling near the Toccoa River,
Vanzant established a trading post that became the germ of a small town
known as the Dial community. Vanzant employed local Cherokee as
builders, engaged in a lively trade with the Natives, and prospered. He
was worth over $16,000 in 1860, with much of his wealth tied up in five
slaves. By the eve of the Civil War, Vanzant's Store was a county land-
mark, and this erstwhile frontiersman was a member of the local elite.[49]

Many North Carolinians followed Vanzant into Union and Gilmer
counties in the 1840s and 1850s. Families named Dickey, Stuart, Woody,
Fain, and Twiggs all moved in from Fannin's neighboring state of North
Carolina. Of approximately 15,000 residents of Union and Gilmer in 1850,
4,800 were born in North Carolina—more than in any other single state,
including Georgia. Some of these immigrants sought a share of north
Georgia's famous mineral wealth. Others intended long-term settlement.
Whatever their motivations, these settlers contributed to a population
boom in the region that caused the Georgia legislature to carve a new
county out of Gilmer and Union in 1854. The new county of Fannin embraced 386 square miles of mountainous terrain and straddled the border
of Tennessee and North Carolina. The county seat was named Morganton, possibly after the western North Carolina town of the same name.
Within two years, the town consisted of a few dozen buildings, a new
brick courthouse, and perhaps 500 people. A few other hamlets sprung
up: Epworth, Hot House, Pierceville, and McCaysville.[50]

From the outset, Fannin's economy was oriented northward. Trading
ties followed the lines of immigration, and Fannin residents engaged in
a lively commerce with Tennessee and North Carolina. Local merchants
moved freely across the tri-state area, setting up shops and stores in Fannin County, Georgia; Polk County, Tennessee; or Cherokee County,

North Carolina, depending on varying economic trends. Sometimes the border was too porous—Fannin's representatives in the state legislature had to propose bills to keep Tennessee livestock from crossing over onto Georgia farms and trampling crops. But the meteoric rise of the local copper-mining industry was too lucrative to ignore, and it fueled the cross-border economy even more. Less sensational than Lumpkin's gold rush, the copper craze that swept Fannin in the 1850s still seemed to hold much promise for pro-development segments of the county. In 1843, large deposits of copper were discovered near Ducktown, Tennessee, just across the state line, giving rapid rise to a mining boom that energized the entire border region. By the early 1850s, copper veins had been discovered in northern Fannin County, and several mining companies had located there. As in Lumpkin County, mining connected Fannin to the outside world. Northern and Southern financiers invested more than $300,000 in mines in the northern part of the county, mines that employed over one hundred people directly or indirectly. Georgia copper was transported north to Ducktown and from there to Cleveland, Tennessee, to be shipped by rail to New York, Baltimore, and other cities. Other Fannin residents crossed over the border to work in the bigger mines in Polk County, Tennessee. Edward Isham, the pugnacious north Georgia mineworker who fought and labored throughout the region, frequently traveled to Ducktown to gamble, work, or hide out from pursuing magistrates.[51]

But extractive industries in Fannin never played the dominant role they had in Lumpkin County. Indeed, many locals resented the mines and their impact on the region. When the Ducktown mines began floating lumber down the Toccoa River to feed the copper-smelting furnaces, the rushing logs destroyed local fish traps, much to the chagrin of Fannin's fishermen (eventually, legislation forbade such traps in Fannin county). And the massive charcoal demands of the mines deforested much of the region and stunted vegetation with harmful emissions. But beyond the mine's destructive impact, the fact was that most local residents were focused on agriculture. The overwhelming majority of Fannin residents were farmers, either working their own land or that of others. To be sure, many of these farmers were doubtless tied to regional markets. They sold surplus produce to feed the voracious miners in the Copper Basin, or drove hogs and other livestock to Asheville, Charlotte, or Savannah. But most of these farmers likely sought a different economic path. Many had immigrated from North Carolina or Tennessee, seeking the Jeffersonian dream of self-sufficiency and economic independence. For the Germain family, this dream came true in the relatively unsettled mountains of Fannin County. One of the Germain children recalled growing up near Morganton during the 1850s in somewhat idyllic terms: "The sturdy mountaineers raised all the food their families ate. Cattle, sheep and hogs furnished the supply of meat. . . . Mother made all our clothing. She cleaned, spun, and wove the wool, the cotton and the flax into cloth. Father tanned the hides of our beef cattle and made shoes for his family, so we were quite independent of any village store."[52]

Independent farmers like the Germains engaged in "safety-first" agriculture that sought above all to provide for immediate family consumption. A key indicator of this economic reality is Fannin County's corn production. At three hundred bushels, the county's annual production of this staple was well below the regional average. There are many other possible explanations for Fannin's low corn output, including poorer land and smaller farms than in many other Appalachian counties. Also, Fannin's relative isolation from outside markets gave its farmers less of a need to produce surpluses to trade.[53]

But these debates were irrelevant to many other Fannin residents. Many could not afford the comparative luxury of owning their own property. Arable land was scarce in the heights of the Blue Ridge, and the wealthiest people soon bought up most of it. In 1860, only 36 percent of Fannin's household heads shared the Germain family's status as landowners. The top 11 percent of Fannin landholders owned over a third of the improved acreage in the county in 1860, and the richest 6.4 percent of the population owned over half the wealth. Almost two-thirds of the county households were landless, compared to 37 percent in the Georgia piedmont and 24 percent in the Black Belt. Most of these propertyless residents worked as tenants, farm laborers, or mining operatives. This section of the Georgia mountains was far removed from the myth of the egalitarian Appalachian community made of independent freeholders. And in this sense, too, Fannin County had much in common with neighboring counties across the border in Tennessee and North Carolina. Most Fannin residents might have echoed the East Tennessee man who recalled this time: "opportunities was bad and it was hard task for a young man to buy a farm or start a business."[54]

Fannin's landholding elite wielded disproportionate power in the community. Elijah W. Chastain was one of the wealthiest and most politically powerful of these elites. He became the patriarch of an influential clan that would play a decisive role in north Georgia's Civil War. Born in South Carolina, Chastain moved to what was then Gilmer County, Georgia, in 1835, settling along the Toccoa River. After earning a military pedigree through service in the Seminole Indian War of 1838 (which caused him to be known in the community ever after as *Colonel*), Chastain read law and became a practicing attorney. By 1850, he was one of the wealthiest figures in the Blue Ridge country, owning over a thousand acres of property and six slaves and having a net worth over $10,000.[55]

He was also a precocious politician. At the age of twenty-one, he was an accomplished stump speaker who energized Gilmer voters with pro-Jackson, pro-Union rhetoric. Due to natural charisma and considerable social and economic influence, Chastain never lost a campaign in north Georgia. At age thirty-nine, he ran successfully for the state senate from Gilmer County, a seat that he held for ten years. Chastain capped a decade of achievement with his election to the U.S. Congress from Georgia's fifth district. He retired from Congress in 1854 to become an instrumental figure in the formation of Fannin County, which he represented in the state legislature. A friend and confidante of fellow Democrat

A poor north Georgia family shucking corn outside their cabin. This lifestyle was the norm in much of Fannin County, and class divisions would play an important role in the region's internal civil war. (*Vanishing Georgia*, rab015, Georgia Division of Archives and History, Office of Secretary of State)

and fellow north Georgian Joseph E. Brown, Chastain spent much effort during the latter 1850s securing electoral support among mountain voters for Brown's successful gubernatorial campaigns. He played a pivotal role in the crisis of 1860 and represented Fannin County in the state Secession Convention of January 1861.[56]

So, on the eve of the Civil War, Lumpkin and Fannin counties embodied many of the conflicts and contradictions of Appalachian society. While similar in many respects, it is too simplistic to label them as "typical" Appalachian communities. Fannin and Lumpkin differed in important respects, including their relationship to the rest of Georgia, their economic structures, their political arrangements, and their demographic compositions. These differences had a significant impact on how each county responded to the crisis of the Civil War, as illustrated by a brief comparison of the two counties as they appeared in 1860.

When Dr. Matthew Stephenson of Dahlonega traveled in 1834 to the land that would become Fannin County, he was astonished at the wild and untamed mountains north of Lumpkin County. It was an attitude that many town-dwellers in Lumpkin seemed to share. To an extent they were correct. Fannin was relatively undeveloped when compared to Lumpkin. Containing over a thousand white and black residents, Dahlonega was the largest town in Georgia's Blue Ridge country, linked to the rest of the state through its gold supply and the U.S. branch mint. Fannin had no towns of any importance and no institutions comparable to the mint. Lumpkin County had a larger class of professionals and merchants than its northern neighbor and more banks, newspapers, and churches. The New York commercial reporting agency R. G. Dun and Company noted twenty-four businesses of various sizes in Lumpkin County during the antebellum decades, ranging from small stores to large, nationally financed mining operations. In Fannin County, the firm's credit investigators found only seven companies worth noting during the same period, all of them small shops servicing the copper-mining operations in Tennessee. Lumpkin was marginally the wealthier of the two counties, with an aggregate valuation of real and personal estate of $933,390 compared to $888,147 for Fannin. Per capita wealth was $222.55 for Lumpkin and $177.77 for Fannin in 1860. Both counties had high numbers of landlessness, but almost half of Lumpkin's farmers owned their own property, compared to about a third of Fannin residents.[57]

For decades, observers allotted geography a determinative role in the constitution of Appalachian society. It was assumed that rugged terrain

isolated Southern mountaineers from the outside world and either re-
tarded their development or protected them from the encroachments of
"civilization," depending on the observer's perspective. This myth has
been overstated, as illustrated by the enthusiasm with which many mountaineers threw themselves into the regional and national markets. Still,
although north Georgia was not exactly "the Switzerland of America,"
geography did affect Lumpkin and Fannin in different ways. Although
the northern half of Lumpkin was quite mountainous, Dahlonega and
the gold-producing region lay on the southern slopes of the Blue Ridge,
within relatively easy contact of Atlanta and Milledgeville, the state capitol. Fannin, by contrast, lay entirely beyond the main line of the Blue
Ridge, separated from the rest of the state by the heights of the Appalachians. Fannin was by no means cut off from the outside world, but
its most substantial economic links were with the copper-mining industries across the state line in Tennessee. The most accessible railhead to
Dahlonega was Athens, Georgia. Fannin's railhead was Cleveland, Tennessee. Moreover, the relative lack of arable land in Fannin led to a more
uneven distribution of wealth and property there and created a larger
class of poor agricultural and mining laborers.[58]

Demographic realities reinforced geographical divisions. As stated
above, a large number of Fannin residents had not been born in Georgia.
Of Fannin's 900 household heads, 739 were born outside of Georgia,
the majority in North Carolina and Tennessee; 38 percent of free Fannin
residents hailed from North Carolina, and fully half had been born outside the state. By contrast, a plurality of Lumpkin household heads were
Georgia-born. Only 26 percent came originally from North Carolina or
Tennessee.[59]

One of the most dramatic contrasts between the two counties was
the relative role of slavery in the socioeconomic structure. Slavery did
not play a dominant role in either county, but it was a presence in both
from the beginning. When George and Hannah Dickey trekked over the
mountains from western North Carolina in the 1830s into what would
become Fannin County, they brought their slaves with them. When
Mrs. Dickey died, the family buried her with in a common cemetery
with her deceased black servants. (The Dickeys of Fannin County were
ancestors of the novelist James Dickey, author of *Deliverance*. In 1999,
Dickey family members restored and rededicated the slave cemetery. A
new marker at the site bears an engraved verse from James Dickey's poem
"The Strength of Fields.") Obviously, slaves and free blacks had also lived

in Lumpkin County from the earliest days of the gold rush. Indeed, Auraria was the vacation home of one of the South's most vigorous defenders of the slave system—John C. Calhoun. In fact, slavery always played a relatively large role in Lumpkin society. In 1850, the waning days of the gold rush, almost 1,000 African Americans lived in the county. By 1860, the number had dropped to 432, but slaves still accounted for 9.3 percent of the population. No other county in the region had a higher proportion of slaves, excepting Hall County, to Lumpkin's south. At one point, Dahlonega was over 30 percent African American. By contrast, Fannin in 1860 contained only 143 slaves—about 2.7 percent of the total population. Thirty-six Fannin residents owned slaves in 1860—which was 4 percent of the household heads—and only 3 people owned more than 10 slaves. The largest slaveholder was James Morris, who owned 20 slaves. In Lumpkin County, almost 8 percent of the household heads owned slaves, and 13 of these owned more than 10 slaves. Daniel Davis, a planter living near Dahlonega, owned 78 servants.[60]

In politics, both counties were solidly Democratic. The dominant local political personalities were almost all members of the party of Jackson throughout the 1850s. Elijah W. Chastain, the virtual founder of Fannin County, was one of the most prominent and devoted Democratic activists in the state. In Lumpkin, rising politicians like Weir Boyd and old hands like Harrison Riley were also Democrats. Fannin and Lumpkin voters were energized by Joseph E. Brown's emergence upon the political stage in the late 1850s. Brown had been born in Union County, and his mixture of populist rhetoric and die-hard southern rights philosophy won may adherents in the Blue Ridge. In the gubernatorial election of 1857, Brown won 71 percent of the votes cast in Fannin and Lumpkin counties. When Brown ran for reelection in 1859, he won 67 percent of the combined vote. The mountains provided perhaps the most reliable base of support for Brown and the state Democratic Party.[61]

But these figures mask important qualifiers, for Lumpkin was less overwhelmingly Democratic than its northern neighbor. Whig or anti-Brown forces garnered 40 percent of the gubernatorial votes in 1857 and 44 percent in 1859. Only about 16 percent of Fannin County residents voted against Brown in either election. There are likely many reason for this disparity, but a large part of the reason probably is Lumpkin's longer history of commercial, pro-market interests, which were typically aligned with the Whigs.[62]

It is possible to overemphasize the differences between these two

Appalachian counties. The majority of Fannin and Lumpkin residents shared similar work patterns, religious beliefs, and political allegiances. Moreover, neither of these counties was a monolithic socioeconomic entity. Each was divided between town and country, mountain and valley, rich and poor, free and slave. But the differences between Fannin and Lumpkin did dispose them toward certain paths. The crisis of war would bring these differences into sharp relief.

William R. Crisson could scarcely believe the transformation wrought upon Lumpkin County in the years since the gold rush began. Crisson had arrived in the upcountry with the first wave of twenty-niners seeking quick fortune. In those wild early days, he experienced the frontier at its roughest, and he seemed to enjoy it. He fondly remembered a time when Auraria and Dahlonega were nothing but rude towns of tents and log cabins, whose residents subsisted on wild game and whiskey. With law enforcement lax and churches nonexistent, gambling, fighting, and epic drinking contests served as daily amusements "in that merry day." But then "the Indians were carried away and the people became more civilized," Crisson recalled somewhat wistfully. New men came to the mountains—judges, businessmen, and, above all, ministers—who were determined to tame the wilderness and "bringeth life and prosperity to both soul and body, and a new and better order of morals." Crisson was ambivalent about the newcomers but conceded that their arrival was inevitable and probably for the best. "The presence of such men, estimable qualities and good morals had much to do with the reforming of the masses," he concluded, which was "a blessing to the people." Crisson numbered himself among the reformed. Although he continued to mine for gold, he soon became a respectable citizen, amassing land, wealth, and status. He even served several terms as justice of the peace in Dahlonega. And when the civilizing elite led Lumpkin County to war in 1861, William Crisson would be marching right alongside.[63]

2 / "*This Unpatriotic Imputation*"

MOUNTAIN IMAGES IN SECESSION AND WAR

On January 19, 1861, Georgia became the fifth Southern state to secede from the Union. In towns and cities across the state, people touched off cannons, fired muskets, rang courthouse bells, hammered on anvils, and shouted in jubilation. In Dahlonega, the anvils rang too. But the celebration was muted by uncertainty. It is doubtful that a majority of Georgians supported secession at that particular time, and nowhere was the doubt more palpable than in the mountain counties. During the winter elections for delegates to Georgia's secession convention, two-thirds of all highland voters had cast ballots against immediate disunionist candidates. Fannin and Lumpkin counties joined their north Georgia neighbors in opposing secession at the polls, and delegates from these counties took the lead in obstructing secessionist forces on the convention floor. However, by the end of 1861, residents of both counties seemed transformed. Hundreds of young men from Fannin and Lumpkin enlisted in the Confederate army, swearing allegiance to a separate Southern republic. Their wives, sisters, and mothers actively contributed to the war effort by making clothing and sending food to the front. Their communities held parades and celebrations for departing troops. What changed?[1]

Any analysis of north Georgia during 1860–61 must take into account the complex political alignments of antebellum times, the real nature of the division between pro- and anti-secession factions in 1860, and the impact of changing events upon the region. During the secession crisis and the first year of the Civil War, north Georgians shifted their loyalties to meet the exigencies of the moment. They would also find their notions of loyalty tested, from within and without. Inside Georgia's mountain communities, individuals struggled to decide to whom and to what they owed their allegiance. Simultaneously, the rest of the state and region sought to gauge the Confederate patriotism of the mountain residents, who had so vigorously opposed secession. In order to deflect charges of Unionism or disloyalty, mountain Georgians embarked on a concerted attempt to prove their loyalty to the Confederacy. Highlanders' battle to shape their public image would dominate local consciousness throughout the war years and after.

Observers have long debated why the South seceded from the Union and invited Civil War. For Abraham Lincoln, the reason was simply that Southerners "would make war rather than let the nation survive." Historians have sought more complex answers. Different scholars have stressed class dynamics, racial ideology, gender conceptions, or other factors to explain why Southerners chose the course they did in 1861.[2] The state of Georgia provides a useful case study on secession, and the upper counties of the state played a key role in the process.[3]

Until quite recently, the mainstream interpretation of Appalachia and the disunion crises was that highlanders were steadfastly pro-Union from the beginning. Local color artists, northern missionaries, and Union army veterans who had visited the mountains constructed this myth of a "Unionist Appalachia" soon after the Civil War concluded. Isolated from the Southern mainstream, hostile to slavery, and sentimentally attached to the Union of Washington and Jackson, the Unionist myth ran, highland people "clave to the old flag" and fought disunion steadfastly. Scholars have challenged this interpretation in recent years, finding evidence of a complex and variegated series of loyalties in the mountains. An analysis of north Georgia's reaction to secession supports the revisionists.[4]

In Fannin and Lumpkin counties, many different social dynamics were at work in 1860–61. Class divisions clearly inspired political behavior. Also, prewar political traditions played a role in how residents interpreted secession. But even though voters in the two counties opposed secession, they defied the *Unionist* label (a more accurate term, and one adopted at the time, is *cooperationist*, which implies that one favored working with the Federal government as long as no overt moves to coerce the South or attack slavery directly occurred). North Georgians voted for many different reasons, and they often changed their minds. Indeed, change was the only defining characteristic during this period in Fannin and Lumpkin history. Voters, legislators, and convention delegates acted in ways that they perceived to be rational at the time, even if those actions appeared to contradict their earlier stances. An analysis of the tumultuous events of 1860–61 in Fannin and Lumpkin evinces all the complexities of Georgia politics and mountain loyalty.

The presidential election of 1860 was the first test of north Georgia's political sentiments on secession. As in the rest of the South, the contest pitted John Breckenridge, a pro-Southern Democrat, Stephen Douglas, the candidate of the national Democratic Party, and John Bell of Tennessee, the so-called Constitutional Union candidate, against each other. Lincoln, of course, was not on the ballot. Most north Georgia Democrats had supported the Union in 1850, but ten years later the story was different. Aided by popular governor and ardent secessionist Joseph E. Brown, the Breckenridge ticket made great strides in the region. Fannin County responded by giving 67 percent of its vote to Breckenridge, compared to only 19 percent for Bell. But Fannin residents also cast 13.5 percent of their ballots for Stephen Douglas, whose reputation was only slightly less egregious than Lincoln's in secessionist circles. In Lumpkin, by contrast, Douglas garnered a bare 30 votes, about 4 percent of the ballots cast. Bell won 53 percent, while Breckenridge captured 43 percent.[5]

These statistics offer few clear answers. Although it is possible that the large vote for Bell represented a stronger cooperationist sentiment in Lumpkin County, this is not the only logical conclusion. A vote for Bell did not necessarily translate into Unionist sentiment, and conversely, many mountain counties that voted for Breckenridge later opposed immediate secession in the convention. It is probable that past party allegiances had much to do with this phenomenon. Even though Fannin was a low-slaveholding area, its voters were also rabidly Democratic and thus sided with those candidates who best represented their past partisan loyalties, namely Breckenridge and Douglas. Lumpkin County, though also majority Democratic, had always contained a healthy minority of Whiggish voters. This reality, when combined with the naturally conservative character of Dahlonega's business community, might explain the county's majority vote for John Bell, himself a prominent Tennessee Whig. These realities seem more salient motivations than any supposed Unionist sentiments.

After the shock of Lincoln's election, Georgia elites began mobilizing for what many saw as the next logical step—disunion. The Georgia legislature immediately announced elections for a statewide convention that would convene in January 1861 to discuss options for Georgia's future. Howell Cobb, one of the most prominent Georgia politicians, immediately took to the mountains to drum up support for disunion. Although he had held office in the Buchanan administration and considered himself a Unionist during previous crises, Cobb now urged north Georgians to "convert" to the cause of secession. He worried that the mountain dwellers would throw their votes behind "submission" if left to their own devices. But Cobb had an even more important ally. Governor Joseph E. Brown, a hero to many north Georgians, played a pivotal role in this movement, especially in the mountains. Indeed, Brown had been selected for his party's gubernatorial nomination largely for his supposed ability to reconcile the non-slaveholding upcountry with slaveholding interests.

Brown hailed from the Georgia mountains, and in the days after the presidential election he appealed directly to the upper counties, urging them to see the common interests linking them to the institution of slavery and to understand how the Republican threat to that institution was a threat to all Southerners. In a series of public letters and addresses issued in the winter of 1860, the governor stirred north Georgians' economic and racial fears. "Every white laborer is interested in sustaining the institution of slavery," Brown wrote, because black servitude invariably would "keep up the price of [white] labor." Brown also played on mountaineers' most visceral racial fears, conjuring images of newly freed slaves who "would leave the cotton and rice fields in the lower parts of our state, and make their way to the . . . mountain region . . . plundering and stealing, robbing and killing; in all the lovely valleys of the mountains." With such rhetoric ringing in their ears, north Georgians prepared to elect delegates to represent them in the secession convention.[6]

Elijah Chastain of Fannin County was one of Governor Brown's chief lieutenants in the mountain region. Like Brown, he was a Democrat and a die-hard defender of slavery. Having just completed a term in the state legislature, Chastain returned to the campaign trail in the winter of 1861 determined to help lead his constituents toward secession. Chastain's career and ideology reflected the complexities of antebellum Georgia politics, and his political evolution sheds some light on the historical and political roots of north Georgia's reaction to the secession debates.

Georgia politicians of the antebellum period had to absorb several competing and sometimes contradictory philosophies in order to fit the local realities of power. Whigs and Democrats could all argue for Union, states' rights, economic development, and agrarian republicanism with equal vigor at different times. Chastain's political soul was Democratic, and during the 1850s he had argued for Jacksonian principles such as hard-currency finance and restricting internal improvements. But as sectional tensions increased in the 1850s, the issues of slavery and Union came to dominate his rhetoric. When the young lawyer from Fannin first ran for Congress in the midst of the Crisis of 1850, he was a vocal Unionist and defender of the Clay Compromise. Chastain swept into office as part of the coalition that brought pro-compromise Howell Cobb to the governor's chair. "Of course I was a Union man," reported one north Georgian in 1850, "and we elected Mr. Chastain to Congress."[7]

But Chastain's Unionism was far from absolute, and his career in Congress evinced a gradual shift toward a Southern rights perspective. A slaveholder himself, he came to see the Federal government as a menace to that peculiar institution. Indeed, Chastain qualified his support for the Federal government from the beginning. He excoriated the disunionists at the 1850 Nashville Convention as "violative . . . of the great republican doctrines of Jefferson, Madison, and Jackson." At that time he denounced secession as "treason" and a "sectional disorganizing movement." In the same breath, however, the congressman attacked Northern Free Soilers for waging "infuriated warfare upon my section of the country" and "trampling with sacrilegious steps upon the Constitution." During the Kansas-Nebraska controversy of 1854, Chastain defended Southern rights even more stridently. In speeches before the House of Representatives, Chastain reviled the Missouri Compromise, defended the right of slaveholders to take their property into the territories, and ridiculed antislavery activists as "fanatical assemblages of Spiritualists and Millerites, . . . men wrapped in the apparel of women." For Chastain, as for Governor Brown, the fate of the mountain counties was inextricably bound up with that of the state and the slaveholding South as a whole.[8]

Due in part to his stature in the community, Chastain won election to the secession convention as one of two representatives from Fannin County. But he was the only one of the four convention delegates from Fannin and Lumpkin counties to advocate immediate secession. Chastain actually ran a narrow second to the other delegate from Fannin, cooperationist William Clayton Fain, who outpolled his secessionist rival 394 to 355 (as the two top vote getters, both men attended the convention). Fain was a thirty-six-year-old attorney with a small practice in Morganton and a fifty-acre farm he worked with the assistance of one slave. Although he lacked Chastain's wealth, he was a considerable political force, especially among residents of the Tennessee-North Carolina border area. Like many Fannin residents, Fain was a North Carolina native, and in border towns like Hot House and Cut Cane, he reportedly had "unlimited influence." The Morganton lawyer served in the state legislature during the 1850s, where he earned a reputation as "a man of considerable prejudices, high temper and an unyielding disposition." He opposed Breckenridge in the presidential election of 1860 and fought secession at the convention. Fain was not afraid to make enemies, and he would be one of Chastain's chief rivals for local power during the war years.[9]

In Lumpkin County, cooperationists won by a larger majority. The leading cooperationist candidate, William Martin, defeated his closest immediate-secessionist rival by a margin of 50 percent. Martin was an important player in the convention, not so much for his success as for his failures. The other representative from Lumpkin, Benjamin Hamilton, also ran as a cooperationist.[10] Both were slaveholders. (Because of the secretive nature of the vote tabulation for the convention, we do not know how many votes Hamilton actually received, but it must have been something greater than the 187 votes garnered by A. M. Russell, the failed secessionist candidate.)

These were the men chosen to represent Fannin and Lumpkin counties in the secession convention, which opened in Milledgeville on January 16, 1861. Mountain secessionists immediately went on the offensive, seeking to convince their delegates to change their minds and support disunion despite the platform on which they had been elected. Andrew Young, writing from Union County, urged secessionist leader Howell Cobb not to take seriously the Unionist rhetoric of delegates from north Georgia. "Our delegates, if properly tutored, will vote for secession by the 4th March—have them flattered and nursed," Young advised, "they can be made to do right." But the cooperationists seized the spotlight early in the convention proceedings when William Martin of Lumpkin rose to speak. When the first resolution for secession was proffered on January 18, Martin sought to delay the debate and call the whole process into question by demanding that Governor Brown provide the members with the exact popular vote in the convention elections (the governor was keeping the voting statistics secret, probably because the anti-secession candidates had garnered so many ballots—indeed, even today the exact figures are not fully known). But the convention swiftly voted down Martin's motion and went directly to debating a secession ordinance.[11]

While William Martin opposed secession in the convention, other north Georgia leaders joined in the fight elsewhere. In the state legislature, representatives from Fannin and Gilmer counties spearheaded a caucus to delay any action on secession until a more accurate popular vote could be held. William McDonald, state senator from Lumpkin, rose from his seat in the capitol to reject secession more explicitly. He proclaimed himself to be "against all revolution and disunion," arguing that "our fathers had fought for liberty, and we should stick by the good old principles which guided them." McDonald feared that secessionists were led by "hot-headed" troublemakers who "were about to rush us into war, the bitter consequences of which could not be seen in full until ruin had spread over the country." But although McDonald opposed disunion, he did so in the most conservative terms. Like many Southern elites, he feared the consequences of fragmenting the Union, especially a war that could disrupt trade and perhaps even the slave system itself. After all, the "the old principles" to which McDonald hearkened back included the principle of protected human bondage, and many Southerners felt that the peculiar institution was safer under the protection of the existing constitutional system than outside. McDonald's comments expressed a cautious concern for the disruptive effect of secession upon the Southern states, not a strident commitment to unconditional Unionism.[12]

On January 19, with William Martin's delaying tactics failing, secession came up for a vote in the convention. The ordinance of secession passed by a vote of 208 to 89, with many of the opposition votes coming from north Georgia. Three of the four delegates from Fannin and Lumpkin voted against disunion. Elijah Chastain of Fannin was the only exception. Chastain, a true ally of Governor Brown, was one of the most vocal secessionists on the floor of the convention, arguing passionately that the mountain counties had as much to fear from Northern abolitionists as Cotton Belt planters did. In one speech, Chastain extolled the virtues of the peculiar institution of slavery, saying that "he thought every man, woman and child in the Southern States should own a slave," and that "the best plan to do so was to open the African slave trade."[13] (For his loyalty, Chastain would gain a plum position on the select committee drafting the official secession ordinance.)

But William Martin of Lumpkin was not through fighting. He offered another resolution on January 22, calling for the issue of disunion to be put directly before the voters of Georgia. Brown's refusal to report precise voting statistics from the January election sowed distrust among cooperationists, who now demanded a direct popular ballot to settle the question definitively. But once again, Martin was defeated. The disunionists quashed his motion and instead passed a resolution insisting that all delegates sign the secession ordinance as a litmus test of loyalty to Georgia.[14]

The behavior of Lumpkin and Fannin's representatives to the secession convention defies easy analysis. On the one hand, most voted against the secession ordinance of January 19, and some, such as William Martin, fought the disunion tide stoutly. But all four of the representatives acquiesced to the will of the convention after the January 19 vote. They all signed the ordinance of secession. None of them bothered to join the six delegates who signed an official protest of the convention's actions. Even William Martin signed the ordinance, although he allowed himself a final sarcasm in a statement issued after the vote: "I came here opposed to secession. My people were opposed to it. But the people of Georgia, in convention assembled, have decided that I was wrong and my people were mistaken. We bow with filial obedience to the behest of that sovereignty which holds our undivided allegiance, and are ready to act upon the supposition that Georgia is right and all else is wrong."[15]

None of the four delegates from Fannin and Lumpkin were "unconditional Unionists," a term historian Daniel Crofts has coined for those few southerners who were strictly and ideologically supportive of the Union. Despite their opposition to the January 19 ordinance, the three men who voted against secession can more appropriately be labeled as conditional secessionists who believed in the right of secession but were unwilling to countenance such action until a more dire threat appeared. As slaveholders, all these delegates believed in white supremacy, hated abolitionists and Republicans, and believed that Southerners possessed a unifying regional integrity. When faced with overwhelming pressure from the rest of the convention to support immediate disunion, they assented. Most would, in fact, go on to play prominent roles in the Confederate war effort. These delegates made the choices that seemed appropriate at the time, and they altered their positions when circumstances demanded it. This malleability characterized the region throughout the war years. For north Georgians, loyalty would remain ambiguous and contingent.[16]

The Fannin and Lumpkin delegates returned to the mountains that winter to wait and see how the North and the upper South would react to their bold action. Within months, the siege of Fort Sumter and Lincoln's call for Federal volunteers to suppress the rebellion pushed the nation into an awkward and undeclared state of war. Fannin and Lumpkin residents tried to put aside prewar politics and mobilize their communities for combat. In Dahlonega, state officials moved in to take over the Federal mint and secure the $50,000 in bullion stored there for Georgia and the Confederacy. William Martin, the erstwhile anti-secession stalwart, turned his attention to raising troops. He spent nearly all the cash he had recruiting and securing equipment for Lumpkin County companies. In Fannin, local leaders barraged Governor Brown with letters seeking authority to raise companies for Confederate service. "I have succeeded in making up a volunteer company . . . I am very desirous to receive marching orders," wrote one eager resident of Morganton. Another asserted optimistically that "I want to go to Virginia. I can complete my company in ten days. I am 55 years old and weigh two hundred pounds and can yet jump a ten rail fence." [17]

Elijah Chastain and Benjamin Hamilton enlisted in the Confederate army as officers. Many other young men joined them, and within the first six months of the war, Fannin and Lumpkin contributed a total of 419 men to Georgia regiments. In Fannin, strong support for Governor Brown translated into solid recruitment numbers. Approximately 25 percent of the county's military-age males enlisted by September 1861. They formed two infantry companies—Company E, 2nd Regiment of Georgia Volunteers, and Company E, 11th Regiment of Georgia Volunteers (to honor the governor, who hailed from their mountains, the Fannin men of the 2nd Regiment named themselves the Joe Browns). Lumpkin also mobilized quickly, sending approximately the same proportion of its fighting-age men into the service. Lumpkin residents made up the majority of Company H, 1st Georgia Volunteer Infantry, and Company E, Phillips Legion of Georgia Infantry.[18]

Communities rallied to support the soldiers. Local officials orchestrated parades and public displays supporting their departing soldiers, ceremonies that were designed to reinforce the commonality of interests among the men, women, and children of highland towns and villages. One of the first Lumpkin companies to form, the Blue Ridge Rifles, marched through the streets of Dahlonega in late June 1861 in an emotional ceremony that drew the entire community into the war effort. First, a local Methodist minister preached a passionate farewell sermon, asking "the God of battles to bless" the soldiers. Each man was presented with a testament "for their counselor and guide on tented fields," a reminder that Dahlonega's departing sons would be expected to maintain the moral laws of the community even on the battlefield. Following the service,

a crowd of townspeople and citizens from the surrounding countryside gathered on the square, where various dignitaries made speeches.
"Flash after flash of patriotic fire electrified the audience and held them
spellbound," claimed the *Dahlonega Mountain Signal* of one speaker,
and "the old man and the young, the woman and the child . . . were
equally moved by his eloquence." The day's activities culminated with
the women of Dahlonega presenting a hand-sewn Confederate flag to
the company. Ida Hamilton, the young daughter of the company commander, rose and recited a moving address for the enlistees. She urged
the soldiers to keep the enemy from invading the community and to
frustrate Yankee plans to "make desolate our homes and firesides." Hamilton continued, "in committing this flag into your hands, all are assured
of the protection it will receive . . . we believe that you will defend it to
the last extremity, and then make it your winding sheet before its folds
shall be polluted with the touch of the northern vandals." While the men
fought on far-flung fields, the women of Dahlonega would do their part,
Hamilton promised. "When [you are] away on tented fields, or charging
the cannon's mouth, our prayers are ascending to the God of Battles in
behalf of our brave defenders." She concluded with assurances of future
glory, pledging that soldiers who returned home with their honor intact
would "return and live like the holy mountain, [with] the admiration,
joy, and praise of all."[19]

Ida Hamilton's presentation on that summer day in Dahlonega symbolized the centrality and duality of women's roles on the southern home
front. On the one hand, women were expected to fill traditional supporting roles for the men going off to war. On the other, the war called for
women to become vital auxiliaries and vicarious participants in combat.
While Hamilton spoke of her "female timidity" and appealed for male
protection for the civilians of the town, she also offered an articulate
and coherent view of Southern nationalism. She made explicit analogies
between the American Revolution and the Confederate cause, called the
Confederacy "the shrine of liberty," and expressed hope for the "liberation" of slave states still in the Union. Hamilton also demonized the
Northern adversary in the fiercest terms, manufacturing vile enemy atrocities with the alacrity of a seasoned propagandist. She accused the North's
"merciless horde of ruffian soldiery" of "the butchery of homeless ladies
and smiling infants." She called on Dahlonega's troops to "avenge with
burning zeal" these wrongs, even if it required sacking Philadelphia and
New York.[20]

Indeed, the elite women of Dahlonega tried to be an enduring source of psychic and material strength for their brothers, fathers, and husbands at the front during the first year of war. Two weeks after the ceremony in Dahlonega, Fannie Boyd, the assertive daughter of prominent Lumpkin attorney Weir Boyd, wrote her soldier brother a scalding letter in which she excoriated the Northerners for being partners in league with "his satanic majesty." Echoing Ida Hamilton's stridency, Miss Boyd expressed indefatigable faith in Confederate victory, proclaiming that "the north means to crush us by superior number but they can't do it." Even if the Yankees did "tryumph at times," she concluded, a righteous God would proclaim on behalf of the South "with a voice louder than the thunder of their grand Niagara." Fannie Boyd and other Dahlonega elites soon added material efforts to their rhetorical patriotism, forming a Ladies Aid Society in town that summer. The group offered aid to returning wounded soldiers and sewed clothing of all sorts for shipment to Lumpkin soldiers at the front. By August, one Dahlonegan could claim that "the women all seem to be busy getting up jeans, socks and anything that will do in the way of clothing" for the troops.[21]

Mobilizing the community for war involved more than men and women organizing in separate spheres. What was going on during the spring of 1861 was a conversation of sorts between men and women, soldiers and civilians, communities and military institutions. The intent and result of these conversations was to unify the community and the soldier, to bring the home front and the front line together and assert the common interests of both in a successful Confederacy. Ida Hamilton reinforced this unity in her speech when she asserted that Dahlonega's females "feel intensely interested" in the fate of Lumpkin's soldiery, proof of which was "this large assembly graced by woman's presence and woman's smile." After her speech, a young Lumpkin private rose and answered Hamilton, concurring with her that "the scenes that present themselves today are of a war-like character, *and of common interest to us all*" (emphasis added). The soldier reminded the listening civilians that "while we are enjoying life, with all its innumerable blessings, our beloved South is invaded by a Northern foe, which threatens to subjugate us and trample us into the dust." Hamilton assured the soldiers and civilians that even though women remained in a separate sphere, they were still vitally connected to the martial world. And by arguing that the war could visit any Southern community at any time, and promising to protect those communities, the soldier reiterated his comity of interests with the civilians in the war effort. In return, soldiers conceded their dependence upon civilian support in order to do an effective job of defending their country. A. J. Reese, a private with Dahlonega's Blue Ridge Rifles, explicitly credited this dependence in a letter to his aunt, Nancy Wimpy, in the summer of 1861. Asking her counsel on a personal matter, Resse asserted, "I know the advice you give me will be for my good and will try to follow it. . . . I never intend to forget you or refuse to take your advice. If I ever did I would feel ungrateful." It was important for soldiers and civilians to acknowledge their common goals and mutual support.[22]

Community organizing did not involve women alone. In fact, leadership on the home front fell to elite men who deferred rushing to the sound of the guns in order to accumulate local power. In Fannin County, wealthy town-dwelling merchants and professionals assumed control of local mobilization. James Morris, owner of a Morganton hotel and the largest slaveholder in the county, helped organize Fannin's effort. Nat Mangum, an influential attorney, worked to organize local forges and blacksmiths into arms manufactories for the Confederacy. William C. Fain, who had resisted secession during the convention, also stayed out of the military, biding his time and building his political power along the border. In Lumpkin County, local power devolved upon other wealthy individuals, notably Weir Boyd and James Jefferson Findley. Boyd and Findley would play vital politico-military roles in north Georgia's civil war, and their leadership of local pro-Confederate forces would have a decisive impact on the region's history.

Weir Boyd's parents had come to Lumpkin with the original wave of white settlers in the 1830s. As a young man, Boyd held a variety of local offices in Dahlonega, and in 1856 he was admitted to the bar. He was a devout Methodist and a leader of the local temperance society—a model member of the town's middle-class establishment. During the prewar years, Boyd split his time between his lucrative Dahlonega law practice and the state legislature, where he served a term as Lumpkin's representative in the house. By 1860, Boyd was a wealthy man who owned property in Lumpkin and neighboring Dawson County. He was also a confidant of Governor Brown's. When secession and war broke out, Boyd sided emphatically with the Confederacy, asserting in a letter to Brown that he believed "in the principle and the theory of States Rights so long sanctioned by the fathers of our country and so ably insisted upon by yourself." The Dahlonega attorney offered his eldest son, Augustus Boyd, to the Confederate military, and his daughter, Fannie, played an active role in the Ladies Aid Society. In 1861, the forty-one-year-old Boyd won election to the state senate from his region. There, he vocally supported the Confederacy but also sought to promote and defend local issues. He actively campaigned for public education funds for his county. He also introduced a bill to allow for the apprenticing of free black children to white masters, an attempt to secure under white control the small but potentially "dangerous" free black population of his home county.[23]

James Jefferson Findley offered a sharp contrast to the polished and pious Weir Boyd. Findley had migrated to the north Georgia frontier from South Carolina as a teenager in the 1840s. He moved to Dahlonega in the 1850s, opened a dry goods store, went bankrupt, then read law, and became an attorney. In 1857, Findley led a small-scale revivification of Lumpkin's declining gold-mining industry. After discovering a rich vein of gold on some land on the Yahoola River, Findley skillfully defrauded the absentee owners of the property and commenced mining with the aid of a few local operatives. To insulate himself from legal troubles, Findley joined in a partnership with prominent local businessman Harrison W. Riley, and together the two ran a mine that ultimately produced $250,000 worth of precious metals. Findley and Riley were of similar background and temperament—ruthless, crude, and often violent men who flourished in the frontier environment of north Georgia. By 1860, the thirty-year-old Findley was a slaveholder, an aspiring politician, and a very wealthy man. (Even in the poverty-stricken post–Civil War South, Findley would still be worth $20,000.) When secession came, Findley also sided with the Confederacy and gained election to the state legislature with Weir Boyd at the end of 1861. Findley enjoyed his legislative service and enjoyed the women of Milledgeville, the state capital. "There are so many [women] who wants me and I cannot marry them all"—he complained happily in one letter—"and they are all so pretty." Apparently at no time during 1861 did Findley consider joining the army.[24]

Men like Findley and Boyd provided the home front leadership necessary for mobilizing their communities for war. In general, they did an effective job. Fannin and Lumpkin counties managed to equip and support four full companies of soldiers for Confederate armies during the war's first year, not counting the many other young men who joined state militia regiments. North Georgia's soldiers performed well in combat in Virginia and Tennessee and maintained high morale about their cause. One Lumpkin private, attached to Robert E. Lee's command in western Virginia in the autumn of 1861, wrote home confidently that "we can whip the enemy . . . if they give us half a chance." Community elites and front line soldiers appeared to present a solid front of support for the Confederacy.[25]

But despite the public and private expressions of fealty to the Confederacy, many Georgians doubted the loyalty of mountaineers. Indeed, one of the first acts of the secession convention was to establish a formal definition for treason. Confederate loyalty was a statewide obsession during the first year of the war, and much of the concern focused on counties like Fannin and Lumpkin. For many outside observers, the history, geography, and racial environment of the mountain counties suggested that their populations could not be relied upon to defend the South. It was a perception that pro-Confederates in the region would have to battle throughout the war.[26]

Suspicions about north Georgia had their roots in history. Many Georgians remembered that the upcountry had been the most reliable bastion of Unionism during the South's last flirtation with secession, in 1850. During that crisis, some residents of lower Georgia worried that the non-slaveholding mountains could launch a class war against the Black Belt. "Is there treason in camp?" asked one Milledgeville newspaper in April 1850, when rumors reached the capital that Dahlonega Whigs were preaching antislavery. The paper charged the upcountry Whigs with stirring up class resentment of poor whites, telling them that "states rights agitation only benefited the lordly slaveholder." It was precisely this kind of sentiment that Governor Brown tried to forestall in his speeches during the winter of 1861, in which he explicitly linked north Georgia's stability to the slave system.[27]

North Georgia's voting behavior during the elections to the secession convention in 1860 seemed to justify further these fears of mountain loyalty. Many delegates wondered about the primarily non-slaveholding areas of the mountains, some of which, like Fannin County, were only tenuously attached to the state apparatus. These doubts were amplified during the ratification election for the new Georgia constitution in April 1861. After voting for the secession ordinance, the convention delegates had set about drafting a new constitution that, among other things, strengthened the political power of slaveholders and limited the possibilities of slave manumission. Although Georgia voters ratified the revised document by a narrow majority, most mountain counties rejected it. Fannin and Lumpkin voted for ratification, but only 18 percent of voters bothered to turn out to vote. Significantly, the pro-ratification vote was much higher in Lumpkin, where slaveholding rates were higher and connection to the rest of the state firmer.[28]

Those who went looking for signs of anti-Confederate dissent in the mountains did not have to search diligently. Although the majority of highlanders seemed to support secession once war broke out, a vocal constituency made clear its opposition to a Governor Brown and Jefferson Davis government from the beginning. "We do not intend to submit to secession," wrote one man from the northwestern county of Walker in early 1861, "which has been out of the hands of the people and has fallen into the hands of Dimegougs and office seekers, pickpockets and vagrants about towns and cities and railroads and depots." In terms calculated to inspire the worst class and racial fears of rich slaveholders, the disgruntled highlander asserted that "It is not the good citizens of our country that owns lands and Negroes," and that he and his neighbors felt "every Negro [should] be set free in this country." The correspondent concluded by promising violent resistance: "we have 2500 volunteers . . . they are sworn to stand to each other . . . we will fight as long as there are men to fight."[29]

Other reports reached the governor from Pickens, Union, and Gilmer counties. "Some of our citizens are the worst sort of Lincoln men," wrote a Brown loyalist from Blairsville, "and they . . . assert boldly that Lincoln would make a better president than old Buck [James Buchanan]." Another mountain Confederate worried that local Unionists had simply gone underground and were awaiting an opportunity to resurface and make trouble. Although "opened and avowed hostility to [secession] has ceased to manifest itself," he wrote, "I am sorry to say the feeling yet exists with many Union men, who constantly predict difficulty and danger to the new Confederacy." One recruiter complained that even in the wake of Fort Sumter, "there is great dissatisfaction among the people of this and adjoining counties and [it is] very difficult to enlist soldiers." Mountain secessionists were unsure how to deal with dissenters in their midst, uncertain whether they should treat them uniformly as a public menace or try them on a case by case basis. "We wish to know what way for us to pursue the case of people talking or acting contrary to the Southern Confederacy," queried one pro-secessionist, "there has some cases . . . which we have acted upon as we thought according to law." Another asked the governor "what is the process to make a suspicious person take the oath, as we still have a few of that sort here that should be attended to."[30]

Anti-Confederate dissent percolated in Fannin and Lumpkin counties as well. When William Martin returned to Dahlonega from the secession convention in the spring of 1861, he found disturbing signs that some of his neighbors might not meekly accept Georgia's departure from the Union. Martin himself had fought secession in Milledgeville, but Fort Sumter had turned him into a Confederate stalwart. His conversion experience made Martin especially intolerant of one his neighbors who had been "an active secessionist, and did everything he could to bring about the present state of affairs," but who was now growing tepid in his support for the war. Other dissenters acted to hinder the war effort by discouraging local men from joining the army. Martin charged A. M. Russell with such activity. "I suppose more than 20 men who have come here to enlist have been dissuaded by him," Martin reported to the governor.[31]

A peculiar incident in Lumpkin County during the peak of the secession crisis seemed to cast further doubt on the county's ideological unity. In the winter of 1861, reports reached Governor Brown that shadowy parties were plotting a takeover of the Dahlonega Mint. "I have heard some talk about the propriety (among some Union parties), of taking possession of this institution and holding for the [U.S.] government," the chief assayer of the mint wrote in January. Rumors continued to fly about the takeover through the spring, although the plotters were never precisely identified. One of them appears to have been the bluff and bellicose Harrison Riley, who was heard to say that he "had as good a right to do so [take the mint] as the Governor did to take Fort Pulaski." Riley was hardly a Unionist, and his bluster was probably an opportunistic attempt to take advantage of a chaotic situation, but the charges were incendiary enough to inspire a group of Dahlonega volunteers to guard the mint building, threatening to "shoot down any man or set of men who should make any improper attempt." The specter of conspirators scheming to rob the Confederacy of its gold fed the perception of the mountains as a hotbed of disloyalty.[32]

In Fannin, the signs were worse for the secessionists. Despite military mobilization and the political dominance of Confederate Elijah Chastain, dissenters were a disruptive force in the county in the months following secession. Some Fannin men openly proclaimed "that they will defend the flag of the old Union . . . and that they will help the North whip Georgia and the South back into the Union." Again, the class resentment imbedded in this dissent was most worrisome. As one Fannin secessionist put it, the actions of many mountaineers seemed to "indicate Union sentiment [and] anti-nigger slavery." Throughout the county, local rebels reported, Unionist "demagogues" were stirring up latent dissent of the "ignorant, honest, unsuspecting" poor classes. These unnamed trouble-makers were agitating the yeoman and poor whites by "telling them that they are not interested in the nigger question, that this fuss was all for the benefit of the wealthy . . . that Bob Towns, Bill [Yancy], Joe Brown . . . and Tom Cobb ought to be hanged." Another north Georgia Unionist claimed that non-slaveholders in his region were "vassals of a system of which they played no part and yet to which they were compelled to yield obedience." The size of the anti-Confederate bloc in Fannin was un-clear in 1861—some local reports claimed that the dissenters were every-where while others estimated that the entire county was loyal except for a few "traitors." Still, the danger that this "small crop of abolitionists . . . shielding themselves in the hysterical garb of Union" might find an at-tentive audience among the county's vast majority of non-slaveholding whites gave further credence to local and statewide fears that upcountry commoners were a dangerous element.[33]

Even after yeoman and poor whites had seemingly established their loyalty by joining the Confederate army in droves during the spring and summer of 1861, doubts persisted. Unsettling demographic shifts further concerned some Fannin secessionists, who worried during the winter of 1861 that "our country is being filled up with the poor from Tennessee" who commenced with "horse-stealing, housebreaking, etc." In towns like Pierceville, near the Tennessee border, the problem was so intense that some feared a revolution unless state-sponsored employment plans were enacted for the emigrants. This connection with East Tennessee doubt-less stirred greater fears among Georgians concerned about mountain loyalty, especially after the abortive uprising of East Tennessee Union-ists in November of 1861. That winter, north Georgia newspapers were filled with lurid tales of the pro-Union terrorists who had burned bridges and attacked Confederate troops just north of the state line. When East Tennessee authorities decorated the roadsides with the hanged bodies of captured Unionists in response, some in Georgia must have wondered whether such scenes would be reenacted in the mountain region of their own state.[34]

Therefore, despite the ceremonies and musters and displays of Con-federate patriotism that occurred in north Georgia during the spring of 1861, an undercurrent of dissent created a perception that the highlands were disloyal to the new order. Mountain Confederates were exceedingly sensitive to this perception and devoted much energy and rhetoric to addressing the situation. Mountain communities hastened to form home guard units to defend against the *Tories,* as white dissenters were beginning to be called. In Hall County, home guards pledged to "try and pass sentence . . . on all suspicious characters [and] keep a strict watch over any one who may be a Lincolnite." In Dahlonega, a chastened Harrison Riley led the local home guard unit, which drilled often on the town square. Guards formed in Fannin as well. These local militias also turned heightened attention to their traditional role in the antebellum South—guarding against slave insurrection. Many upcountry whites took seriously Joseph Brown's threats of a black "invasion of the mountains. Their fears were fed by rumors like the one recounted by the *Clarkesville Herald* in November 1860. Reportedly, "several slaves and one free negro" had been overheard planning "to seize Mrs. 'M' and throw her into a well." Such worries resonated sharply in slaveholding counties like Lumpkin, where groups of blacks were arrested for suspicious activity at least once in 1861.[35]

Upcountry secessionists worried that the voting results in the convention elections indicated deep-seated and dangerous opposition to their cause, and they were also concerned that the perception of disloyalty would taint the entire region. In places like Dahlonega that were heavily connected to the rest of the state politically and economically, such doubts could be fatal. To address the problem, some mountain elites encouraged enlisting massive numbers of local men into the Confederate army. Sending more mountain boys into Confederate service would achieve two purposes. First, it would tie upcountry communities directly to the war effort by giving them a concrete interest in the outcome. As one mountain rebel wrote, "our people are not as sanguine in the cause as we would like to see them, and every man that enters the service gives us the stronger ties and sympathies of our people." Second, high enlistment numbers would prove to the rest of the state and the South as a whole that mountaineers could be trusted, and that rumors of disloyalty were unfounded. As one north Georgia newspaper trumpeted, "the people of this section were . . . fiercely denounced as Lincoln men . . . the manner in which they have rushed to the field shows what sort of 'aid' they are willing to give Lincoln." Others even felt that recruitment in the mountains would boost statewide enlistment, and that volunteers from the supposedly "Unionist" mountains would shame others into joining the cause.[36]

In addition to the concrete actions taken to address dissent, highland secessionists also embarked on a propaganda campaign designed to replace perceptions of their region's disloyalty with images of a unified, pro-Confederate north Georgia. Upcountry newspapers came to the defense of the mountain inhabitants and criticized those who interpreted the region's electoral behavior during the secession convention as treasonous. The editors of the *Athens Southern Watchman* allowed that "while the question of secession was an open one, a large majority of the people of the upper counties . . . opposed precipitate action," but now that the question was settled, they asserted that mountaineers would rally to the cause with more verve and vigor than other Southerners. Upcountry Confederates urged Georgians to forget the anti-secession vote from the mountains in January and to have faith that highlanders had simply "clung to the flag of the Union as long as there was . . . hope that a returning sense of right in the North would save the Constitution." Once that possibility died, mountaineers wholeheartedly agreed with other Southerners that secession was the same divine right that "Old England had denied to the colonies" during the American Revolution. Mountain Confederates decried efforts to use their section's reputation for disloyalty as an excuse to keep highlanders out of sensitive military and political posts and argued that perpetuating this "tory" image of north Georgia would lead to an enervating internal division at a time when the state needed unity against its Northern enemies. One North Georgia representative to the secession convention encapsulated the impulse of many of his colleagues to defend his section. Responding to accusations of disloyalty late in 1861, after hundreds of north Georgians had proved themselves in battle, he said: "I hail from the mountains of Cherokee Georgia, and am proud of it. When down here last winter [for the secession convention] I was asked whether in the event Georgia seceded, it would be necessary to send up troops to coerce our people into acquiescence. This unpatriotic imputation has been gloriously met by . . . our hardy and valiant fighters." [37]

An interesting facet of this propaganda campaign was the way in which its creators used some mountain stereotypes to counteract others. The most frequent example was the myth of the savage, supermasculine, and combative highlander, which had first arisen during the gold rush days. North Georgians now capitalized on this image in order to defuse accusations of their disloyalty to the Confederacy, arguing they were not only loyal but also endowed by culture and temperament with fighting skills that would make them the most valuable weapons in the South's arsenal. "Where can better material be found . . . for a regiment than in Northeastern Georgia? Not even in the highlands of Scotland can furnish braver or heartier men!" argued one regional newspaper, comparing mountaineers to the supposedly "naturally" combative ethnic Scots. Other accounts portrayed mountaineers as a "hardy, brave and patriotic rural population," not too sophisticated or intelligent, but strong and loyal enough to fight for the cause.[38]

The *Dahlonega Mountain Signal* agreed and countered rumors of mountain disloyalty with images of mountain ferocity and devotion. The *Signal's* editors compared their community's recruits with the brave Appalachian riflemen of the Revolution and promised Georgia that "the past fame of our mountain boys will be maintained at their hands." The paper made the most of Lumpkin's frontier background, proudly calling one local company the "Rough Diamonds" and touting their soldiers as the "most daring and untiring devils in the army." Dahlonega propagandists emphasized the violent character of mountain life and used this as an argument for the value of mountain troops. "No company from the state is better qualified for destructiveness," boasted Lumpkin's Blue Ridge Rifles, "as they have been from their earliest boyhood used to the rifle and shut one eye when they shoot, and every time they pull the trigger a man will fall." Such depictions instantly transformed every north Georgia male into the kind of violent backwoods killer that local color artists had portrayed during the 1830s and 40s—an image that Dahlonega elites had adamantly rejected at the time in favor of the genteel, progressive society they wished to create. But in order to assure others of their allegiance to the Confederacy, Dahlonegans embraced stereotypes they had spent decades trying to suppress. This preoccupation with the mountain image, this desire to shape the way in which their society was perceived by others, would do much to determine the wartime behavior of north Georgia Confederates. Mountain rebels were at once possessed by a desire to overcome stereotypes of their region and an eagerness to manipulate the stereotypes when convenient to their cause. This duality would have bloody consequences in the years following 1861.[39]

Fannie Boyd spent the spring and summer of 1861 actively and vicariously involved in the Civil War. After the Dahlonega volunteers, including her brother Augustus, had marched out for the front in July, she followed their every move in the newspapers. She wrote Augustus encouraging letters, offering political and military opinions, advice, and moral support. Fannie was bored by school and spent as much time as possible either reading about the war or doing volunteer work with the Ladies Aid Society. In July she received a disturbing letter from an aunt in Lincolnton, to the southeast. During a town military muster, Fannie read, a drunken man had shouted that he would "fight for Lincolnton or something to that effect." Apparently, due to the man's inebriated slur, locals misinterpreted him to mean that he would fight for President Lincoln. A mob immediately took the man up, and "if it had not been that he was drinking and his friends interceded for him . . . he would have bin hung." Even though Lincolnton was far from Fannie's home, the story must have offered a chilling picture of what could happen in a divided community, where the fear of disloyalty made people consider monstrous deeds. She could not know that similar events would be happening in Lumpkin County within the year.[40]

3 / Rebels, Traitors, and Tories

LOYALTY AND COMMUNITY IN NORTH GEORGIA, 1862–1863

On January 25, 1863, Colonel George W. Lee led a mixed column of Confederate cavalry and Georgia militia into Dahlonega after a grueling week-long march from Atlanta through the cold and snow. As his tired soldiers trudged through streets of Lumpkin County's seat, Lee reflected on his mission. The colonel normally commanded the Confederate post at Atlanta and was chiefly responsible for policing the city and keeping order. But directives from Governor Joseph E. Brown and Confederate Secretary of War James A. Seddon now brought Lee out of winter quarters and into the mountains in the middle of a north Georgia winter. Lee's orders were simple. He was to "to suppress any insurrectionary movements, to capture deserters, and generally to restore tranquility to this part of the country." In short, the colonel and his troops were to coerce the loyalty of a mountain populace that many Georgians increasingly saw as treasonous. In these hills, grim divisiveness had replaced the staunch Confederate unity of 1861. Lee's troops marched in stark contrast to the local boys who had paraded proudly through town during the war's first spring.[1]

In the spring of 1861, the young men of north Georgia marched away from their homes as soldiers, committed to fight for Southern independence. In the fall of 1862, many of these volunteers came back home—with a vengeance. The Confederate Conscription Act of 1862 changed the face of north Georgia, setting off a chain of events that left highlanders more divided than ever. When the draft went into operation, many erstwhile Rebel troops from Fannin and Lumpkin counties deserted their units and flooded the familiar mountains of home, joining others who had not yet enlisted in the army and who now faced conscription. These dissenters hid in the hills, defying the state and Confederate governments as well as their secessionist neighbors. In reaction to the increasingly restive dissenters and deserters, whom locals called Tories, mountain Confederates faced a new challenge—suppressing the dissenters in their midst and retaining social order.

The years 1862–63 were volatile for the people of mountain Georgia. It was a time of preparation for the guerrilla war that burst into full fury in 1864. It was a time during which residents gathered forces, chose sides, and debated the meaning of loyalty. Secessionists and anti-Confederates alike found their allegiances tested by multilayered ties of community, region, and nation. Ultimately, neither group could escape the localism that defined their existence.

Like the vast majority of Americans in 1861, north Georgians expected a nearly bloodless war. Rarely have events so thoroughly destroyed so universal an expectation. In those first desperate, deadly battles, highlanders learned that the war would not only last longer than expected but would also test their society to the utmost.

Each of the four infantry companies from Fannin and Lumpkin counties experienced combat in the war's first two years, and in general, each unit fought effectively. The first troops to enlist from Lumpkin County, Company H, 1st Georgia Volunteer Infantry, marched to western Virginia in the summer of 1861. Its men served well but had the misfortune to fight in some of the Confederacy's early defeats, including Robert E. Lee's Cheat Mountain Campaign. Before the unit was mustered out in the spring of 1862, some of its young men were buried in Virginia towns like Winchester, Staunton, and Greenbrier. The other Lumpkin company, the "Blue Ridge Rifles," was attached to Phillips Legion, a combined infantry and cavalry unit designed to operate quickly and independently. The men of the legion took part in some of the bloodiest fighting in the Eastern Theater, including Antietam, Fredericksburg, Chancellorsville, and Gettysburg. In late 1863, elements of the unit went with James Longstreet's corps of the Army of Northern Virginia to East Tennessee to fight in the Chickamauga campaign.

The Fannin County companies raised in 1861 also saw action in the Eastern Theater during the war's first two years. After decamping from Marietta, Georgia, in the summer of 1861, Fannin's young men suffered through severe combat at the Seven Days Battles, Second Manassas, and Gettysburg. Almost a third of the county's volunteers were killed, wounded, or captured in the first two years of the war.[2]

When it became clear that the war would continue beyond initial expectations, north Georgia mobilized more of its young men to feed the Confederate war. Dahlonega attorney Weir Boyd helped organize the new 52nd Georgia Volunteer Infantry in 1862, a unit composed largely of recruits from the mountain counties. Lumpkin men made up two companies in the new regiment, assigned to the Confederacy's Army of the Tennessee. Fannin men filled out three new companies in 1862 and 1863, joining the 52nd and another new regiment, the 65th Georgia Volunteer Infantry, also assigned to the Western Theater. These units fought in East Tennessee and the Perryville campaign in Kentucky before being captured and paroled by Grant's Union army at Vicksburg in 1863. Considering north Georgia's performance on the battlefield, therefore, mountain Rebels seemed justified in their claims to Confederate patriotism. By the end of 1863, almost 60 percent of the military-age men in Fannin and Lumpkin were serving in the Confederate military, not counting those serving in the state militia.[3]

But despite north Georgia's heavy commitment to the war effort, the region did not present a united front. By 1862, highlanders were beginning to feel competing community and national pressures. For many on the home front, local problems began to assume precedence over the war effort. Some soldiers began to criticize their communities for lacking commitment to the cause; others found their concerns about community gradually overriding their nationalism. Soldiers and civilians began to factionalize into pro- and anti-Confederate camps.

To be sure, north Georgians had divided loyalties from the beginning of the secession crisis. A few had resisted the Confederacy aggressively and consistently from the outset. But such dissension was limited until the Confederate Conscription Act of 1862. "With the enforcement of this act began the oppression and exodus of the Union men of North Georgia," one Tory later recalled. The draft, and the measures adopted to enforce it, was the true catalyst for the kind of deep-seated disaffection that ultimately led to internecine guerrilla warfare in the region.[4]

Arguably the most revolutionary act the Jefferson Davis government ever took, the Conscription Act of April 1862 mandated military service of all Southern white men between the ages of eighteen and thirty-five (with the exception of vital operatives and, later, large slaveholders).

Under the act's provisions, all men in the military were bound to service for the duration of the war, regardless of the terms under which they had originally enlisted. The act provoked widespread dissension in north Georgia. Newspapers reported "unanimous . . . denunciation of *Monsieur Conscript*" and editorialized that the draft would leave "the old men, cripples, invalids women and children to till the productive lands of the upcountry." Some highland counties petitioned the governor opposing the act on these very grounds, complaining that too many able-bodied mountaineers were already in the service, leaving the crops untended and families uncared for. When north Georgia soldiers heard the rumblings of dissent from home, many reacted with indignation. "I think if they attempt [to avoid military service] they ought to be . . . considered as cowards, as enemies," wrote one Lumpkin infantryman. Another regretted hearing "of so much disaffection among the citizens at home" and promised that "desertion will soon meet its just reward." A. J. Reese remembered one former neighbor who had enthusiastically supported secession but who now was avoiding military service. "I have thought of old Isaac and how he said he was willing to shoulder his rifle anytime his country needed him and still I do not hear of [him] volunteering. We have too many such 'patriots,'" Reese noted sarcastically. Augustus Boyd, sitting in camp near Vicksburg, speculated that those who avoided military service would regret their actions. "How hard the deserter would feel in that day when the true soldier is receiving the honor that is due him."[5]

But such sentiments did not prevail among all soldiers and civilians. Many began to see local needs increasingly coming into conflict with national ones. As the war dragged on, Fannin and Lumpkin residents sent numerous petitions to the Confederate secretary of war, asking draft exemption for personnel performing vital services to the community. The petitions all had a similar ring: "Discharge John Cox . . . blacksmith for our district, for it is impossible for us to get our farming work done"; "We petition that . . . Dr. E. B. Moore be relived from service . . . there being no other physicians in this county"; "Discharge . . . Elias J. Kelly . . . we are in great need of a shoemaker in this portion of the county." Shoemaker or physician, these individuals played necessary community roles, and they were being kept from these roles by the Confederate government. Other north Georgia soldiers were receiving direct pressure from family members to leave military service and return home to their beleaguered communities. William Lyle's father repeatedly urged him to desert his state militia unit and return home to Lumpkin County, promising his son that "I could lay out about home and never be caught." And Curtis Oliver's wife wrote reminding him that "you said you was agoing to try and get a furlough to come home and cut your wheat and I want you to try . . . pretty much all the men that went from here is agoing to try."[6]

Increasingly, north Georgians did try to get home—legitimately or not. A number of factors combined to generate a massive outflow of soldiers from mountain regiments in late 1862 and 1863, but preeminent among them were soldiers' growing concerns about home and community. The draft, by keeping men away from their homes, increased the bifurcation between local and national perspectives among soldiers. In 1862 and 1863, poor weather and insufficient labor devastated the crops in north Georgia and left many civilians destitute. In the spring of 1863, Weir Boyd informed Governor Brown that Lumpkin County had a "scarcity of bread [which] is subjecting our people to great suffering . . . corn is $4 per bushel and very little to be found at that. Every nerve is stretched to the utmost tension in trying to raise subsistence." Another Lumpkin man worried that "the soldiers wives, widows, and children of this county . . . will be obliged to suffer unless some steps are taken for their welfare." A Hall County man frequently saw "one child attending to two or three more little ones and their mother working in the fields and fed on bread only." By the end of 1863, the situation was so bad that both Fannin and Lumpkin earned the dubious status of "destitute county" requiring food aid from the state government. Word that loved ones at home were suffering poverty and hunger was too much for many upcountry soldiers. As one upcountry civilian wrote, "can the authorities expect men to go into the service and remain there when they know their families are suffering for food and clothing? It is more than men can do." Another concurred, stating harshly that "it is not worth while to prosecute this war while our families are starving." Local officials tried to address this problem by affording social welfare disbursements for soldiers' families. Weir Boyd made a direct connection between home front poverty and desertion when he proposed a bill for statewide welfare payments while he served in the state legislature, writing that "under these circumstances it is hoped their will be no more desertions by Georgians."[7]

In addition, military defeat itself discouraged many mountaineers in the service. Lumpkin and Fannin troops in the Army of the Tennessee endured numerous reverses on the battlefield in 1863, contributing to

defeatism and disaffection. In the hard winter following the defeat at
Chattanooga, A. J. Reese grumbled about the loss and wished fervently
that the war would end. "Our company has bin unfortunate ever since we
came into the service," Reese complained. After the surrender of Vicksburg, many of its north Georgia defenders saw no point in continuing.
"A great disaffection arose among the Rebel soldiers," one remembered;
"there was sometimes four, six, eight, or ten wanted to go [home] in
companies from Habersham, White, and Lumpkin." One winter morning soon after Chattanooga, private Oliver Strickland awoke to find
"nearly all of the 52nd Ga. regiment is runaway and going home . . . 25
went home last night." Defeat compounded the increasing pressures calling soldiers home. Men who found it difficult to resist the urgent pleas
of destitute family members to return home felt even less sanguine about
continuing the fight when the cause seemed a losing one.[8]

Enduring defeat and worrying about problems at home, many north
Georgians did desert in 1862 and 1863. Fannin County units suffered especially high absentee rates. In 1863, the captain of Company E, 65th Georgia Infantry, resigned his commission on the grounds that his command
"was reduced by desertion to three men." In both Fannin companies of
the 65th Georgia Infantry, desertion rates exceeded 50 percent, and at
least one quarter of all Fannin men who enlisted in the army deserted
at some point during the war. Lumpkin companies, in general, suffered
much lower rates—less than 10 percent of Lumpkin soldiers deserted
during the war. But desertion was still enough of a problem in Lumpkin
units to make Augustus Boyd applaud the strict punishment of a comrade
who tried to leave the regiment in 1863. Watching the man hobble about
with a ball and chain attached to his leg, Boyd mused, "I hope he will
be a warning to all deserters." By the end of the year, resistance in the
mountains was so widespread that Governor Brown suspended the draft
in nine north Georgia counties, including Fannin and Lumpkin.[9]

When erstwhile mountain Rebels began to return home in late 1862,
they would usually band together in groups and "lay out" in the mountains, concealing themselves from conscription agents, visiting their
homesteads for hurried, secretive reunions with family and friends. Their
numbers grew so steadily that by the winter of 1863, a north Georgia editor estimated that "over one half of the men who went into the service
from the Northeastern counties were at home without leave." Regional
newspapers ran frequent advertisements listing the names of deserters
and urging the local populace to turn in the shirkers. Startlingly simi-

lar to the notices for runaway slaves, the ads described the individuals physically—"sandy hair, blue eyes"—and promised monetary rewards for their arrest or detention. Some highlanders were doubtless motivated by patriotism or pecuniary reward to help find the missing soldiers, but deserters also found many natural allies among two groups of disaffected citizens: men of military age who had not joined the army and now faced the draft, and highlanders who had been victimized in some fashion by the state or Confederate governments. These elements joined the deserters in the mountains and, together with a small number of avowed Unionists, formed the basis of the Tory opposition to the Confederacy in the mountains.[10]

Fannin and Lumpkin counties had mobilized most of their men of military age, but almost 45 percent of white men between eighteen and forty-five years of age were still at home in 1863. With the draft law in effect, one observer noted, "a scattering out of boys" who intended to avoid military service began hiding in the nearby mountains. Others resorted to more drastic measures. When the conscription agents came into Ennos Brown's neighborhood in the mountains of Towns County, Georgia, the man reportedly cut off his big toe with an ax, to make him less palatable as cannon fodder. (He was drafted anyway, but this did not keep some other mountaineers from resorting to self-mutilation to escape the army.) Draft dodgers—the term is modern, but accurate—could be quite persistent and determined. Some, captured and recaptured by conscription agents, deserted again at the first opportunity. Others endured imprisonment, only to escape with the help of family or fellow Tories. Still others consented to the draft physically but refused to do so psychologically. When Robert Woody was arrested at his home in north Georgia and forced into the service, he refused to swear the requisite oath to the Confederacy, substituting instead a defiant "so help me God I won't!" This kind of dogged resistance caused Huldah Fain of Gilmer County to wonder if mountain women alone possessed the power to shame the malcontents into obedience. "I think if it were left to the ladies they would take them [the deserters] up."[11]

Solomon Stansbury's story illustrates the practical, generally nonideological motivations of most north Georgia draft evaders. Stansbury had migrated to north Georgia from Tennessee in the 1850s, settling along Hot House Creek, just across the state line in what would become Fannin County. Like many of his neighbors, Stansbury looked to Tennessee, not Georgia, for his livelihood. In the decade before the war he made a rather lucrative living manufacturing and providing charcoal to the Ducktown Copper Mines, and by 1860 he owned a 200-acre farm worth over $4,000—he was a prosperous yeoman farmer. Stansbury's neighbors recalled that "before and at the commencement of the war [he was] a rebel sympathizer," but his patriotism dimmed when he was called upon to make personal sacrifices for the cause. Stansbury did not enlist in the army, and when conscription agents knocked on his door he claimed exemption on the grounds that he performed vital services to the Ducktown mine and, by extension, the Confederate war effort. His pleas went unheard, and in 1863 conscription agents arrested him and escorted him down from the mountains of Fannin to Atlanta, where authorities kept him imprisoned for a month. Stansbury finally gained release through the personal intercession of J. E. Raht, the superintendent of the Ducktown mine, who had paternalistic concern for his operatives and who wrestled with Richmond throughout the war to keep his workers exempt from conscription. Solomon Stansbury had earned a temporary reprieve from the army, but he was permanently soured on the Confederacy. He began speaking out publicly against conscription and urged his neighbors "to stay home and take care of their families" instead of submitting to the draft. (Stansbury appears to have suffered from a congenital obstreperousness. At least once before the war broke out, he was sued for "uttering slanderous words.") He soon became a leading Tory in Fannin County and played an important role in the guerrilla war that erupted a year later.[12]

What motivated people like Solomon Stansbury to resist the Confederacy? The loose collection of deserters, dissenters, and Unionists who flooded the mountains of north Georgia had various rationales for their behavior; but they are difficult to analyze because so few anti-Confederates left contemporaneous records explaining their beliefs. However, in the years following the Civil War, many former Tories testified in lengthy depositions before the federal government's Southern Claims Commission, set up to evaluate the claims of Southern Unionists for reparations stemming from the war. An analysis of the north Georgia claims reveals that multiple motives applied. A handful expressed avowedly pro-Union ideas, hid runaway slaves, and even fled the state to enlist in the Union army. The vast majority, however, were little concerned with the Union or slavery and were too focused upon their communities to consider defecting. Most simply felt the Confederacy was an intrusion and a threat to local autonomy. Those whom the secessionists branded

Tories all shared basic concerns with community, family, and local justice. The Confederacy's perceived infringements upon all three were the roots of dissent in upcountry Georgia.

Conscription was the most obvious threat to community autonomy, a direct example of the central government reaching into the household and seizing men for service on far-flung fields. Because the Richmond government took direct control of the draft, conscription agents were often seen as outsiders intruding upon the community. Some conscription agents added to this negative image with their ruthless fervor, hunting down men with hounds, jailing people summarily, and dragging captives in chains through public streets. One dissenter later remembered that "Conscript officers were everywhere, making arrests . . . holding drumhead courts, and driving whole neighborhoods of the Union men along the highways and through mountain passes and streams, to the nearest conscript station or camp, there to be enrolled, arbitrarily, in some organization . . . the selection of which they were not . . . permitted to have the slightest choice." In Gilmer County, a Confederate official named Spregg acted with single-minded fury to force one Jeff Miller into the service. When Miller escaped from prison, Spregg took the deserter's two sisters as hostages, threatening to jail the whole family if Miller did not turn himself in by the next day. By attacking the deserter's vulnerable sisters, Spregg and by extension the Confederacy were making war on the family itself. Some families tried to resist this intrusion and maintain the integrity of the household at all costs. Mothers and fathers went to great lengths to keep their sons out of the army, hiding them in the mountains, pleading with conscription agents, and writing to state or national authorities to ask for clemency. Sometimes parents took great personal risks to free children from the military, sneaking into the mountains and avoiding the omnipresent patrols to supply their sons with food and clothing. One Lumpkin County man sheltered his two deserter sons in his home and openly defied conscription agents sent to gather up the boys, saying "he would shoot anybody that tried to arrest his sons." Martha Ledbetter forged birth documents to convince military officials that her son was too young to be drafted. James Wilson made a dangerous trek across the north Georgia mountains to a Confederate military post in Tennessee to seek the release of his son, then imprisoned for draft evasion. Wilson's attempt was successful, but not without cost—his son was released, and he himself was forced to take his son's place in the army. But for many north Georgia parents, these risks were worthwhile to keep families intact.[13]

In addition to conscription, dissenters objected to the increasingly voracious demands of the Confederate government upon private property and resources. By 1863, Richmond had resorted to impressment and tax-in-kind policies to sustain the army. The impressment laws allowed designated agents to seize needed supplies from citizens with minimal compensation, while tax-in-kind obligated farmers to give one-tenth of their produce and livestock to the government. Now north Georgians had to fear more agents of the central authority eager to extract even more from the community. Between losing their crops and their sons, highlanders had sacrificed much to the war. It was a sacrifice many were unwilling to bear. Conscription, impressment, tax-in-kind, were all material drains upon mountain families, and these policies increased the daily strain to survive. But dissenters did not oppose these intrusions on the grounds of simple economic self-interest. They perceived the centralizing impulses of the Richmond government as a direct assault upon the community. Men who were needed at home were taken away. Crops and livestock that had once been used to serve the community were now extracted for the army's use. At base, dissenters saw these actions as violations of common justice, and they considered the agents of the Confederacy to be lawless brigands preying upon the helpless. As one north Georgian put it simply: "I became embittered against [the Confederates] because they robbed me."[14]

Such convictions had substance. By 1863, impressment officials were acting aggressively in the mountains, and some took Richmond's new policies as a license to plunder at will. For one local Unionist, it seemed as though "a veritable reign of terror prevailed. . . . The homes of these people were repeatedly plundered by armed bands, calling themselves soldiers, and the defenseless women and children were often reduced to conditions of extreme suffering." North Georgia civilians accused agents and troops of taking livestock and crops without remuneration, breaking into homes, and stealing personal belongings. Soldiers looted smokehouses, took horses and saddles, and emptied corncribs. One farmer was forced to watch as a group of Confederate soldiers parked a wagon in his cornfield and piled it high with his harvest. Another recalled that rapacious agents "almost stripped my people of everything." Confronting impressment agents could be a harrowing experience for a household, as one mountaineer found out one day when agents and soldiers entered his home looking for booty. "Taking and destroying everything in the place did not satiate them . . . but the fiends must literally strip and ill treat my children mere infants, my eldest boy but six years old, took the hat off his head and the shoes from his feet." Experiences like this were all the more frightening because civilians did not know where the boundaries of legality lay in the transformed environment of war. As one highlander asked in a plaintive letter to Governor Brown, "suppose a forage master . . . comes without an order? Would it be safe to resist him and how far would resistance be justified? I also wish to know what is a legal order? What officer must issue it?" In his search for answers, this north Georgian illustrated a growing conviction in the region that the Confederacy was transgressing the limits of the law.[15]

Impressment agents often justified their actions by claiming their victims were in some way disloyal to the Confederacy. When one mountaineer objected to the looting of his house, the officer in command stated that "I was a tory and they had a right to take stock or anything else from them sort." Another upcountry woman recalled that soldiers left her neighbors' houses untouched, but ransacked her farm because it was known that she had tried to keep her son out of the Confederate army. Impressment authorities thus put dissenters beyond the pale of civilized treatment, justifying illegality toward them on grounds of disloyalty.[16]

Obviously, impressment hit the poor the hardest, since they had fewer surplus goods to offer the state, and issues of class certainly prevailed in Tory thinking. Some dissenting highlanders directly connected their fate to their poverty and the unequal distribution of wealth and power symbolized in the slave system. A Union County dissenter thus explained his resistance to the Confederacy by stating "we had no land or Negroes to fight for." In Hall County, John Bryson complained to the governor in 1862 that "our county haint no slaves to tend our farms. You have slaves to help you. Please look to the poor class of people as well as the wealthy." However, class was not always a determinative factor in establishing loyalty. Many of the poorest north Georgians volunteered enthusiastically for the Confederate army. By the same token, some of the upcountry's most active dissenters were wealthy slaveholders—in Fannin County, for example, affluent elites like William C. Fain, James Parks, and William Umphrey led the anti-Confederates.[17]

The important point is that many mountaineers saw the Confederacy's policies as essentially illegal. In the name of secession, authorities invaded homes and violated the sanctity of property and family. The traditional arbiters of law and order—constables, soldiers, government officials— had transformed into brutal agents of state-sponsored terrorism. Even some pro-Confederates realized the dangerous implications of the impressment policy. One north Georgia secessionist asserted that "these seizures are not impressments. Impressment is a legal power of the government. . . . Any other violent seizure without legal warrant is robbery." He warned that this "cruel oppression" created a "profound sense of injustice and injury" among the populace that could lead to widespread disaffection.[18]

Sion Darnell summarized this state-as-criminal rhetoric perfectly. Darnell was a north Georgian who opposed the Confederacy and who eventually joined the Union army in 1864. In a postwar speech to the Grand Army of the Republic, Darnell told the story of mountaineers like himself and compiled a long list of Confederate transgressions to justify his Unionism, including such crimes as "robbery, plunder, and destruction." He charged that the Confederate authorities had known no law but "the law of force," and that "those who exercised authority in the region appeared to have lost all sense of reason and humanity."[19] Tories like Darnell found motivation for resistance in the belief that his enemies had violated citizens' fundamental rights to legal protection by (and from) their government. When the Confederacy abandoned these protections, it lost legitimacy. For the deserters and others who dissented from the Confederacy, the Southern military represented a destabilizing force that disrupted communities, abused authority, and violated common understandings of justice. These feelings of the illegitimacy of Confederate authority drove dissenters to increasingly violent resistance as the war continued.

Therefore, it is clear that north Georgia's Tories were driven to resist in reaction to the policies of the Confederate government. What does not appear in the records is any strong evidence of ideological Unionism among the dissenters. Just as a vote against secession in 1861 did not necessarily delineate unconditional pro-Union sentiment, the desertion, draft evasion, and resistance of 1862 and 1863 were not a comprehensive demonstration of any well-defined commitment to the abstract ideals to which so many Northerners subscribed. Although a few "unconditional Unionists" doubtless inhabited north Georgia's mountains, it seems evident that dissent sprang from less philosophical, more contingent causes.

Again, the Southern Claims Commission records are instructive. When in the 1870s diligent commissioners sought to quantify the loyalty of thousands of Southerners asking for restitution, they devised a comprehensive questionnaire designed to force claimants to explain and substantiate their Unionism. The answers that north Georgians provided to these questions reveal mostly a profound alienation from the Confederacy and a preoccupation with local conditions among the former Tories.

To be sure, some highlanders expressed deep-seated Unionist sentiments to the federal investigators. One insisted that at the beginning of the war he steadfastly opposed his Confederate neighbors on the grounds that he "wanted the government of his fathers and of Washington." Another echoed these sentiments, saying that "his fore fathers had fought for his independence and he would never fight against the United States." A few claimed to have spoken out in favor of Lincoln's election—one recalled saying to neighbors that if the Southerners would "let Lincoln alone and he would have made a good a president as we ever had." Some mountaineers even claimed antislavery credentials. Pinckney Howell of Murray County said he was something of a closet abolitionist during the war and had supported the Emancipation Proclamation. His neighbors substantiated his claims, telling investigators that Pinckney was "opposed to human slavery and always said he wanted the slaves free" and colonized in Africa.[20]

However, such statements were relatively rare and often smacked of invention (after all, these people were trying to convince the federal government to give them money). Other accounts ring truer and speak to a pervasive but ill-defined disaffection with the Confederacy rather than a commitment to the Federal cause. When asked for proof of her Unionism, one upcountry woman responded not with patriotic rhetoric but with the simple story of how she had petitioned to have her son released from the Confederate army. "I did this because I was opposed to his fighting for a cause I believed to be unjust, and I regarded this as doing a service to the Union," she recalled. Other claimants said their "Unionism" consisted of joining the home guard so they would not have to enlist in the Confederate army. "If I had not gotten an easy position [in the militia,] I would have deserted," one such claimant asserted. Others confessed that they had been effectively neutral during the hostilities, but they still interpreted this as Unionism. When asked what he had done to actively support the United States during the war, Moses Simpson answered honestly: "I don't know I did anything for the Union cause . . . but I know I did nothing against it" (such simple truth probably cost Simpson his claim).[21]

Even if they had been ideologically Unionist, social pressures constrained north Georgians from expressing or following up on such beliefs. As more than one claimant remembered, "Confederate laws were rigidly enforced and it was dangerous for people to talk against the war . . . the country was in a state of terror." Another Unionist asserted that dissenters were "given over to public hatred and, in many cases, public vengeance. There was not only no liberty of speech, but the very THOUGHTS of men must . . . be suppressed." Public pressure to conform extended to the pulpit as well, as one mountaineer recalled that "Ministers of the Gospel were regarded as disloyal to the cause of the Confederacy if they refused to pray for its success. And they were required to do more than that. They were expected to make fervent and persistent supplication to a throne of divine grace for the destruction of the Union Armies and the government for which they fought." Women dissenters also deferred speaking out because of the strong pre-existing social prejudices against females being involved openly in political issues of any kind. Martha Ledbetter eschewed public events such as meetings and barbecues and insisted that she was "a quiet woman" who "knew but little of politics."

Rebels whipping a man for expressing Union sentiments. (Page 274.)

Anti-Confederate Tories in north Georgia suffered harassment, intimidation, and assault from the Confederate power structure during the Civil War. (From William Gannaway Brownlow, *Sketches of the Rise, Progress, and Decline of Secession: With a Narrative of Personal Adventures among the Rebels.* Philadelphia, George W. Childs, 1862, p. 168)

Susan Davis, a widow living near Dahlonega, echoed these sentiments, stating that as a noncombatant, she had no "political sympathies." Finally, some dissenters were restrained by a real sense of community with their secessionist neighbors. Susan Davis may have lacked political sympathies, but she did claim that "her natural sympathies were with those of my neighbors who were suffering." James Baily concurred, stating that even though he privately rejoiced at the news of Union military victories, "I had sympathy for my friends in the South." [22]

What does come through in dissenters' testimony is an abiding war-weariness that superseded political or ideological belief. When asked to re-create their wartime state of mind, dissenters invariably responded with statements like: "my feelings and sentiments were opposed to the war"; "the war was wrong"; "I thought it [the war] would ruin us." These people, like many Americans in 1863, were simply tired of the privations and violence of war. To the extent that they blamed the Confederacy for bringing on hostilities and for victimizing its own people, the dissenters can be called anti-Confederates—but not "Unionist" in the strictest sense. For north Georgians, "Unionism" could mean pacifism, defeatism, self-interest, or neutrality. But rarely did it mean a philosophical commitment to the ideals of national unity, free labor, or anti-slavery. A later generation of observers would try to transform the image of the Civil War mountaineer into that of the simple, loyal backwoodsman, mystically attached to the Stars and Stripes and the legacy of Washington, Jefferson, and Jackson. The Southern Claims Commission agents who interviewed these people in the 1870s knew better. [23]

Not all north Georgians grew to oppose the Confederacy. Many, perhaps most, continued to call themselves secessionists and supported the war effort through 1863 and beyond. What motivated these mountaineers? What role did they see themselves playing in the war effort, and how did they perceive their enemies? Mountain Rebels were more firmly connected to broader political and economic trends than the Tories, but still interpreted the war through a localistic framework. Many continued to believe in the rhetoric of states' rights and proslavery. Residents of commercial towns like Dahlonega linked their economic and political interests with the Rebellion and sought to maintain close ties with state and national authorities. Upcountry Rebels were indignant about their region's reputed Unionism and went to great lengths to prove their adherence to secession by serving in the armed forces and supporting the war on the home front. But a strong undercurrent of localism always underlay Confederate nationalism in the mountain counties. Even as they offered fealty to Joe Brown and Jefferson Davis, highlanders who called themselves Confederates also worried about the growing instability on the home front and came to see their primary goal as defending the local order. These local objectives were not separate from their Confederate identity, but part of a conglomeration of interests and allegiances that bound highland Rebels to the cause.

North Georgia mobilized much of its populace in support of the war effort in the first two years of the war. By 1863, most of the men of Fannin and Lumpkin were in the military, fighting on fields from Mississippi to Pennsylvania. Indeed, during 1862 and 1863, many of these soldiers strove solidly to maintain the Confederacy. For many of them, patriotism and ideological commitment to states' rights and slavery were powerful and sustaining motivators. An analysis of the writings of north Georgia soldiers partially substantiates the theory of Civil War scholars such as James McPherson, who argue that American soldiers of the 1860s fought for deeply held ideas. Many of north Georgia's fighting men performed their duty to the Confederacy according to nineteenth-century expectations of manhood, and most civilians acted out supportive roles.[24]

Lumpkin County soldiers wrote passionately about their patriotism in their early letters home, expressing pride in the Confederate cause and assuring their families of their commitment to victory. A. J. Reese, a private in the Blue Ridge Rifles, wrote his aunt early in 1862, saying that even though "a great many of us would like to be at home," he devoutly supported the cause. "If [we] have to sacrifice the lives of many of our best and most dear friends let [us] do it. It is better to die freemen than live as slaves," Reese exclaimed. Other north Georgia soldiers echoed the rhetoric of their national political figures and reiterated the political arguments of the secession crisis. One wrote that "I offered my life as a sacrifice for my country's defense and I am sure that cause is just," adding, in the language of the fire-eaters, or proslavery extremists, "I don't think I can ever reconcile myself to live under black republican government."[25]

Neither did this commitment necessarily fade after the first taste of battle. A year of campaigning in Virginia did leave A. J. Reese a bit more sober, and in late 1862 he confessed that "I would be glad to see this war come to a close. I have seen enough of fighting to do me." Still, Reese seemed willing to continue the sacrifice and boasted that although "The Yankees seem hard to convince that we intend to be free," the enemy would "find out in the end that the subjugation of the South is not as easy a thing as they suppose. It is costing us dearly but it only makes our men more determined to live freemen or die fighting."[26]

These same sentiments motivated Weir Boyd to leave the comfort of home in 1862 for the battlefield. Boyd had observed the first year of war from the sidelines, dividing his time between his farm, his law practice, and the state legislature in Milledgeville. But even though the Dahlonega attorney was eager for the war to end and "for peace to prevail," he was no pacifist. "I have concluded the best way to bring [the war] to a close is to convince the Lincoln government that we are all ready to fly to arms in defense of the country. Therefore, I have obtained leave to raise a regiment in North Eastern Georgia," he told his daughter. Together with James Jefferson Findley, another Dahlonega lawyer and home-front leader, Boyd marched off to war that spring. Boyd's son, Augustus, who was already in the service, shared his father's nationalism. When he proudly recounted for his sister Fannie his first test in battle, he professed that his resolute faith in the Rebel cause had bolstered his courage. "The shells fell as thick as hail, several of our boys were knocked down," Augustus recollected, but he insisted that "I was not in the least frightened. I went into the fight as cool as I am now. . . . I knew that if I fell that I was not the only one that had fallen in defense of their country." Even while lying in the miserable trenches around Vicksburg in 1863, the younger Boyd continued to cleave to Southern honor and Confederate patriotism. "I will still keep fighting until we gain our independence," he wrote soon after the Battle of Chickasaw Bluffs, "and if I fall I will die in a glorious cause." And if the Confederacy did by chance lose the war, Boyd concluded, "no one can point his finger at me and say that I never done my duty."[27]

But north Georgia soldiers felt as bound by localism as they did nationalism. A powerful web of relationships and loyalties connected them to their communities and intruded upon their every thought and action. Like soldiers throughout time, north Georgians constantly asked for community gossip, inquired about the crops, and requested information about siblings, parents, and sweethearts. Underlying this common concern with the mundane detail of home life lay a pervasive interest in community affairs that was inseparable from other loyalties. Soldiers evinced this in extensive letters home in which they actively engaged in local issues. Benjamin Sitton, a Lumpkin County private serving in Virginia, did not let military concerns keep him from inserting himself into local politics in Dahlonega. He wrote long letters from the front to colleagues back home seeking to mobilize political support for increased school funding, urging his friends to lobby the town for higher teacher salaries. Another north Georgia soldier spent his spare time collecting on debts owed to his family by his fellow soldiers, and kept meticulous records on those in arrears. While serving as colonel of the 52nd Georgia, Weir Boyd spent almost as much time managing his Dawson County farm long-distance as he did seeing to his troops. Conversely, when home on sick leave, Boyd tried to run his command via the mails, dashing off notes to his subordinates regarding promotions and other military issues. Men like Boyd were never fully at home or fully in the field—their duties were inextricably intertwined. Indeed, for many, national and local duties were one and the same, at least early in the war. Thus, when one Lumpkin County soldier wrote his family in 1862, he cast his patriotism in terms of home and family. "I still intend to do my duty and never disgrace that family of my good and noble parents," he stated. Soldiers' letters manifested a transcendent concern with the home front that sometimes complemented, and sometimes complicated, their allegiances to the army and the Confederate Republic.[28]

Pro-Confederate civilians possessed the same dualistic loyalties. On the one hand, those who stayed at home were committed to the Confederate nation. Just as Ida Hamilton had promised in her speech to Dahlonega's departing troops in 1861, the women and men who remained at home identified with the soldiers and the cause for which they fought, and performed the vital supportive duties required by the state and central governments. In towns like Dahlonega, where commercial ties encouraged residents to look outward, people linked their fate to that of Georgia and the Confederacy. Every domestic chore took on broader significance, as women knitted socks and made uniforms and packaged food for their soldiers. Church sermons, friendly discussions, and idle gossip naturally focused upon the war. Civilians praised or damned national political and military figures in their correspondence and speculated about the intentions of the enemy and the proper dispositions of Confederate troops.[29] Civilians participated substantively and vicariously in the war effort. In Dahlonega, Fannie Boyd eagerly followed military and political news, rejoicing after Confederate victories, stoically accepting defeats, and criticizing her neighbors' flagging patriotism. She determined to leave school so that she could contribute to the Ladies Aid Society full time. "I don't expect to see the inside of a school room this year," she wrote with solemn pride, "duty points another way." Like many women strongly committed to the war effort, Fannie fantasized about being allowed to fight the enemy herself. "If the Yankees get all over the Confederacy, then they will learn what trouble is," she wrote, "for the women and children will have a chance to hurt them and they will soon be glad to let us alone."[30]

But even civilians who deemed themselves loyal Confederates often felt conflicted when local conditions loomed larger than national events. Although they supported the war effort, they felt that Richmond had lost sight of what it owed to the communities it claimed to defend. When he heard rumors of another draft beginning, a loyal Confederate in Union County wrote that "if this be done the people must starve for there is not enough men left," and he urged authorities to see that "these upper counties have done their duty manfully" already. When Weir Boyd asked a Lumpkin County colleague to enlist in his regiment, the man declined on the grounds that "I can be of more service to my distressed country at home." Increasingly, mountain Rebels requested that they be allowed to serve their country closer to their communities. The commander of a recently formed Fannin County regiment asked "if we would . . . be permitted to occupy some position in the Western part of Georgia or on the Tennessee line" because his men "would much prefer that location as being nearer their homes." And when the officers of a Fannin County militia unit heard that they were about to be drafted into Confederate service in 1863, they insisted that their current duties were vital to the Confederacy. "We . . . have taken up nine deserters and . . . sent them to their command at Knoxville," they noted proudly, suggesting that they be allowed to continue serving the Confederacy in their own, localistic manner. A north Georgia woman melded her local and national loyalties in a letter to Governor Brown: "I am a poor lone woman. I have two sons in the Confederate service. . . . I am about out of means. I thought I would ask you . . . to help me to some money. Fifty dollars would do me. I think the government [ought] to help me . . . I done a great deal of work making clothing for the soldiers [helping] the fight for liberty in our country."[31] This mountain woman asserted her loyalty to the Confederacy by offering concrete evidence of her patriotism—her sons and her sewing. She also expressed a fundamental belief in a social contract, by which central authority owed assistance to localities in return for their support.

Perhaps the ultimate example of mountain Rebels' bifurcated allegiances was the changing behavior of its elite men as the war progressed. In Fannin and Lumpkin counties, planters, lawyers, and professional men had taken the lead in forming and leading companies in 1861 and 1862. Elijah Chastain, the wealthy Fannin lawyer who had been so instrumental in securing the mountain counties for secession, served as colonel in the 1st Georgia Volunteer Infantry. Other Fannin elites, such as attorney William A. Campbell and merchant Stephen C. Dobbs, also enlisted early. In Lumpkin County, Weir Boyd and James Jefferson Findley left their Dahlonega law practices to become officers in the 52nd Georgia regiment in 1862. But by the end of 1862, all these men, and many others, had resigned their commissions and returned home. Some, like Boyd and Campbell, served in state or local government. Others, like Dobbs and Findley, assumed control of local militia forces in north Georgia. This outflow of Confederate officers evinced the shifting priorities of secessionist elites as the war began to impact the home front more directly. Increasingly, upcountry Rebels saw the community's interests intertwined with the nation's. Thus, when James Jefferson Findley left Confederate service to command local militia, he had two missions: to provide "for the defence of the people against Disloyalists" and to fight in support of Confederate Army of the Tennessee. For Findley and his men, the balance must have seemed about right—"when not needed to repel raids or stop robbing in their own section, or for an emergency in aid of [Confederate] General Hood's operations, they will remain at home in the discharge of their ordinary business." [32]

Why would these men abandon prestigious military careers during wartime to assume less glorious roles as municipal functionaries? Several factors pulled these men homeward. Many of these officers were slaveholders, and the growing strains upon the slave system generated anxiety for the stability of the household and community. From the very beginning of the conflict, the paternalistic system enforcing slavery was in crisis. Slaves were, of course, immediately aware of the conflict and the disorder it wrought within the white power structure. Indeed, with masters and overseers gone off to war, the traditional lines of authority on the plantation were weakened. When Mollie Tate's master left for the Confederate army, he told his slaves to look after his wife and children. This must have seemed a peculiar role reversal—masters were supposed to protect and care for their own families, not to depend on their slaves for this duty. For many slaves, the war broadened their horizons and gave them a glimpse of life beyond their homes. Stephen Connelly of Murray County took an epic buggy ride from north Georgia into Tennessee to help fetch back two of his master's sons from the battlefield. As Union forces approached, other mountain blacks were sent away from their farms to hide in the mountains, where they fended for themselves without white supervision. This loosening of the geographic ties that normally bound the slave to the home location further disrupted the system. Even those who did not move from home found their lives altered. Slaves cautiously took advantage of the situation to lighten workloads, ignore tasks, resist orders, and even run away. Rumors of slave violence increased, and whites grew increasingly fearful of their enslaved population. In one mountain community, four of the wealthiest local slave owners died violent, mysterious deaths during the course of the war, and slaves were reportedly involved in at least some of the killings. And in Habersham County, in northeast Georgia, local whites claimed to have discovered "a hellish plot among the negroes." The ringleaders were captured and tortured into revealing the plan before it could be carried out, but the terror within the white community was irreversible.[33]

Residents of Lumpkin County, with its relatively high slave population, were especially vulnerable to these concerns. Weir Boyd did not own any slaves, but he hired some and agreed to temporarily house others who belonged to friends. With both Weir and Augustus Boyd gone to the army, Fannie Boyd frequently wrote worried letters asking for guidance and complaining about having to house and care for slaves. The absence of patriarchal control on the plantation caused Boyd's father-in-law to complain to the secretary of war on Weir's behalf: "He has no man on his place. He has eight hands and volunteered for the war." Some masters tried to resolve this problem by taking some of their slaves with them to the front. Tom Singleton, a Lumpkin County slave, went to war with his master: "I waited on him, cooked for him, an' went on de scout march wid him, for to tote his gun, an' see atter his needs. I wuz a bugger in dem days!" But this did not assuage white fears. Another soldier from Dahlonega, A. J. Reese, found his body servant Henry a constant source of worry. A few months after going off to war, Reese asserted that military life did not agree with Henry. "I wrote uncle that I didn't want Henry any more. . . . I think the service will ruin him. I think it advisable to sell him." Reese's aunt and uncle worried about Henry, too, especially as military service brought him into contact with Union soldiers and with his family in Tennessee. "I fear he will run away from you now he has got so near his wife," Mrs. Wimpy mused. Indeed, Mrs. Wimpy had cause to worry, and about matters even closer to home. Only a few months after she wrote her nephew, three slaves ran away from Alston plantation along

Shoal Creek. They eventually made to freedom behind the Union lines. Thus, realistic concerns over the viability of the slave system doubtless caused many highland elites to see their duties to the Confederacy in a more localistic light.[34]

But an even more important reason why men like Boyd, Findley, and Chastain left the battlefield was the growing conviction that the real war was not in Virginia or Tennessee, but raging at home in north Georgia. By late 1862, the Georgia mountains brimmed with deserters and dissenters. Armed Tory bands roamed the countryside, subsisting off the land, looting farms, stealing weapons, terrorizing pro-Confederates. This enemy posed a more direct threat to the community than the Union army did in 1862. For mountain elites, preserving law and order was paramount, the first line of defense of the Confederacy. For this reason, they returned home in 1862 to find not peace, but a new brand of warfare.[35]

A rhetoric of law and order permeated Confederate highlanders' statements and writings. In Fannin County and especially in Lumpkin County, secessionists labeled dissenters as anarchists and common criminals who willfully defied legitimate authority and used the war as a pretext to prey upon the helpless. In letters to Governor Brown, secessionists portrayed a battle in north Georgia between the forces of stability and legal authority and those of revolution and criminality. In Lumpkin County, Josiah Woody reported that a "line of robbers extends from Rabun County to the west of the Cohutta Mountains." Equating dissenters with criminals, Woody lumped all the disaffected into three synonymous categories: "tories and deserters and thieves." The main sin of those Woody called "Union men" was their lawlessness. Woody reported that "they are robbing soldiers families. They broke open many houses and stole rifle guns and money and clothes and provisions to a great extent and the soldiers wives . . . and even ministers of the gospel have been threatened and badly abused." Most frightening was the fact that the Tories seemed to rejoice in their outlaw activity. "The tories . . . says they will do as they please, for there is no law nor men to keep them from living better than they ever did." Other mountain Confederates repeated these charges. James Findley's brother Walter said the Gilmer County Tories were "killing and destroying the beef cattle . . . taken off what they could carry, leaving the rest for buzzard fowl." Elijah Chastain wrote that Fannin's Tories were imitating the organized thievery that impressment officers had previously visited upon them. "They are [raiding] . . . every night, 'pressing' as they term it, every gun that can be found."[36]

Confederates worried chiefly about the impact of these criminal assaults upon families and emphasized the victimization of women and children. Letters and reports were filled with tragic images of lawless Tories preying upon helpless dependents, abusing the weak whose fathers, brothers, and sons were in the army and unable to offer protection. A group of Blairsville secessionists feared that "all the mountain region will be overrun and our crops destroyed and our women and children brought to destruction," while a Gainesville man begged the governor for soldiers "for protecting the women and children." Josiah Woody in Lumpkin County put the matter starkly: "In behalf of defenseless women and children . . . to whom shall we look for protection but the Governor?" Just as dissenters opposed the destructive impact of impressment and conscription upon the family, so too secessionists feared for families' stability in the face of Tory raids.[37]

Some Confederates understood the commonalties between Tories' actions and the lawless actions of their own government. Although these individuals remained loyal to the Confederacy, they did question the policies of impressment and the draft. One Lumpkin County militia officer reacted angrily when Confederate troops came through his neighborhood in 1863, "stealing everything they can get their hands on." He asked the governor to send him some "pamphlets on the law" to distribute to the visitors and remind them of proper behavior. Huldah Fain, a Rebel woman in Gilmer County, felt that impressment encouraged the lawlessness of the Tories by teaching the poor that thievery was justifiable. When hungry women rioted in the streets of Milledgeville, looting stores and shops, Fain was not surprised. If the state legitimized seizing private goods for the war effort, how could authorities criticize needy women for taking food and goods? "I don't believe in 'pressing' unless suffering," Fain wrote, "[but] then I say take if it is to be had." Thus, the implications of impressment came home to roost.[38]

But despite these doubts, most upcountry Confederates argued that the Tories presented the chief threat to law and order in north Georgia. The question was how to handle the dissenters. For the first few years of the war, mountain secessionists generally eschewed extralegal violence against their "criminal" enemies and tried to adhere to the formal channels of protest and peacekeeping afforded by the law. Even if the Tories were outlaws, they had to be dealt with according to the due process of the law. Highland Confederates bombarded the governor's office with requests that he delineate the "proper" treatment of dissenters, insisting all the while that communities would observe strict legal proprieties when dealing with alleged traitors. Even Josiah Woody, who wrote panicked letters to Governor Brown reporting on the "deserters and thieves" in Lumpkin, worried that some of his Rebel compatriots were getting over-zealous in their approach to the Tories. "The good people of this section have in many places formed mob crowds and have taken up the Union men and made them take the oath of allegiance," Woody noted with concern. "It is right to make them take the oath, but I have doubted the propriety of forming mobs. Let us have a legal organization, and all we do let it be lawful and right." While Confederates feared Tory lawlessness, they remained committed to prewar legal procedure when dealing with their enemies during the first two years of the war. Indeed, north Georgia secessionists would never totally abandon a certain legalistic pretense, even after the stress of war gradually eroded the boundaries between the legal and the extralegal.[39]

Therefore, upcountry Rebels acted out of a complex combination of overlapping beliefs and allegiances. To a greater degree than the anti-Confederates, they focused outward and oriented themselves toward broader political and economic trends. They consistently professed Confederate patriotism even when facing the rigors of combat. Historians who see Confederate nationalism and ideology as durable motivating forces can find much supportive evidence in the behavior of Fannin and Lumpkin secessionists. However, even though mountain Rebels seemed firmly committed to the Southern polity, they never stopped being a part of their communities, never totally subsumed localism into nationalism. For the first two years of the war, these two forces complemented each other rather well. But as the war dragged on, Confederates increasingly saw the two come into conflict, and they would have to work harder to reconcile the growing dichotomy in interests and loyalties.

The year 1863 was a time of shocks in Fannin and Lumpkin counties. A series of events disrupted communities and destabilized the political and social order. Growing Tory activity prompted invasion by Confederate troops sent to reestablish order, an intrusion that outraged dissenters and offended the honor of local Rebels. A series of trials brought anti-Confederates to the bar of justice to answer for the "crime" of dissension. Finally, disloyalty and rumors of disloyalty caused a virtual witch hunt in Fannin County, targeting anyone tainted with charges of disloyalty. These events evinced the growing divisions among north Georgians and served as a watershed that determined a more violent course of events in the future. As a result, the region was much closer to internal civil warfare at the beginning of 1864 than it had been a year earlier.

In January 1863, the Confederate States of America seemed as viable as ever. Bloody repulses of Union troops at Fredericksburg and Murfreesboro and initially at Vicksburg kept Southern military hopes alive, while Jefferson Davis's mobilization policies seemed to be maximizing Southern resources. But in north Georgia, Confederates had much to worry about. In Fannin and Lumpkin counties, anti-Confederate bands roamed the hills, stealing weapons, food, and livestock and occasionally ambushing conscription and impressment agents. The draft was largely moribund, and pro-Confederate civilians began to fear for their property and their personal security.

In the hills near Dahlonega, Confederates reported during that winter, "an armed band exists mustering 50 who have deserted from the army . . . openly proclaiming to resist the laws . . . and threaten[ing] to burn our village." Sometime around New Year's Day, the band burned the shop of a local secessionist named Perry and fired rifles into his house. Another squad of dissenters set fire to the home of Confederate minister Josiah Woody the following week, and Woody's own brother was arrested inside the city limits of Dahlonega scouting out the site of the prison for a planned jailbreak to free the draft-dodging inmates. The Tories evidently intended to emulate a recent raid in nearby White County, in which 40 Tories attacked the Cleveland jail to free a deserter. Dahlonegans had reason to fear such activity, for six months earlier a group of Tories had broken into the Lumpkin County jail and freed Jefferson Anderson, a violent criminal and deserter who now victimized secessionists throughout the region.[40]

In Fannin County, Confederates felt besieged. The secessionists were weaker in the border county, and dissenters were more assertive than in Lumpkin. W. A. Campbell, who had recently resigned his Confederate army commission, returned home to find that "a very large majority of the people now here, perhaps two-thirds, are disloyal," and that "not 1/2 dozen men have gone into the service" in the heavily anti-Confederate district of Hot House, bordering Tennessee. Campbell charged that "a secret organization of disloyal individuals," was conspiring to disable the conscription act in the county, refusing to enroll able-bodied men and protecting dissenters from military service with false exemptions. Led by "influential individuals" such as Solomon Stansbury (who had spoken out against conscription) and William Fain (the Morganton lawyer who had fought secession in the 1861 convention), this "Union party" sought to sabotage the Confederate conscription apparatus in the county.[41]

Some highland secessionists tired of waiting for outside support and began to take spontaneous local action to suppress the Tories. Soon after dissenters burned down Josiah Woody's corncrib, a secessionist mob formed and went looking for retribution. The "rebel crowd went twelve miles in the country from Dahlonega where Lewis Fricks lived, busted open Fricks' feather bed and mixed molasses with the feathers and then burned down his house." Elites acted to contain mob violence by forming a Committee for Public Safety to decide "the best means for our defense from outlaws." The committee first tried moral suasion, sending representatives to meet with the dissenters and urging them "to reflect upon the infamous course they are taking and the consequent disgrace they will entail upon their families." When this failed, squads of home guards rounded up dissenters and imprisoned them in Dahlonega.[42]

As increasingly frantic reports of north Georgia disloyalty reached the capital that winter, Governor Brown felt compelled to respond. Brown was sensitive to the political realities surrounding the situation—north Georgia was a bastion of electoral support, and he could not risk alienating his constituents. Using his own mountain upbringing and his impeccable populist credentials, the governor used both the sword and the olive branch to bring the Tories to heel and return the deserters to the army. In a public decree, Brown offered amnesty to any deserter who voluntarily surrendered to authorities, while at the same time threatening that anyone who committed "any overt act of treason" would face severe penalties. To enforce his proclamation, Governor Brown sent the militia troops known as the Georgia State Line into the mountains on January 17, 1863. But the soldiers were under strict orders to observe the legal niceties:

> The duty your detachment will be called upon to discharge is a delicate one and the Governor desires . . . your officers and men to regard strictly the laws and the liberty and individual rights of the people. . . . Deserters from the Confederate armies will be delivered to such provost marshals as Gen'l Johnson may indicate . . . taking receipts therefore. Citizens who may be disloyal and such as harbor deserters . . . are to be dealt with as the Civil Laws direct, they not being amicable to Military Law. In such cases, make complaint to

the nearest local magistrate, and acting under his orders as a proper course takes, deliver the offender to the Civil power to be tried by the laws of his country. The Governor relies upon your intelligence and discretion, and wishes you to instruct your command well, so that while protection is given, the Civil Laws shall be respected.

At the request of Secretary of War James Seddon, Confederate troops from Atlanta joined the column, and the expedition was put under the overall command of a Confederate officer, George W. Lee.[43]

Five hundred troops arrived in Lumpkin County during the last week of January. The soldiers in the column were nervous. "It is reported that wee will be sent to Delonegay to fight the Georgia conscripts," one wrote before the mission, "it is reported that there is between 900 and a thousand if there is that many it will be a hard fight." The troops were also uneasy about their assignment. "I am glad to get back to Georgia," wrote a Confederate soldier, "though I don't much like to fight georgians." Lee established headquarters in Dahlonega, and quartered his soldiers in private homes and churches in town. The *Dahlonega Mountain Signal* grumbled that "so many troops and horses find it difficult to find accommodations," but the paper insisted that the troops were welcome. Lee's first act was to make a public speech promising leniency for contrite deserters but warning those who continued to evade the draft that "my men will be ordered to fire on them, and at all hazards to capture the last man, until this treasonable movement is completely suppressed." Lee's soldiers at once went to work. Detachments probed from Dahlonega into the surrounding counties, including Union, Gilmer, Hall, and Fannin, "arresting deserters and all lawless persons and all parties who have advised resistance to the laws." The troops had direct orders to forage supplies liberally from "disloyal parties" and to "visit those who violate the laws . . . with the retribution due the crimes of which they are guilty." In Dahlonega, Lee obtained the names of dissenters from the Committee for Public Safety, summarily jailing all he could catch. Within a week, Lee proclaimed his mission a success and returned to Atlanta, satisfied that "the people had been enlightened in regard to the duties they owe their government." His soldiers stayed to enforce order. Lee's expedition had forced over one thousand deserters and draft dodgers into the Confederate army. Fifty-three people were sent back to Atlanta for trial on charges ranging from "aiding and abetting treason" to being a "citizen in arms." Echoing the rhetoric of law and order, the *Dahlonega Mountain Signal* stated that the arrested Tories deserved their punishment, and wondered why "men of good sense should place themselves in the humiliating position of felons."[44]

But Lee's invasion also left smoldering resentment in its wake. Dissenters grew even more restive in reaction to the use of force, and many who had been neutral now took up active resistance to the Confederacy. A Lumpkin Confederate reported that "there are a good many disaffected families in the county that have become greatly incensed at the home guards of Dahlonega for . . . confining them to jail." One Lumpkin draft dodger who was unlucky enough to be captured remembered vividly the painful humiliation of being arrested by Lee's troops, "handcuffed and tied hand and foot with chains" and marched through the streets of town. Others were jailed or even had the letter "D" branded into their hips with a hot iron. In Fannin County, Lee's invasion spawned even more hostile reactions. Dissenters were now "very buoyant and defiant generally, more so than usual." Local Confederates worried that the enraged Tories, "exasperated by the punishment of their relatives and friends will doubtless seek revenge, especially upon those who . . . assisted in the execution of their just punishment." In late February, anti-Confederates held a mass meeting at Hot House, in the northern part of Fannin County. The featured speakers were William Umphrey, James Parks, and Nat Mangum, three wealthy Fannin professionals and slaveholders who were also rumored to be Tory leaders. The three had been arrested and taken to Atlanta by Lee's troops, only to be released soon afterward. The guests of honor captivated the crowd with stories of their horrific imprisonment, of dissenters being tortured, "beaten with rods on their bare backs 'til they had no sense." Then a petition circulated claiming that Lee had "acted here without law or right and had acted shamefully." The gathering may not have been the "general uprising" that local Confederates claimed it to be, but it did evince the heightened tensions Lee's invasion caused.[45]

Even pro-Confederates in the upcountry were uncomfortable with the invasion, and their reaction to Lee's expedition exposed the fault lines in Confederate nationalism in the mountains. Secessionists were at once thankful for outside assistance and uneasy about the continued presence of Lee's troops, for the soldiers served as physical manifestations of all the doubts about mountain loyalty to the Confederacy that had possessed Georgians and Southerners since the secession crisis. Lumpkin's Confederates were especially conflicted, for it appeared that all their efforts to assure others of their loyalty and patriotism were now threatened by the presence of a Confederate colonel who presumed to lecture them on "the duties they owe the government." And even though some Dahlonegans had been eager to see the troops arrive, many were quick to urge their hasty departure. Dahlonega Confederates got up a petition a week after Lee's arrival, asking the governor to replace the Confederate soldiers with a local military unit under James Kelly. Locals were perfectly capable of defending themselves, the citizens argued, and besides, Lee's troopers were beginning to be a drain on the community they were supposed to protect. "They [Lee's troops] are obliged to take nearly all our supplies, corn, and fodder is very scarce. . . and the sufferings of the poor will be great" the petitioners warned.[46]

When the Lumpkin County Grand Jury convened for its February term, Lee's troops still roamed the streets of Dahlonega, and the jurors felt compelled to make some statement about the loyalty of north Georgians. "For the first time in the history of the county," the jurors noted, "its roads are patrolled by a military force." Although the jurors rejoiced in the restoration of order and agreed with the punishment of the "band of outlaws and traitors," the continued presence of the soldiers deeply offended the honor of the community, for "the good name of the county is hearby tarnished and its reputation lost." The Lumpkin jurors went on to remind all about their county's dutiful service and deny the taint of disloyalty:

> Against this stain upon her honor Lumpkin County protests. Her people are not traitors or disloyal. The number of her brave sons and citizens already in the field at their country's call equals the enrolled vote of the county before the war. . . . From the highest and most patriotic motives her citizens promptly met and defied this scoundrel force [the Tories] when it first organized against her and to their vigilance and courage it is that the court now finds a house to set in or the military comfortable quarters for their reception. Lumpkin County greatly acknowledges the service rendered by the military power but let it be remembered it was in her hour of need and not of shame.[47]

Grand jury statements were normally mechanical documents filled with mundane community details of interest only to local people. But this statement was different—it was truly intended for all Georgians who doubted the loyalty of mountaineers. Although Lee's invasion had been necessary to maintain the Lumpkin elites' power, they resented it deeply, and the incident made Dahlonega Confederates all the more defensive about their patriotism. They were indignant at the blow to their honor implied by Lee's expedition and humbled by the fact they had needed help to maintain law and order. The grand jury statement was, therefore, an interesting expression of the dual loyalties held by mountain Rebels. On the one hand they asserted the primacy of Confederate nationalism by defending the patriotism of their citizens and reminding others of the region's contributions to the Confederate military. On the other hand, Lumpkin's secessionists maintained their right to police their own community and claimed that the local actions of the Committee for Public Safety had actually been the key to defusing the whole crisis. They were Confederates, but they insisted upon constructing their Confederate patriotism locally. This dichotomy—the desperate need to prove loyalty to the nation while at the same defending local prerogatives—would dramatically affect the way Lumpkin secessionists would deal with the upcoming crisis of guerrilla war.

The north Georgia press concurred with the Lumpkin jurors and campaigned against the traitorous characterization of the mountain counties. Reporters and editors minimized the crisis that occasioned Lee's invasion and argued that only a few "malcontents and deserters" existed. "It is unjust to denounce the whole county as tory because there exists a small band of tories within its limits," asserted the *Athens Southern Watchman,* concluding that "we have known all the time that the cock and bull stories about great numbers of tories in Northeast Georgia were gross exaggerations." Another writer singled out "the women of Northeast Georgia" as having "made greater sacrifices than any," for sending their men to the battlefields while they stayed home and bore the brunt of domestic production demands. "It is hard, considering the sacrifices made by the people of northeast Georgia," the article concluded, "that editors who ought to know better continue to prate about the alleged 'toryism of the ignorant people of the mountains.'"[48]

Meanwhile, Lumpkin's Confederates set out to prove they could keep order in their own house. After Lee's troops departed, Lumpkin's court system sprang into action against dissenters in two high-profile court cases. The Committee for Public Safety had arrested James Payne and John Woody in January on charges of treason, and both cases came to trial later that year. Witnesses claimed Payne had conspired to avoid the draft with two of his sons, Thomas and Asbury. The three men were seen walking though the streets of Dahlonega on January 5, armed with "guns, sticks, Knives and pistols," when they were approached by the sheriff and some conscription officers. The elder Payne, according to some accounts, leveled a rifle at the lawmen and threatened to kill "anyone who tried to arrest his sons."[49]

The Woody case was more sensational. John Woody was a prosperous yeoman farmer and brother of one of Lumpkin's most prominent secessionists, minister and governor's confidant Josiah Woody. John Woody had been captured while leading a squad of Tories toward the Lumpkin County jail, presumably to free two of his sons, imprisoned for desertion. In the course of the treason trial, various witness claimed Woody avoided the draft by hiding in the mountains until he was over forty-five years old (the upper age limit for the Confederate draft). Others heard Woody assert that "he did not believe the war was right," and that "it was not right to take the men out of the country." The dramatic high point of the trial came when the defendant's own brother testified for the prosecu-

A family divided by war. Josiah Askew Woody, shown here in his Confederate military uniform, testified against his own brother, John Wesley Woody, in a sensational treason trial in 1863. (*Vanishing Georgia,* lum191, Georgia Division of Archives and History, Office of Secretary of State)

tion. Josiah Woody briefed the court on several incriminating conversations he had had with the defendant before the incident and asserted that the two brothers had often argued about the war. John Woody had said that "secession was wrong and had brought the war upon us," and that "he wished the Confederacy to be subjugated and that we should be whipped." During one heated exchange, John Woody threatened that his brother "would be burned out, that the army was all deserting and coming home and [the Tories] would soon be the strongest." When the defendant's turn came to testify in his own defense, he did not confess to any treason, but he did boldly oppose the Confederacy and the war effort, looking directly at his accusers and saying "he did not begin the war and would not fight if he could help it." [50]

John Woody was acquitted of treason, and the James Payne case never went to trial. Pro-Confederates also failed to obtain convictions against two Lumpkin men accused of harboring runaway slaves. The combined impact of these legal failures must have shocked Lumpkin's Confederates, who had been committed to working within the legal system to pros-

John Wesley Woody and his wife after the war. After being acquitted of treason in 1863, Woody crossed the border into Tennessee and joined the Union army. (*Vanishing Georgia*, lum193, Georgia Division of Archives and History, Office of Secretary of State)

ecute the Tories. Now that system had failed to punish dissenters. Adding to the disillusionment, several of the men Lee's forces had taken away to Atlanta for trial began coming home in February, apparently judged innocent. Taken together, these cases gave Dahlonegans reason to doubt the efficacy of legal action and also taught them to look within their own communities for traitors and enemies.

In Fannin County, secessionists faced even worse troubles. Not only had the Lee invasion enraged local dissenters, but it also had failed to discourage more desertion. By June, papers reported that "some of those who were forced into the army last winter have returned with government arms and ammunition." The deserters added industrial terrorism to their activities, attacking and destroying threshing machines, ironworks, and other targets vital to the Confederate war effort (a class element doubtless existed here, as the owners of these industries and machines were wealthy local elites). Fannin Tories also began ambushing conscription agents that summer. In June, Stanley Rickles and some compatriots fired on a group of conscription agents in the process of taking his father away for the draft, killing one officer and wounding two others. These incidents led even some north Georgia papers, previously defensive of mountain loyalty, to label Fannin a hotbed of Unionism.[51]

Things worsened as the summer of 1863 wore on. In August Elijah Chastain reported that three hundred Tories roamed Fannin's mountains every night, stealing "every gun that can be found in the county, threatening . . . every man from whom they take the guns that if he attempts to have them or any other deserter arrested, that they will hang him to the first limb of a tree they can find." With Lee's troops gone, the local sheriff stood alone against the deserters. Chastain begged for outside assistance, claiming that "so soon as they get all our guns . . . this county will be over!" The authorities responded to the call, sending George W. Lee into the mountains again in September. The soldiers cracked down hard upon the Tories, but Lee conceded that he faced a more difficult job. "There is considerable trouble in North Eastern Georgia," Lee wrote, "especially in Fannin County. . . . Supposed to be one hundred and fifty tories and deserters in a body and camped. They are plundering and burning."[52]

Not only did dissenters increase their active resistance, but a power struggle within the Fannin elite created an atmosphere of fear and accusation in which no one's loyalty was above suspicion. In the wake of Lee's invasion, Elijah Chastain, recently home from the war, prepared to fight the war on a new front. With the help of James Morris, the wealthiest man and largest slaveholder in the county, Chastain organized Fannin County's Committee for Public Safety to manage the Tory problem. The committee soon moved beyond this original mandate and began to act as the arbiter of loyalty, branding any who opposed it as Tories and Unionists. In June, the committee sent a letter to the Confederate secretary of war naming names and flinging charges of treason against several influential Fannin citizens. The letter accused W. A. Campbell, William C. Fain, and the local conscription officer of engaging in a vast conspiracy to deprive the Confederacy of men and resources. Campbell, the writers claimed, "has proved to be a traitor . . . he makes false statements to Capt. Starr thereby obtaining [draft] exemptions for this who are not entitled." William Fain, of whom the committee was already suspicious because of his anti-secession stand in 1861, assisted this distrust by deliberately employing disloyal and incompetent men at his ironworks, thus depriving the Confederacy of needed iron and winning false draft exemption for his traitorous workers.[53]

Nothing much came of these accusations. The War Department sent an investigator to the scene who concluded that the committee had made "accusations without substantiating them" and that the entire controversy resulted from "a most bitter personal and political feud" that inspired "the most prominent citizens of Fannin County [to engage] in civil war of the most ridiculous character." W. A. Campbell, who himself had previously made frequent, hysterical denunciations of fellow residents, dismissed the committee's charges against him and asserted his undying loyalty to the Confederacy. As for William Fain, Campbell concluded, he was at best a "semi-Unionist" whose worst crime was making a political enemy of the influential Elijah Chastain. After a secret meeting with Fain, Campbell claimed the Morganton attorney offered his promise to dampen Tory activity in return for more lenient treatment of dissenters.[54]

The Fannin controversy may indeed have been "of the most ridiculous character," but it revealed the intense dynamics of loyalty in the region. The deserter influx, the Lee invasion, and the Lumpkin treason trials had created an atmosphere in north Georgia in which even elite slaveholders could not agree on what constituted loyalty and disloyalty. In this increasingly unstable environment, mountain Confederates began to look at every neighbor as a potential traitor and also grew ever more eager to prove to others that they themselves were loyal. This earnest concern would soon grow to paranoia when guerrilla warfare struck the region in 1864.

During 1862 and 1863, Fannin and Lumpkin counties endured internal division, social disruption, and outside invasion. But as residents of both counties reacted to the crisis of loyalty in the mountains, certain differences emerged between the two localities. Fannin County's young men deserted the Confederate army in much higher numbers and at a higher rate than their Lumpkin County counterparts (27 percent of Fannin's soldiers deserted, compared with less than 5 percent of Lumpkin men). Fannin's dissenters were more active and its pro-Confederate elite less stable and united. Lumpkin's establishments tried to utilize the judicial system to keep order, whereas by the end of 1863, all Fannin's Rebels could do was call for more troops.

Perhaps nothing exemplified the growing divergence more accurately than the Georgia gubernatorial election of 1863. Joseph Brown ran for an unprecedented fourth term that year and was depending on mountain voters to support him as they had since the 1850s. Brown's suspension of the draft in north Georgia and his relief programs for the mountain poor doubtless helped his chances of victory, but the governor was still uneasy and constantly asked his confidants for readings of the political barometer in the upcountry during the autumn of 1863. George W. Lee, whose direct experience in the upper counties was limited to the role of policeman, was optimistic; "my observations . . . lead me to believe that the result of the election will afford gratifying evidence of the regard in which you are held . . . in that portion of the state." In Fannin County, Elijah Chastain was not so sure, and he predicted severe electoral problems for the governor. As it happened, Joseph Brown won his fourth term with a solid percentage of the mountain vote, including a secure majority of Fannin's electorate. Brown lost decisively in Lumpkin County, where the former Whig Joshua Hill beat the incumbent by a count of 331 to 121. But the truth lay behind the numbers. Even though Lumpkin rejected Joseph Brown, most people there probably still supported the Confederacy. In Fannin, Brown may have won the election, but fewer than 300 people voted—about 29 percent of the voting-age population. Over 50 percent of Lumpkin men voted in the election. Thus, while most Lumpkin residents opposed Brown and the way he was conducting the war, they still were invested enough in the system to participate. In Fannin County, the vast majority of voters simply opted out of the system entirely—their silence spoke volumes about political sentiment in the county. As Elijah Chastain stated after the election, "If the entire strength of the tories had been polled, I believe they would have carried the county . . . and unless troops are kept in the county they [the Tories] will take the county."[55] Fannin and Lumpkin counties were reacting very differently to the continuing crisis. In the year to come, these differences would lead to civil war between the two counties.

After he was acquitted of treason in January 1863, John Woody found life intolerable in Dahlonega. Harassment from authorities and his pro-Confederate neighbors soon drove Woody into the mountains, where, like many other dissenters, he "lay out" to avoid conscription agents. According to family lore, he lived in a dugout in a cane break near his home while waiting for his wife to give birth to their sixth child. But soon authorities closed in on Woody and forced him out of his hideout and deeper into the mountains. In late 1864, he crossed the state line into East Tennessee and finally decided to take a drastic step. Union military forces were based nearby, and Woody decided to join them. In November of 1864, he enlisted in the 10th Tennessee Cavalry, U.S. Now he was protected by the power and authority of the Union military, power that he could use to fight his secessionist enemies and drive them from Lumpkin County. But before John Woody left for Tennessee, a family story goes, he made one last secret trip home to see his wife and their newborn baby, a boy. They named him Abraham Lincoln Woody.[56]

4 / *Hellish Deeds in a Christian Land*

THE SOCIAL DYNAMICS OF VIOLENCE
IN NORTH GEORGIA'S GUERRILLA WAR,
1864–1865

In October of 1864, U.S. Army Captain John Azor Kellogg escaped
from a Confederate prisoner-of-war train and fled through the Southern Appalachians toward the safety of the Union lines in East Tennessee.
On his journey he found refuge with a small colony of anti-Confederate
guerrillas in north Georgia. The Tories quickly acquainted the Northern
officer with the cruel realities of their own civil war, regaling him with
horrifying tales of daily atrocities and merciless combat with Confederate
authorities. One of Kellogg's hosts told of a deserter whom Rebels had
captured: "[they] tied him hand and foot, mutilated him in the most hor-
rid manner, and then, bleeding as he was, they hung him to a tree in sight
of his own house." There could be no compromise with such implacable
and ruthless enemies, the Tories claimed: "it was a war of extermination
between them. No prisoners were taken by either side." Kellogg sympathized with his hosts' plight and was grateful for the assistance of these
"generous, hospitable, brave . . . Union men." But the kind of warfare
they engaged in shocked his Victorian sensibility, and although Kellogg
was a seasoned combat veteran, he found it difficult to accept that "such
hellish deeds could have been enacted in a Christian land."[1]

In the mountains of north Georgia, this Northern sojourner traveled
through a realm of violence utterly alien to him, violence that he thought
even more senseless and barbaric than the killing fields of Antietam or
Fredericksburg. However, to those who lived in the region, north Georgia's guerrilla war had an explicable source and a logical, if brutal, rationale. By 1864, the years of accumulated tensions between Tory and Rebel

burst into intra-community combat. Factions became polarized by the Union army's entry into the region, as dissenters turned to the approaching army for assistance and Confederates embraced ever-harsher methods to suppress "traitors." The crises of 1863 laid the attitudinal groundwork, but the continuing dynamics of Appalachia's shadow war also exacerbated the situation, and the progression of events encouraged north Georgians to ever more extreme actions. As each side reacted to the other's abuses, the scale and intensity of violence increased—from destruction of property to symbolic attacks on persons to vigilantism and summary execution. Atrocities ultimately were committed by both sides. By the war's final months, few ethical barriers to brutality remained, and violence became a casual, causeless affair.

Although their methods changed, becoming less restrained and more violent, north Georgian's goals generally remained the same. Tories and secessionists fought because of their concerns over community, family, and law and order. Both sides proclaimed a broader allegiance—the Tories clung to the Union army and the Confederates to the tottering Jeff Davis government. But beneath these loyalties, the local always lurked, strong and unavoidable. Guerrilla warfare only amplified the community-level concerns that had always prevailed in the region.

Toward the end of 1863, elements of the Union army penetrated the extreme southeast corner of Tennessee and for the first time came within striking distance of north Georgia. This introduced a new dynamic into the ongoing struggle in Georgia's mountain counties, presenting new options for the Tories, while increasing Confederate fears that dissenters represented a dangerous fifth column.

Some north Georgia anti-Confederates fled as early as 1862, but when Federal forces occupied Cleveland, Tennessee, just across the state line, the flood of refugees swelled. Now, the thousands of deserters, dissenters, and Unionists "laying out" in the Blue Ridge had a haven and a potential ally in their fight against the Confederate power structure. In Lumpkin County, dissenters realized the approach of the Union army changed the equation. When one unhappy Confederate draftee wrote home of his plans to "run away and go off to the Yankees," his brother urged caution. "If I was you I would hold on a while . . . for I think the Yankees will run our army back before long and if they do there will be a good chance then." But in Fannin County, very near the Union base at Cleveland, not all Tories were willing to wait for the approach of liberating Northern arms. The effect was almost immediate. One observer noted that "there is a great many families leaving . . . and moving to the yankees," and estimated that "a third of the citizens of Fannin County will go to the north." The route was difficult. Refugees traveled on foot, horseback, and wagon. They had to follow the twisted course of the Toccoa River as it wended through deep gorges and thick forests, or take narrow mountain trails clinging to the sides of steep cliffs. Soldiers and militia patrolled escape routes constantly. To avoid them, refugees depended upon the "grapevine telegraph," a system of pilots and safe houses that guided and protected the members of the Tory exodus through northern Georgia to Union lines. The network included some local government officials friendly to the anti-Confederates, who would sometimes write false travel passes to fleeing men, authorizing them to leave the state, allegedly in pursuit of lost livestock. After crossing the state line at Copperhill, Tennessee, refugees endured a rugged forty-mile wagon road used to haul copper to the rolling mills at Cleveland. Even here fleeing Tories were not safe, for the road passed through an isolated countryside pockmarked

By 1864, Tory refugees like the ones depicted in this wartime engraving were flooding across the border from north Georgia to the relative security of East Tennessee. Many of these Georgia mountaineers would later join the Union army. (From *Harper's Weekly*, September 19, 1863, pp. 600–601)

with abandoned mining tunnels, perfect lairs for bandits and guerrillas. One defector recalled that "all avenues of escape were closely guarded by armed bands of the most bloodthirsty and irresponsible men" who robbed and murdered the refugees, leaving "their bleaching bones in some mountain gorge." Even so, thousands of north Georgians made the trek. As the Union army penetrated deeper into Georgia, more mountain dissenters "refugeed," as they called it, to the area of northwest Georgia organized under the Federal military's District of the Etowah.[2]

Some of those north Georgians fleeing to the Union lines were runaway slaves. Like African Americans throughout the South, mountain blacks took the opportunity to gain the freedom offered by the Emancipation Proclamation whenever Union troops neared. Slaves in north Georgia faced particularly arduous obstacles in their paths. Since large Union forces never actually penetrated the mountain counties of the state, enslaved persons were forced to hike through miles of rugged terrain and cross the state line to even get near Yankee units. In the process the runaways had to pass through a skein of Confederate troops, state militia, bushwhackers, and slave patrols sent to retrieve them. For some, this proved an insurmountable obstacle. Two north Georgia slaves were recaptured while trying to escape in April 1864 and were imprisoned in Dalton, where one died of frostbite. But many made the hazardous journey despite the risks. James Cowan fled his master's farm in Murray County in the dead of the winter of 1864 and successfully reached the Union base in Knoxville, Tennessee. Scipio Henry slipped across the border from Fannin County and made it Chattanooga, Tennessee. And in the spring of 1864, three slaves escaped from the Alston farm in Lumpkin County. Isaac, Julius, and Robert Rucker traveled almost two hundred miles to Knoxville, where they joined the 1st U.S. Colored Heavy Artillery. Sometimes slaves did not need to escape. When one north Georgia slave was traveling with his master from Atlanta to Knoxville, a Union patrol swept up the pair and liberated the black man.[3]

Once behind Union lines, north Georgia refugees of both races worked on railroads, hauled wood, drove wagons, and performed other auxiliary services for Federal forces. Several hundred enlisted in the Union army. Tennessee governor Andrew Johnson sought to take full advantage of the new source of manpower offered by the refugees, and Union army officials actively recruited among Georgia's exile population during the summer and fall of 1864. A few recruiters even infiltrated north Georgia, encouraging dissenters to travel to Tennessee and enlist. Several Union units formed in this fashion, including the 5th Tennessee Mounted Infantry, of which north Georgians composed approximately half of the total enrollment. Scores more enlisted the 1st Georgia State Troops Volunteers, which formed after Sherman's forces began their march to Atlanta and was the only official all-Georgia regiment to serve in the Union army during the Civil War. At least 121 white men from Fannin and Lumpkin counties served in these or other Union army units during the war. Many African Americans also served. By April 1864, enough black north Georgians had gathered in Chattanooga to help fill out the ranks of two infantry regiments—the 42nd and 44th U.S. Colored Troops. Some of these black men had run away from their farms in north Georgia seeking freedom and military service. Others were dragooned into service by roaming enlistment squads of Federal recruiters. One black mountaineer remembered sadly that "one regiment took my oldest brother, John, away and we never heard from him for several years after the war." But some of these black draftees seemed jubilant about army service. "The niggers was mighty glad to have the Yankees take them," one recalled, "they wanted to get out from under that rough treatment. Georgia was about the meanest place in the world. They would knock you and kick you around just like you was dogs." Whatever their motivation, black men faced an uncertain fate once in Union uniform. General Sherman himself had little use for black soldiers and assigned them a disproportionate share of fatigue duty. When black north Georgians did get into combat, they faced horrific risks. At the Battle of Dalton in autumn 1864, several soldiers of the 44th U.S. Colored Troops were shot after surrendering to Confederate forces under General John Bell Hood. Most of the rest were re-enslaved after the fight, and as a result, the 44th USCT ceased to exist.[4]

For mountain blacks, the reason for running away to the Union army seemed obvious—they wanted their freedom. For whites, the reasons seem a bit less clear. What motivated these refugees, who in a later age might have been called "defectors?" Why would people who were so focused upon the community abandon their homes for strange places and unknown allies? A variety of factors influenced the refugees, including economic security, family stability, and the continuing oppression of Confederate authorities in north Georgia. For many dissenters, these issues outweighed the benefits of staying in north Georgia. However, leaving home did not mean leaving concerns about home behind. Even in exile, they defended their notions of community.

Refugees felt pulled by the economic allure of federal employment and pushed by increasingly desperate poverty at home. Poor crops and absence of farm labor impoverished upcountry homesteads even before impressment agents arrived to take their measure of produce and livestock—Confederate requisitions only heightened the problem. "Bread in this and other sections is very scarce," wrote one Fannin Confederate who sympathized with the Tories' plight, if not their choice of allies, and another mountain Rebel admitted that hunger forced dissenters into "selling out and moving to Tennessee or Kentucky, for they say . . . their families must perish [otherwise]." A Confederate officer passing though the mountain counties was shocked by the poverty of a region that he called "a perfect waste, worse than any portion of Virginia, the people almost entirely destitute, the women and children begging for bread." Refugeeing to the Union could mean the difference between survival and death for many mountaineers, and for others, it simply meant a dramatic increase in their standard of living. When James Withrow left Fannin County and secured a job working for a Union quartermaster, he was stunned at his $40-per-month salary, which was substantially higher than what he had earned as an operative in a Confederate copper mill. Jacob White of Pickens County went to work on a Union bridge-building crew; John Shelton and his mother moved from Towns County to Sweetwater, Tennessee, where he supported her with his $10-per-month salary for railroad work; Edward O'Kelley secretly returned to his north Georgia home to give his family a portion of the money he earned as a federal laborer in Tennessee. For these and many other refugees, economic needs demanded migration to Federal lines.[5]

While some migrants like O'Kelley left family behind, many others fled as family groups. If the residential community had to be left, than at least the basic unit of community, the family, would be preserved. Refugeeing plans often involved entire clans or extended kin groups, with women and children laying away food and stores for the journey while the men scouted the route or went beforehand to establish safe houses. Sometimes the women and children traveled the main roads with wagons and supplies, acting as decoys for the men, who followed along hidden mountain trails. Such arrangements were natural extensions of previous Tory survival networks, in which men "lay out" by day and parents, wives, and children supplied them with food and clothing. Family refugeeing also was a practical precaution, since bandits and pro-Confederate guerrillas often littered the mountain trails refugees used to escape Georgia. Family thus remained central to dissenters' motivation.[6]

It is somewhat more difficult to discern the motives of those north Georgians who enlisted in the Union army. Joining the Federal armed forces was a notably assertive anti-Confederate statement, indisputable treason against the Jefferson Davis and Joe Brown governments. If any dissenters truly earned the label Unionist, it would seem these men did. They took a formal oath to the United States, joined an army pledged to the destruction of slavery and restoration of the Union, and took up arms to destroy the Confederate nation. But in actuality, multiple motives acted upon the mountaineers who joined these Federal units, and nationalism was perhaps the weakest of them.

The first issue for Tories was survival—material and physical. Economic factors were important, just as they were for all refugees. John Azor Kellogg remembered that the mountain dissenters he met in Georgia were eager to join the army, if only to "procure good arms and clothing" issued to Lincoln's soldiers. Many received cash bounties for enlisting, like the Parris brothers of Fannin County, who each collected $30 when they joined the 5th Tennessee Mounted Infantry. Recruiters who penetrated north Georgia communities were aware of the poverty there and often lured the destitute residents with federal greenbacks—one highlander remembered that a Union recruiter "gave my father the first government money he ever had—a $20 bill."[7]

But cash bounties and new clothes only went so far in motivating men to risk their lives in the military. North Georgians also joined the army in order to exact revenge upon Confederate authorities and to defend the communities that continued to suffer impressment, conscription, and state-sponsored violence. The ranks of Federal units like the 5th Tennessee and the 1st Georgia were filled with mountaineers who had personally experienced examples of Confederate intrusion. Some were Confederate conscripts, like the Lumpkin County soldier who described to a comrade his intention to "go home and lay out and if they [the authorities] fooled with him he would go to the enemy." Many more had not yet been drafted into the Rebel armies but feared the imminent prospect. These men had managed to avoid Confederate military service for the first three years of the war but feared that the continual pressure of conscription agents would soon force them into the Southern armies. As one mountaineer remembered, "The Confederate authorities were hunting for me all the time. I was not allowed to remain at home . . . I slept in the mountains nearly all winter of 1863 and 1864. . . . Finally in summer of 1864 I went through the lines at Cleveland." Another Tory explained that Union service was the best of several bad options available. "Union men either had to leave or go into some sort of Rebel service, lie out, and be shot if they was caught." Other Tories recalled being imprisoned without trial or having family members abused. Lemuel Chambers endured the humiliation of being chained and handcuffed by conscription agents and then dragged to a Confederate unit for service. He promptly deserted and defected to Federal forces.[8]

Many men living in the Fannin County town of Hot House, along the North Carolina border, feared the Confederate draft. They had enjoyed exemption from military service because they worked at the Confederate copper works in Ducktown, Tennessee. But in 1863, rumors began circulating that the exemption would be revoked. One Hot House woman remembered "quite a bunch of men working at the copper mines quit and refugeed" to the Federal army. Solomon Stansbury was one such exile. A substantial farmer and community leader in the Hot House region, Stansbury supplemented his income with a thriving charcoal business that depended on the patronage of the Ducktown mine. Stansbury had endured harassment and imprisonment in order to stay out of the army and maintain his economic position, but with the draft looming, he fled to Tennessee in late 1863 and joined the 13th Tennessee Cavalry. He returned in 1864 to play a key role in the region's civil war.[9]

Mountaineers feared the prospect of the draft, but they especially despised the prospect of serving in Confederate units that victimized their own communities, such as conscription squads. W. A. Campbell expressed particular frustration at the behavior of Fannin County Tories who refused to participate in police actions against dissenters. When called to service by the Confederate enrollment officer to arrest deserters and "suppress the insurrection then in our county," Campbell noted, many citizens "wholly refused to . . . obey the order," and simply "left the command and went home of their own accord." Some Fannin men, like William Long, accepted assignments as conscript agents only to suffer guilty consciences. When Long was detached from the 65th Georgia Infantry and ordered to help arrest deserters in his home county of Fannin, he quickly tired of hunting down his own neighbors and friends. Long deserted the deserter-hunting business in 1863 and ultimately enlisted in the 10th Tennessee Cavalry, U.S.[10]

But it took more than anger at personal indignities or fear of the draft to push north Georgians into Federal service. Increasingly, mountaineers saw joining the Union army as a way to defend their families and communities, to prevent the kind of abuses William Fox suffered when draft agents came to his house in 1864. When soldiers came to conscript Fox, they brutalized his father before taking Fox off to the army. Fox remembered that Rebel soldiers had captured his father, "robbed him, taking two horses . . . and drove the old man from his house at night," after which he died of exposure. At the time Fox was helpless to protect his family, but when he joined a Federal cavalry regiment in the winter of 1864–65, Fox gained a new ally with the power to secure his family's stability. When Jacob White fled north Georgia for the Union army in September 1864, he had similar goals. White later said he wanted to "push the war off of North Georgia" and to help protect "those that was trying to defend themselves and property against the . . . Confederate Cavalry." North Georgians who served as Union recruiting officers took the same position. They not only enrolled fellow highlanders into the Federal forces but took advantage of their positions to aid the Tories. James G. Brown, a Murray County native who helped organize the Union's 1st Georgia State Troops, saw defending community and family as his primary goal. Although Union army officials authorized Brown only to recruit soldiers for Federal service, he also funneled weapons to highland dissenters and organized Tory home guards in the mountains, ordering them to "arrest all Rebel soldiers, deserters or citizens . . . committing any outrage upon the community." Another U.S. recruiting officer from Lumpkin County claimed he was fighting to protect "the many loyal sufferers of north Georgia."[11]

Many mountaineers sought atonement for the real or perceived injustices committed by secessionists and wanted to use the Union army to wreak vengeance upon their enemies within the community. When one deserted the Confederate army and appeared at a federal post in Tennessee, he demanded he "be mustered into the service of the United States, because some of his men had ben captured by the Rebels and summarily executed." A Fannin County dissenter smoldered in anger because he "had a brother killed by rebels," while another Tory claimed "he wanted to kill the rebels who were trying to run him off from his home." James G. Brown seethed over the pro-Confederate guerrillas who sacked his father-in-law's house, and although he insisted "I have no wish to retaliate" against his enemies, he admitted that "I do most earnestly want to get [those] who are desolating the homes of those men who remain true to their country." Tories who had endured similar abuses for three years joined the Union army to strike back at their local enemies.[12]

Not all highlanders reacted in the same way to these crises. Almost twice as many Fannin men joined the Federal armies as Lumpkin men, bearing out a growing dichotomy. Of the two mountain counties, Fannin was poorer, had fewer slaves, and had a higher proportion of household heads enrolled in the Confederate army by 1863. This caused more disruption on the home front and resulted in many Fannin men deserting the Southern armies (at least 16 percent of Fannin's Union recruits were Confederate deserters). Fannin also had preexisting economic, social, and demographic ties with other disaffected regions of the Southern Appalachians. The vast majority of Fannin's Union recruits had been born outside of Georgia, mostly in western North Carolina. Many others living in the northern part of the county, like Solomon Stansbury, worked in the Ducktown mines and oriented their household and community economies toward East Tennessee. For them, the wild river gorges and mountain trails connecting Georgia to Tennessee were well-known avenues of commerce and migration, which they exploited when the time came to refugee to Federal lines. The majority of Fannin men who enlisted in the Federal army lived either in these border settlements or in the more rural areas of the county. The border village of Hot House, for example, provided nearly a quarter of the county's Union recruits, while less than 6 percent of the county's Confederate soldiers came from this district.[13]

Community support networks were vital in supporting Tory guerrillas. With dissent widespread in Fannin County, anti-Confederate fighters could rely on sympathetic locals to provide them with food, clothing, and assistance. In addition, Fannin's dissenters had an influential group of community leaders to which to turn for protection. Some of Fannin's elite, like Elijah Chastain and W. A. Campbell, were committed secessionists who used all their influence to secure the county for the Confederacy and for Governor Brown. But they had rivals for power who opposed the Rebellion—wealthy slaveholders like William Fain and James Parks and prominent yeomen like Solomon Stansbury. These leaders served as epicenters for protest and offered other dissenters a measure of security. And when some of these leading citizens, like Fain and Stansbury, eventually joined the Union army, others followed.[14]

Lumpkin offered a contrast. It was wealthier and had a larger town population, and its military units maintained very low desertion rates (less than 10 percent). More of Lumpkin's military-age men stayed at home during the war and, with the help of a substantial slave population, managed to forestall some of the home-front economic problems that disaffected so many Fannin families. Over two-thirds of all Lumpkin soldiers were born in Georgia and lived in the Dahlonega area. They looked southward for their political and commercial economic leadership. Lumpkin dissenters, on the other hand, were more isolated geographically from Union invasion routes than Fannin dissenters and faced more difficulties in reaching Federal lines. Moreover, they could not look to community leaders for protection, for the solid core of Lumpkin leadership remained pro-Confederate. Men like Weir Boyd, Archibald Wimpy, and James Findley successfully secured the reins of power for the Confederacy and used that power efficiently against the Tories.[15]

Of course, most north Georgia dissenters did not flee the state or join the Federal army. They stayed at home and resisted pro-Confederate authorities at the local level. Deserters continued to hide in the Cohutta Mountains and among the peaks of the Blue Ridge. Tory bands, like the one that John Azor Kellogg stumbled upon, continued to resist conscription agents, rob secessionist civilians, and harass state militia units. Some north Georgians joined a paramilitary group of raiders based in western North Carolina and led by one Goldman Bryson. Bryson's men roamed

Armed bands of Tories seeking refuge in the north Georgia mountains frequently skirmished with pursuing militia and conscription agents. (From Junius Henri Browne, *Four Years in Secessia: Adventures within and beyond the Union Lines.* Hartford, CT: O. D. Case, 1865, p. 346)

the border area, as one veteran remembered, "protecting loyal citizens from being impressed by the conscript law . . . and giving aid to loyal men through the Federal lines when they could no longer withstand the hardships of the rebels." The band made raids on Murphy, North Carolina, and on northern Fannin County in late 1863, freeing imprisoned deserters and striking terror into the hearts of pro-Confederates as far south as Dahlonega. A few of Bryson's men later served in organized Federal units, but in general the group "stayed at their homes, and got together when the occasion required."[16]

Whether they remained at home or went into the Federal armed forces, north Georgia dissenters essentially pursued a common goal—defending the community. True, those who crossed the lines, swore the oath to the United States, and put on a blue uniform were abandoning their homes, forsaking their state and joining the army that was killing their neighbors and relatives. But even though these highlanders risked everything to escape their homes, they did not try to escape their responsibility to their communities. They saw the Federal army as a tool to use against their local enemies. A few Tories espoused the rhetoric of the Union and claimed to be serving the broader interests of the United States. James G. Brown often wrote of his love for the Union, insisting "there is no rest for me until this Rebellion is crushed," and asserted that "it will always be a source of gratification when my humble services can aid in establishing our government." And Sion Darnell claimed that he and his highland neighbors joined the Union armies because "they had imbibed sentiments of freedom, and a patriotism high enough, and broad enough, and deep enough, to embrace the whole country, and the whole Union—not of certain states, but of all states." But for most anti-Confederates, army service meant something less ideological, more concrete and limited. Many dissenters who fled north Georgia in 1864 for the Union army would later be killed while trying to return. Others deserted the Union army when it no longer served their local purpose, or when Federal missions threatened to remove them from north Georgia. As the guerrilla war in north Georgia escalated, Tories remained focused on the local situation.[17]

For mountain Confederates, the year 1864 brought with it a host of changes that threatened their established order. Tory defections, growing violence, slave resistance, and the concrete threat of the Union army gave upcountry Rebels even greater cause to fear for their community. As dissension grew, the search for internal enemies left many secessionists willing to strike back at the neighbors and former friends they viewed as disloyal. In this atmosphere, extreme measures were embraced as necessary to defend the established order.

The wave of Tory defections represented a new crisis of confidence among mountain Rebels, stronger evidence that dissenters were overtly treasonous and a threat to the Confederate nation. In March 1864, Lumpkin Confederates were again scandalized when several young men from that county were court-martialed for conspiring to desert from their Georgia militia unit and defect to the Union army. At trial, the deserters admitted being absent from their command, but they steadfastly rejected the charge of "going off to the Yankees." They had simply been war-weary, the erstwhile soldiers insisted, not traitors. They wanted to return home to care for sick parents or visit with friends. Francis Tumlin, the group's ringleader, asserted in his defense that "I had no intention to go to the Yankees," and sharply rebuked a prosecution witness, insistently asking "do you believe I am disloyal to the South?" But the authorities presented intercepted letters between Tumlin and his brother, also in service, in which the two discussed joining the Union forces. The brother of another deserter actually testified against his sibling during the trial. In the end, the men were found guilty of the lesser crime of simple desertion, punished with corporal and financial penalties, and returned to their units. But like the civil trials in Lumpkin the previous year, these proceedings highlighted the deepening community divisions and even familial strife over loyalty in the mountains. And once again, Lumpkin County's pro-Confederate population had to sit by as the traitors in their midst were exonerated or let off lightly by legal authorities. The perceived inability of the justice system to deal with disloyalty was beginning to change the minds of highland Rebels with regard to the proper treatment of the Tories. No longer would the law be the option of first resort.[18]

But other upcountry Confederates were relieved to see the troublemakers leave the state, and they even encouraged Tories to migrate—"go to your friends the Yankees," one dissenter remembered state militia shouting at him as they looted his home. And when a pro-Confederate woman watched her neighbors flee from north Georgia to the Federal lines, she wrote "I hope that [all] may get off that wants to go. It only serves to unite the true-hearted . . . in striving for their just rights." Others, however, worried that the steady drain of upcountry refugees would weaken the forces of law and order and contribute to instability. Fannin's militia commander fretted that "many in this county who owe military service to the state are moving off to Tennessee within the enemies lines," and another local secessionist said with disgust, "I think they are 'driving their flock to a bad market.' for I have no love for the Yankee thieves." Rebels thought that crossing the lines to the enemy proved that dissenters were not simply desperate victims of war and poverty, but dangerous fifth columnists now showing their true traitorous colors as the Union armies approached. S. C. Dobbs of Fannin County admitted that economic hardship forced many to leave north Georgia, but he felt that going to the Unionists evinced something more insidious than just material need. "They might and ought to move in some other direction besides going to the Yankees," he complained to the adjutant general, "which in my judgement is a matter *of their own choice.*" [19]

But although they denounced Tories for fleeing north, many secessionists abandoned the region as well—going in the opposite direction. The Tory migration North was mirrored by a parallel Confederate outflow to the south, as those loyal to the Rebellion sought ground safer than the increasingly hostile mountains of north Georgia. One mountain woman noted in 1864 that "most all the secesh is moving," while another reported that "all of our true men of the county have had to go South . . . and every Southern man from Morganton. There are only two [Confederate] families left in Morganton." Fannin's Confederate population thinned drastically as the Federal army neared and emboldened Tories intensified their raids. Some, like Martha Williams, fled "the tyrannies of the bushwhackers" in Fannin County only to find themselves in the path of Sherman's invading armies further south, and they were forced to move yet again. And with the pro-Confederates forsaking the region, those secessionists who stayed in the area were even more vulnerable to the Tories. Huldah Fain watched with alarm as her neighbors left her one by one, and she worried that "I began to think a while that we would be left alone among the bushwhackers . . . I never want to be left among such an atrocious set." Others complained that the flight of the elite left them without protection from dissenters. With many of "the wealthy southern men" leaving the area, one petition read, "a number of true soldiers' wives and widows are here yet who have not the pecuniary facilities of removing south . . . [and] are subject to all manner of injury and insult by Tories." [20]

Abandoned by their allies, increasingly fearful of their enemies, highland secessionists began to worry more than ever about the specter of disloyalty in their midst. Slaves had been a source of anxiety and distrust for whites since the beginning of the war, and the increasingly unstable situation on the home front only added to the tension. One north Georgia white woman watched with disgust as interracial recruiting gangs from the Union army marched through her county in 1864. "I don't know what to call them," she wrote, "though part of them was black and the other white but to say the least of them I guess they have black hearts." As more slaves ran away to the Union lines in 1864, masters focused on the most obvious threat to the security of the white household—a rebellious servant. Ironically, masters both depended on and were suspicious of their slaves, as one Fannin County slave named "Uncle Jake" found out when Tories raided his master's farm in the middle of winter. When the raiders stole his master's mule, Jake was sent to investigate. He "sneaked around the barns and in the chimney corners to eavesdrop at the homes of those he suspected of being disloyal to the Confederate cause." Jake finally tracked down the stolen animal but was immediately swept up by the local sheriff, who presumed the elderly slave was taking the mule and refugeeing to Union lines. Similar incidents had recently occurred in nearby Floyd County, where runaway slaves had seized mules and horses to aid in their defection to the Union forces. Jake steadfastly maintained his loyalty, claiming he was merely "serbing my white folks by getting back what is deris. Dis mule was stole by some po' sinner what don't know the scriptures." Eventually, the elderly black man was released, and he took the mule back to his master's farm. What Jake's real intentions were is impossible to tell. Perhaps it was an abortive escape attempt, perhaps not. But in the divided communities along the Georgia-Tennessee lines, masters felt they had to be wary of every potential threat to the slave system.[21]

In this environment, even mundane features of everyday life took on sinister connotations, as north Georgians looked for evidence of treason within the community and even within the family. One example was the debate over state aid to destitute families. Since 1862, the state had authorized funding to assist the families of soldiers with food and supplies. The local county inferior courts were in charge of disbursing this welfare fund, and they drew up lists of eligible recipients and schedules for "public corn" distributions. As food shortages grew in 1864, and more families faced potential starvation, controversy broke out about the proper distribution of the welfare funds. Inevitably, in the divisive environment of north Georgia, debates over loyalty and disloyalty were superimposed upon this issue. Families accused each other of being unworthy of state aid. One Gilmer man wrote that "I am the agent of this county to distribute the government corn . . . and if they are with the Yankeys their families are not entitled to it." And in Dawson County, a Confederate asked "is it right for deserters' families who has been laying out for twelve months and upwards to participate in the public corn?" Another claimed that "some draws corn that ought not . . . the meanest characters who don't try and make anything." In Lumpkin, the court openly refused to distribute aid to "disloyal" persons, inspiring one Dahlonega man to protest to the governor. "I had the honor of raising the first and finest company that ever left Georgia," Alfred Harris proclaimed, "and yet the Inferior Court refuses to let me have any of the public corn." Harris stoutly defended his secessionist credentials, listing a long litany of service to substantiate his claims to public aid and denigrating the patriotism of others who unjustly profited at the public's expense. Harris not only defended his own loyalty but impugned the inferior court's, the members of which, in his view, favored Tories and "allowed other men not so old as myself . . . and who never served a day in the army in all their lives to draw corn, thread, and money." [22]

Others echoed this charge of disloyalty in high places, criticizing the inferior courts for "want of energy, incapacity, misapplication of the public fund." In Fannin County, dueling factions used the language of loyalty in a wrangle over the constitution of the inferior court. W. A. Campbell organized a petition asking for the removal of court officers for authorizing "provisions for the families of men who have gone over to the Yankees." A rival group answered with charges that the court's critics were "evil persons . . . who wish to gratify their own prejudice," and claimed that at least one petitioner was guilty of "carrying deserters' wives through the lines." [23]

With starvation looming, north Georgians were bound to fight over limited food resources, but interestingly they framed their arguments in terms of loyalty. Three years of divisions and the recent introduction of the Union army had taught highlanders to suspect the allegiances of even close neighbors, and to cast their own identities in terms of fealty to the Confederacy. This accusatory impulse sometimes intruded within the family circle, dividing siblings, husbands and wives, parents and children. No component of the community was immune to charges of disloyalty. On March 18, 1864, the Georgia State Legislature approved a bill originally proposed by a senator from northwestern Georgia that pitted highland families against each other. The bill amended Georgia law to allow for "a total divorce in favor of any loyal female" if her husband was "in the military service of the United States . . . or is voluntarily within the lines of the enemy, furnishing them aid and comfort." It soon became widely known in north Georgia that Tories' wives could seek divorce on grounds of a husband's disloyalty. Many women did so, and in the process, they illustrated the divisions within their communities. In the spring of 1864, Emma Roberts of Lumpkin County charged her husband with adultery and being "forgetful of his marital obligations," but she also accused him of treason. She claimed her husband deserted the 52nd Georgia Infantry in March 1864 and "being actuated by unpatriotic and traitorous designs . . . did abandon his government and is now within the lines of the military authorities of the people of the United States, giving them as enemies aid and comfort . . . against the people of the said state of Georgia and of said Confederate States." Jane Duckett's husband Henry also left his wife and "went and joined himself to the public enemies of the Confederate States," helping in "prosecuting the present war against the people" of Georgia." Some Fannin women made similar charges against defecting men.[24]

These women took the spirit of the proposed divorce act to heart and cast their personal crises in the language of loyalty. Jane Duckett explicitly equated Henry Duckett's adultery with his disloyalty to the Confederacy and, in her deposition, coupled his treason with his failures as a husband. The wording of her deposition evince this linkage: "her hopes were soon blighted by infidelity and the traitorous conduct of her said husband"; her husband had "wholly disregard[ed] his marital obligations . . . and his allegiances to his own native country"; he had "unlawfully abandoned and deserted your petitioner and wickedly and traitorously deserted . . . his own country." Although the precise motives of these women are unclear (they were likely trying to lay claim to their ex-husbands' property), it is clear that, in the polarized environment created by dissension and desertion, all social relationships were colored by the ongoing debate over loyalty in the mountains. And the family, which in general served to unite members, also was vulnerable to the growing atmosphere of suspicion.[25]

With Tories fleeing to the enemy, the Union army approaching, and neighbors, husbands, and wives doubting each other's loyalty, pro-Confederates became more harsh in their attitudes toward "traitors" and less restrained by the notion of legalism that had bound much of their behavior through 1863. Mountain Rebels' hearts hardened in 1864, and a growing conviction took hold that the enemies of the community should be treated mercilessly. The bitter progress of events left its mark on north Georgia, and the change was increasingly manifest in the thoughts, writings, and actions of upcountry secessionists.

The process of "othering" Tories and Unionists clearly had impetus from the highest levels of state government. In addition to the aforementioned divorce bill, the state of Georgia also moved to place dissenters beyond the pale of legal protection. On March 10, 1864, Governor Brown urged the legislature to pass an extraordinary series of measures designed to strip the disloyal of their property and rights. Brown asserted that north Georgians who refugeed to the Union lines in Tennessee "have never been loyal to the cause of the South" and were trying to "unite with the enemies of their State." The only just treatment for such defectors, Brown said, was for the state to confiscate their property and use the proceeds to support "loyal citizens of the same section, whose property has been destroyed, by raids of the enemy, or by armed bands of tories." As for those highlanders who actually joined the Union army, the governor had nothing but contempt:

> I am also informed, that some disloyal persons in that section, have deserted from our armies; or avoiding service have left their families behind, and gone over to the enemy, and are now under arms against us. I am happy to learn that the number of such persons is very small. I recommend the confiscation of the property of this class of persons also, and in case they have left families behind, that are a charge to the county, that no part of the relief fund be allowed them; but that they be carried to the enemy's lines, and turned over to those in whose cause their husbands now serve. I also recommend the enactment of such laws as shall forever disfranchise and decitizenize all persons of both classes, should they attempt to return to this State.[26]

By thus defining Tories and their families as unworthy of citizenship or state assistance, Brown was encouraging Georgians to treat dissenters as a separate class of untouchables, whose property, family, and very existence was unworthy of civilized treatment. And many upcountry Rebels were quick to take the implications of the governor's statements. Those who actively fought the armed Tory bands were among the first to embrace ruthless methods against dissenters. Andrew Young of Union County had served bravely in the Confederate army during the war's first years, but as dissent increased, his cavalry unit was assigned to north Georgia to aid state militia in keeping order and hunting deserters. Young quickly grew frustrated with his mission—Tories were elusive, the local citizenry often hid offenders from his troops, and dissenters received aid and intelligence from compatriots across the border in Tennessee and North Carolina. Complaining to the governor, Young asked for authority to treat Tories ruthlessly, asserting that "no temporizing plan will succeed here. Action emphatic [and] quick" was necessary. For Young, "action emphatic [and] quick" apparently included the summary execution of any Tory who put Confederate lives at risk. "As to deserters, persons absent without leave, persons aiding deserters . . . if they shoot any of my men I will wait for no order but dispose of all I capture." [27]

Upcountry Confederate soldiers serving at the front also worried about the stories they heard about dissent at home and became increasingly determined to see Tories destroyed. Soldiers grew ever more frustrated that internal enemies were victimizing civilians while they fought the Confederacy's external enemies on the battlefield, and such frustration drove many almost to desperation. Stories of Tory violence in Gilmer County were almost too much for M. C. Briant to take as he sat in the trenches around Petersburg. He wrote his fiancée of his fears that "the country is over-run by tories and marauders and that you are subject to the barbarity of a worse than savage and brutal foe." Briant worried that "you will be mistreated by the disloyal fiends and ruffians" and swore "eternal vengeance to the man that does it." In another letter, Briant voiced disbelief that the very thing he was fighting for, "home with all its endearments," was being "endangered and trodden down and insulted by such a vile enemy as a tory." He urged his relatives and friends in Gilmer to exhaust "every honorable means" to end the Tory threat. A. J. Reese of Lumpkin County was less charitable. When he heard of more highlanders deserting their regiments and returning home, he asserted that "about half of them ought to be shot." And Reese seemed eager to do the shooting. He urged that his company be assigned to its mountain homeland to "skirmish out those mountains and run [the Tories] in their holes and smoke them out. Our boys swear eternal vengeance against them." Other soldiers dehumanized the Tories in their everyday language, employing animal imagery by referring to dissenters as "Federal Mules" or "hogbacks." [28]

Pro-Confederate civilians also voiced unforgiving sentiments about their Tory enemies. Many secessionist women were even more strident than the men in advocating remorseless pursuit and destruction of dissenters. When state militia attacked a band of Tories in Fannin and Gilmer counties, Huldah Fain noted approvingly that "they have killed lots of . . . bushwhackers that should have been killed long since." And when Confederates shot eight local Tories, including a woman, Huldah Fain's mother could only express regret that the soldier had not finished the job. "Dock got away from them," Mrs. Fain lamented. "It would have been a good deed if they had got him too." In Dahlonega, Nancy Wimpy also grew callous to the fate of dissenters. After enduring continuous alarms and rumors of Bryson's Tories victimizing secessionists, Wimpy seemed eager to embrace the harshest possible measures to ensure the safety of her community. In a letter to her nephew, Wimpy related matter-of-factly that "some of the state troops shot a deserter night before last by the name of Seabolt. He is one of the tories that was taken up last winter [by George Lee's troops]." Totally supportive of the militia's actions, she wrote that "I think all deserters from the State service ought to be shot, for they know nothing about hardship and suffering yet." And Wimpy hearkened back to an old cultural stereotype of savage Native American warriors when she advocated unleashing the Cherokees against the Tories. "It would be a good thing if they could get those Indians in N.C. after them," she mused, "they would treat them just about right." Her anger at her local enemies also inspired Wimpy to preach hard war against the North. She urged Confederate troops raiding in Pennsylvania to destroy as much private property as possible. "I think everything ought to be left in ruins. Let them feel the war at home as our people have felt it." For these civilians, merciless warfare was the only way to vanquish dissenters and their Northern allies. Indeed, many female rebels seemed to have more stomach for harsh measures than their men. Nancy Wimpy's call for deserters' blood contrasted with the sentiments of some north Georgia soldiers who had witnessed such events. One northwest Georgia soldier was quite disturbed by the public killing of a captured deserter from his unit, asserting that it was a crime to execute a man "unless he has proven himself a traitor.[29]

The steadfastness of some of the region's elite Confederate women seems to dispute the analysis of some scholars who argue that Southern women gradually lost the will to continue the war and, in so doing, turned Southern soldiers against the Confederacy as well. To be sure, many north Georgia women saw their patriotism erode in the face of Tory attacks at home and military reversals in lower Georgia. The women of Dahlonega evinced the same war-weariness and longing for absent husbands, fathers, and sons that plagued most Southern women. They surely felt abandoned and beset by the consequences of the war their men had wrought, as they strove to deal with the devastation on their doorsteps. But for many of these women, the solution to the crisis was not surrender but rather an increased commitment to the cause and sterner measures against its enemies. Rather than urge their men to desert the fight and return home, these women professed a continuing faith in armed struggle despite overwhelming evidence of Confederate defeat. Even as the final battles around Petersburg sealed the fate of the Robert E. Lee's forces in Virginia in early 1865, Huldah Fain urged continued resistance. "I believe Old Bob's army will have to do the fight another year and believe they are willing and able, for I believe among you there are but very few whose love of self has prevailed over their love of country."[30]

The hardening attitudes of mountain women, and civilians in general, toward enemies of the Confederate cause had important consequences. Upcountry Confederates began to move away from strict concepts of legalism that had previously bound their behavior against Tories. Since the unsuccessful Dahlonega treason trials in 1863, secessionists seemed to have less faith in the ability of the judicial system to deal effectively with dissent. Few mountain Rebels complained, therefore, when Confederate soldiers captured and summarily executed seventeen of Bryson's band in North Carolina toward the end of 1863, including the Tory leader himself. "Thus ended the inglorious career of this tory chieftain," the *Athens Southern Watchman* editorialized, "who has made a name and fame by the side of which that of Benedict Arnold stands in enviable contrast." A few days later, White County militia captured another Tory, Jake Wofford, accused of murdering a local secessionist. A mob formed and forced Wofford to stand on a platform with a rope around his neck while officers interrogated him, but a bystander grew impatient at the process. "Finding he was very obstinate and would not answer any questions propounded to him, some person in the crowd yanked the plank out from under his toes and . . . launched him into eternity," an eyewitness reported. Many other north Georgia Rebels were growing impatient with the formal justice system, and as guerrilla war escalated its intensity, they embraced extralegal violence to serve their conceptions of justice.[31]

On March 6, 1864, William Fain made a choice. The prominent Fannin County dissenter had spent three years cautiously resisting Confederate authorities and local secessionist rivals. Fannin's Committee for Public

Safety had castigated him as a Tory and tried to have him arrested for disloyalty the previous year. Four of his brothers were serving with the Confederate armed forces, and a cousin, Ebenezer Fain, was a key Rebel leader in neighboring Gilmer County. Through it all Fain was careful not to commit any overt acts of treason to the Confederacy. However, as the Union army neared and offered Georgia dissenters an opportunity to defend themselves, the Morganton attorney decided to embrace new allies. Fain gathered his wife and family and crossed over the state line to Cleveland, Tennessee, a town already teeming with Georgia refugees. There he sought out a Union colonel, told him of the willing pool of potential volunteers in north Georgia, and won authority to recruit Federal soldiers from the border area. Later that month, Fain returned to his native county, armed with the power of the U.S. government and determined to convince other Fannin dissenters to join him. In doing so, he fired the opening salvo in a regional civil war.[32]

Once word spread that Fain was "on his way to Yankeedom," other Fannin dissenters followed suit. Several joined Fain's mission, and by late March a small party roamed the county, looking for more Union recruits. Confederates were terrified, and rumors spread. Some claimed that Fain had twenty-five men with him, while others said the Tories numbered almost a hundred. Ominous stories circulated that Fain held secret communiqués from Federal commanders in Tennessee, which contained orders for "tory friends" in the region. The letters, according to local newspapers, were calculated to appeal to "the most ignorant and degraded of mankind" to join the Union forces and "commit all sorts of depredations upon defenseless women and children." The local militia commander wrote that the Tories were "robbing and stealing everything they can find" and had even raided Morganton, Fain's hometown and the county seat. Others worried that Fain intended to hold and secure Fannin County as a Union enclave by dispossessing and evicting pro-Confederate citizens. "They have caused nearly all of our true southern men to move south, and they fully intended to drive out the true men from the county," reported a pro-Confederate from neighboring Gilmer County.[33]

The most disturbing and persistent news reaching Fannin's Confederates that spring concerned Fain's recruiting activities among the black population. In March, several of Fain's men, dressed in Federal uniforms, attacked the two-thousand-acre plantation of one of the county's wealthiest slaveholders, James Morris. The Tories reportedly either captured or "induced to leave" four of the Morris slaves, as well as three other black men from adjoining farms. "W. C. Fain was seen in the company of the Negroes as they went on to the enemy, conducting them through," one rebel reported. Soon thereafter, Fain's men struck the Mangum farm, killing the owner and "taking his negroes." These stories must have frightened mountain Confederates on several levels. Not only was Fain stealing thousands of dollars of slaveholders' "property," but his "inducing" blacks to leave implied that the Tory raids would inspire local blacks to defect en masse, or perhaps even to revolt. To many slaveholders, this fit into a larger trend of black refugeeing, as evidenced by the formation of units like the 44th U.S. Colored Troops. Moreover, the fact that Fain, a slave owner himself, engaged in such activities made him a traitor to his class and a dangerous example for others.[34]

Mountain Rebels were also shocked at the violence of Fain's expedition. In the attack on the Morris plantation, the eldest Morris son tried to resist the raiders, and Fain's men shot him through the bowels. When two of the Morris women tried to assist, the Tories knocked them to the ground with rifle barrels. Fain's recruits reportedly killed, wounded, or shot at several other secessionists while on their mission, and the violence of the raid incurred swift reaction from the authorities. By April, troops and secessionist civilians were scouring the mountains of Fannin and Gilmer counties. There were several skirmishes with Fain's recruits, with Tories using guerrilla tactics to fight off their better-armed and organized pursuers: "The Tories with their squirrel rifles pick off our men from behind rocks and trees and all manner of hiding places. In this way they have killed six or eight of our soldiers," the local press reported.[35]

On April 6, Fain and his recruits began crossing back into Tennessee, heading for Cleveland, where they could officially enroll in the Federal service. Militia from the Governor Brown's Georgia State Line followed, under orders to quell the "maraudings of Tories and deserters" in the mountains. At Edwards Ferry, a crossing on the Toccoa River in northern Fannin County, a squad of militia captured Fain and one of his recruits. What happened next is unclear. Some witnesses claimed that Fain tried to escape and was shot as he ran. Other accounts make no mention of escape. Fain's wife was watching her husband cross the river from the Tennessee side, and she reported that the militia captured Fain, led him away on a horse, and shot him in the back of the head, "the ball . . . coming out on the right front side of his face." Possibly the soldiers were so enraged at Fain's raid that they simply killed him on the spot—other defectors reported that angry soldiers were shooting refugees on sight. The militia's treatment of another recruit they captured that day bears out their rage. Locals found Henry Robinson the day after Fain's murder, tied to a tree with some twenty bullet wounds in his lifeless body. Pro-Confederate civilians shared in this anger and felt the means used to stamp it out were justified. When Ebenezer Fain heard of his cousin William's execution, the Gilmer County Rebel noted with satisfaction that the soldiers who carried out the killing were "the rite sort of men for this country."[36]

Fain's raid was the most serious, organized threat upcountry secessionists had yet faced, and they escalated their own violence in response. In the spring, state militia and Confederate Cavalry made another expedition from Atlanta, this time launching strikes into Tennessee and North Carolina as well as north Georgia. The soldiers arrested a few deserters but found the Tories more resistant and more eager to fight than previously. In the wake of the raid, impressment agents and conscription officers also became even more ruthless, and those dissenters who stayed in their communities suffered for the actions of refugees and defectors like William Fain. Invading soldiers and militia increasingly viewed north Georgia as a land apart, where no rules applied and where, by implication, force could be used without restraint. One officer compared Fannin County to the bowels of hell and claimed that "this place is to all intents and purposes a den of thieves and is the known resort of all outlaws of the land." The records of the Southern Claims Commission reveal that Tory civilians fell victim to a gradual escalation of violent attacks by authorities as the war approached its final year.[37]

Violence had always been implicit in the behavior of impressment officers, but as dissenters became more closely identified with the approaching Federal armies, state and Confederate officials were quick to embrace all kinds of violent means against those perceived as disloyal. Some officials relied on threats to intimidate their victims. One Tory recalled that militia had "threatened to have a dozen bullets shot into me," and another reported that soldiers told him that "I ought to have my brains knocked out" for his anti-Confederate sentiments. "I was threatened to be hung and have my head cut off," remembered yet another civilian with vivid clarity, while another reported that "they threatened to shoot me off my horse if I did not give him up." The threats often involved a victim's family. When one dissenter heard some soldiers "threaten to shoot my wife if she didn't open the smokehouse door," he quickly complied. And when militia approached the house of a Tory woman whom they suspected of funneling supplies to a group of deserters, they "gave her 'till the next morning to leave the county, if not they would burn the house." Often authorities would make implicit threats by referring to other violent acts they had perpetrated. The troops who killed William Fain bragged about it to a Tory woman in Morganton soon after the incident, and another dissenter remembered being spared by an armed Confederate who claimed he had "already killed a lot of men that day." These threats and rumors frightened some north Georgians into refugeeing—Hosea Hopkins of Pickens County said that he had heard of "several Union men [being] killed and we went north to avoid the same lot."[38]

Authorities also employed symbolic and psychological violence invoking terror that was all too real upon dissenters. Troops looted Tory homes in the most invasive ways, killing livestock and other animals, breaking down doors, and invading the most personal spaces of individuals. In Gilmer County, soldiers reportedly "broke open trunks and carried away ladies clothing," and other Tories claimed that Confederates had taken the clothing off the backs of their children. At other times, troops played cruel games with civilians: aiming and cocking their weapons at victims only to relent at the last second; hauling Tories before firing squads; letting them stand terrified, expecting death, and then releasing them to their families; shooting at the feet or near the heads of victims.[39]

Tories had reason to fear these threats and symbolic attacks, for soldiers often punctuated them with action. When Stanley Rickels resisted the impressment squad that came to his Fannin County farm, the troops responded brutally—"all his daughters [were] knocked down and badly hurt, his wife and children badly abused," one witness stated. Soon after the Fain raid, vengeful militia made a dawn visit to the house of Albert Ward, a Gilmer Tory. Hearing the crowd outside, Ward came to the door and reached out to shake hands when he spotted a familiar face, only to be "jerked out of the door." The troops then fired indiscriminately at Ward and into the house. "They shot seven balls into him . . . [and] they shot his wife's thumb off in shooting at him," witnesses reported.[40]

Notably, both these incidents involved women victims, which was one measure of the war's escalating violence. Although most accounts report that a different standard of violence applied to women—"Union men were killed; women were insulted," recalled one Tory—violence eroded the gender barriers as Confederates became increasingly frustrated with disloyalty. In part, mountain Rebels were simply retaliating for previous

Tory actions such as the beating of the two Morris women by Fain's recruits in March. In addition, Confederates knew that women and children formed a vital part of the support network that dissenting men used to continue their resistance. By striking at dissenter's mothers, sisters, and daughters, Rebels were cutting the root of the anti-Confederate resistance. One Confederate officer noted that noncombatants were integral to the whole defection process and implied that stern action must be taken against civilians to stem the flow of north Georgians to the Union lines:

> Wagons are loaded and started across the lines carried along by women and boys while the men who are making their way to the enemy skulk around the mountains and go to the wagons after they have reached the enemies lines. By this means they are continually deserting and carrying their property to the enemy, thereby strengthening them and weakening us. I would rather burn up the property than permit it to go over to our enemies. . . if the Gov. permits the blockade to be run in this way . . . a great many will escape who might otherwise have been deterred from going.[41]

Moreover, many secessionists were so embittered by the years of Tory "lawlessness" that they were willing to take such measures. In their minds, dissenters had first begun to violate sanctions against attacking dependents in late 1862, when Tory bands started preying on the populace. Secessionists like M. C. Briant blamed the Tories for making war upon "home and all its endearments," while the Rebels were selflessly fighting for home and family. In this view, attacking dissenter families seemed like just punishment. And Rebels were unwilling to show tolerance for the families of an enemy who was so ruthless himself. Nancy Wimpy fully expected to be physically attacked if Tories ever took Dahlonega—"I don't expect any mercy from them if they come here," she wrote in 1864. Why extend mercy to a merciless enemy, Wimpy must have wondered.[42]

If William Fain's raid increased the bitterness and anger of mountain Rebels, subsequent events only compounded the tension. Fain's death did not stop the Federal army from recruiting in north Georgia, and as Sherman's forces marched deeper into the state, more U.S. agents infiltrated into the mountain counties. In the summer and early fall of 1864, two more Federal officers crossed the mountains from Tennessee and entered Fannin County, intending to capitalize upon the region's tradition of dissent and the Tory outrage inspired by William Fain's murder.

William Lillard and William A. Twiggs operated independently of each other, but both had orders from the commander of the 5th Tennessee Mounted Infantry to enroll as many highlanders as possible. Their activities would touch off the next bloody round of guerrilla combat in the region.

Lillard was a native of Polk County, Tennessee, and he knew the border region and its people well. Like many Tories, he was conscripted into the Confederate army. He deserted in the spring of 1863 and hid in the mountains with a band of dissenters. After several of his band were imprisoned or killed by Confederate soldiers, Lillard enlisted in the 5th Tennessee Mounted Infantry. Friends remembered that the ambitious Lillard was "anxious to become an officer" in the new regiment, and he volunteered for a recruitment mission into north Georgia in the spring of 1864. He spent the summer and fall slipping back and forth across the border enlisting handfuls of north Georgia recruits on each trip. Secessionists heard rumors of the invasion by a party of "torys and rouges" from Tennessee; home guard units kept alert for Lillard's men but were unable to capture him.[43]

In September, one of Lillard's recruiting missions took him to the outskirts of the Fannin County seat of Morganton, where he met Nathaniel Parris, a poor tenant farmer and wounded veteran of the Army of Northern Virginia. Two of Parris's sons, Peter and James, were Confederate deserters who were active in a local band of Tories that allegedly "murdered and robbed inoffensive persons without any reason or conscience." Using the Parris cabin as a base, Lillard arranged for two of the Parris sons and several of the women to flee to Tennessee, where the men would enlist in the 5th Tennessee. Peter Parris agreed to stay behind and help recruit another group of Fannin men for the Union army, which he would lead to Tennessee when the opportunity arose.[44]

Meanwhile, a second Union officer entered the Blue Ridge country. William A. Twiggs was a thirty-three-year-old yeoman farmer from North Carolina who had migrated to Fannin County in the 1850s. In 1862, he was conscripted into the Confederate 52nd Georgia Infantry and served a year before deserting, like many north Georgians, soon after the Battle of Vicksburg. He enlisted in the 5th Tennessee Mounted Infantry in 1864, gained a commission as captain, and entered his home county in September to recruit a company of Union soldiers. But his mission soon evolved into much more than an enlistment drive. Twiggs had family and friends in the region, and he knew firsthand the difficulties and privations Tories suffered there. When the Union recruiter met with Solomon Stansbury and Iley Stuart, two local dissenters, the three planned a new mission that would strike at local Confederates in the region.[45]

Stansbury and Stuart were anti-Confederates of long standing. The Tennessee-born Stansbury was a vocal opponent of conscription who had been imprisoned on at least one occasion for his resistance and eventually joined the Union army in the winter of 1863–64. Stuart was a fellow yeoman farmer, who migrated to Fannin from western North Carolina before the war. In the ensuing years he attained moderate prosperity and became a leading civic figure in Pierceville, along the Tennessee border. His wife and friends remembered him as "a Union man from the first" who "cursed and abused the rebels for doing as they did." This "made him obnoxious" to local authorities, who singled him out for punishment and harassed him and his family constantly. Stuart also defected to Tennessee and enlisted in the Union 11th Tennessee Cavalry in 1863.[46]

But Stansbury and Stuart both deserted the Union army within months of their enlistment, and by the summer of 1864, they were back in Fannin County. On the surface their choice seems puzzling. Both men had aggressively resisted the Confederate draft, had spoken out against the secessionists, and had made the seemingly irrevocable decision to turn their backs on their state and join the Union army. But Stansbury and Stuart's behavior illustrates the continuing power of localism to define mountaineers' interests. Just as Weir Boyd and James Findley abandoned the Confederate armies to fight for order in their community, the two Fannin Tories decided to leave a conflict that did not involve their direct interests to fight for Fannin County.

Stuart and Stansbury were ill served by their new Union allies when they first defected to Federal lines. Soon after swearing in the recruits, U.S. troops confiscated their horses and other personal items. (Indeed, Georgia Tories often reported such abuses by their ostensible "allies." Several recruits stated that William Lillard foraged liberally among Union families when looking for enlistees in the mountains. And Susan Davis, a Tory woman from Lumpkin, claimed that recruits stole her livestock on a raid.) After Stuart deserted, he told a friend that he would not go back to the Federal troops because "they had not treated him right." More importantly, Stuart and Stansbury realized that the war they were fighting in the Union army only drew them farther away from their homes and from their local enemies. While Fannin dissenters endured Confederate abuses in Fannin County, Stuart and Stansbury suffered assignments to far-removed posts in Knoxville and Nashville. This was not the war they enlisted to fight, and so both men deserted and returned home to organize a home guard and take the fight to the local pro-Confederate forces.[47]

When William Twiggs came through Fannin on his recruiting mission in September, Stuart and Stansbury were already mobilizing the forces of dissent. The Union recruiter soon decided to expand his mission to assist in launching a local rebellion against pro-Confederates, organizing Fannin dissenters into a force that could "give protection to the Union people" and pursue retribution against secessionists. They traveled throughout the county that autumn, wearing their Federal uniforms to add legitimacy to their mission. They gave public speeches in Morganton and other villages, asking citizens for assistance, with appeals to justice and localism. The raiders promised to "drive out the rebels who were robbing the citizens" and to "protect their homes" from impressment officers, conscription agents, and militia. If Fannin Tories acted together, the three Unionists claimed, nothing could stop them from "driving out the Confederates and holding the country."[48]

Appealing to local resentment over Confederate intrusion, Twiggs, Stansbury, and Stuart gathered a band of recruits and went into action in October. Gathering horses was the first priority, for Twiggs had been ordered to have his men furnish their own mounts. The Tories enthusiastically set about liberating mounts from "enemies of the government." The mission soon degenerated into a destructive spree, as the recruits "took the opportunity of repaying past injuries, if not on those [who] inflicted them, on their abettors." A later government report blamed the resultant atrocities on lax recruiting officers who had failed to keep their charges "under the proper control." But it is likely that no control could have kept these men from lashing out at pro-Confederates. For three years, Rebel authorities and their civilian sympathizers had made virtual war on the dissenters and their families. Now they were back in the midst of their homes and kin, armed and empowered, and the emotional intensity of the moment was irresistible. The Tories sought their own form of justice through indiscriminate violence of the most brutal kind. When a group of Union recruits encountered a Confederate sympathizer named Bird McKinney, they captured him and took him off toward Cleveland, Tennessee, as per the orders of their sergeant. But after a short time the enlistees decided to deal with the prisoner in a different way. They summarily executed him with a bullet to the head and then mutilated the body. One Unionist cut an ear off the corpse, which he carried with him back to Tennessee to show his comrades, saying that "it was a damned Rebbel ear and he wanted all the boys from Gilmer County to come and see it." By engaging in this savage exhibition, the Union guerrilla sought the validation of his peers and reminded them that any means were justified to suppress and take revenge upon those who had persecuted their homes and families.[49]

The news of revolt in Fannin struck Lumpkin County Confederates at a time when tensions already ran high. Secessionists reported that "no citizen is secure on his life liberty or property . . . our best citizens [have been] killed in cold blood." Elijah Chastain admitted that "my section . . . is almost entirely overrun with robbers and tories." The Tory raids of 1864 culminated a series of crises that forced the county's Rebels to become even more preoccupied with law and order and to look on their northern neighbors with a suspicion born of insecurity. These factors propelled Lumpkin County down a violent path that ended in a wave of military-sponsored vigilantism against Unionists in the autumn of 1864.[50]

The Vigilance Committees, treason trials, and military intervention of 1863 had traumatized Lumpkin County, but it did not leave Confederates feeling any safer. It was evident that the problem of disloyalty was not eradicated, and in fact it was intensified by the approach of the Union army and the growing number of defections to the enemy. Lumpkin militia commander James Findley complained in January 1864 that "deserters and tories and rouges" still ran unchecked through the county, "stealing horses . . . and cattle" and making it impossible for farmers to tend their crops. Worse, some of Findley's militia were refusing to muster for duty, especially "the disloyal and the tories of which I regret to say we have many." By the summer, dozens of Lumpkin men had escaped the state and joined the Union army, while local Tories intensified their activities. Word of William Fain's raid and the infiltration of more Union recruiters into the mountains only heightened the Confederates sense of surrounding anarchy. Nancy Wimpy grew weary of the constant alarms of Union raids and Tory crimes. "Every two or three weeks we hear they [the Tories] are coming," Wimpy wrote, "[and] every man that are not for the Yanks get their guns and go make ready for them." The alarms often proved false. But the constant threats contributed to a growing sense of insecurity and helplessness among Lumpkin Rebels.[51]

Matters worsened with the virtual collapse of the local justice system in the summer of 1864. In August, Judge George Rice of the Blue Ridge circuit court suspended meetings of Lumpkin's superior court, owing to "unsettled conditions in this peculiar crisis." Rice canceled court again in October, leaving Lumpkin residents without the legal machinery to address the Tory threat and inspiring Weir Boyd to plead with the governor to order Judge Rice to "meet his appointments . . . that Law and Order may prevail." This compounded the mistrust with which local Confederates had regarded the court system since the treason trials of John Woody and James Payne the previous year and persuaded many Dahlonegans to look to the local military authorities to keep order.[52]

In addition, Lumpkin Rebels were feeling even more insecure about perceptions of their loyalty and were eager to shift the label of treason onto other mountain counties to prove their allegiance. Lumpkin still resented the "stain upon her name" against which the grand jury railed after Lee's invasion in 1863, and in their eagerness to substantiate their commitment to the Confederacy, local Rebels accused neighboring mountaineers of being the true traitors. It was a pattern that developed soon after Lee's first expedition, when pro-Confederates felt the need to deflect criticism of their region onto others. Thus, one Dahlonega correspondent asserted that "some might suppose that the chief troubles lay in Lumpkin County; but such is not the fact. The malcontents and deserters belong to nearly all the counties in this region of the state." The indignant Dahlonegan compared his town's record favorably with that of nearby White County, saying, "let it be remembered that though these lawless men succeeded in breaking a jail in a neighboring county, when they attempted to do likewise in Dahlonega, they found citizens in arms and ready for them, and wisely desisted." When William Fain raided Fannin County in the spring of 1864, the *Dahlonega Mountain Signal* emphasized the traitorous actions of their northern neighbor and highlighted the violence and barbarity of the "ruffians" with Fain. Indeed, to Dahlonega elites, Fannin County must have seemed everything they were not—undeveloped, unsophisticated, and full of disloyal backwoods highlanders who had no history or commerce to tie them to the state of Georgia. When Weir Boyd conjured his worst fears for Lumpkin's future, he thought of the current state of affairs in the northern county. "Our county is rapidly approaching anarchy . . . and unless a favorable change soon occurs will become *like Fannin* . . . on our Northern and Western border."[53]

Continuing Tory activity, the perceived breakdown of law and order, and the heightened sensitivity to charges of disloyalty against mountain people all contributed to a siege mentality among Lumpkin Confederates. Therefore, when news reached Dahlonega that Twiggs, Stansbury, and Stuart were raiding in Fannin County, "stealing horses and robbing houses," Lumpkin militia sprang into action, determined to stamp out the latest manifestation of treason. James Findley ordered a detachment of his militia under Captain Francis Marion Williams into Fannin to "capture the party or drive them out." Williams's troops set out on October 18 and crossed the border into southern Fannin County, on a direct intercept course for the Unionists. Twiggs's raiders were heading for Stock Hill, Twiggs's hometown, in the southeastern part of the county, where he could hope to raise more volunteers. At some point, Stansbury, Stuart, and a few other men separated from the main group of Tories and stopped at a blacksmith's in Dial to shoe the horses and mules recently captured from pro-Confederate civilians. There the Lumpkin militia surprised and captured the entire group. Some witnesses later claimed that the militia initially intended to shoot all the Tories on the spot but were dissuaded by the fact that the raiders wore Federal uniforms and thus were due some consideration as prisoners of war rather than common criminals. That same day the militia led their captives back toward Dahlonega, forty miles away. On October 22, the column reached the town, where Colonel Findley ordered the prisoners jailed in the courthouse. Meanwhile, William Twiggs and the rest of his recruits escaped back across the state line to Tennessee.[54]

For Findley and many other pro-Confederate Dahlonegans, the proper punishment for the prisoners seemed clear. They were traitors in alliance with Federal officers who had victimized Rebel civilians in a violent raid. Because they were not from Lumpkin and instead were from an isolated and underdeveloped part of the Appalachians, they could become examples for other Tories. Lumpkin Rebels could prove their loyalty to the Confederacy and their commitment to law and order by executing the three Tories, who were, after all, from a county widely portrayed as treasonous. Moreover, the public mood seemed to endorse harsh measures. Lumpkin Confederates lived in almost daily terror of Tories and had endured a series of disturbing, violent events in which some of their own citizens had been implicated as traitors. Now the "savages" of the Blue Ridge threatened to spread more disorder. No measures seemed too extreme to prevent this disintegration.

James Findley saw no reason to offer the prisoners a trial. On October 22, he ordered William R. Crisson of his command to "take the following named of those prisoners—Solomon Stansbury, Iley Stuart, and William Witt—and have them shot for being bushwhackers." Stansbury and Stuart were obviously key anti-Confederate leaders in the region, but it was unclear why the third man, a recruit they had picked up on the raid, was also selected for death. Whatever the reason, a seven-man firing squad took the prisoners out to a small knob called Bearden's Bridge Hill, overlooking the Chestatee River, on the evening of the 22nd. There, Findley's soldiers shot the three men to death. The bodies were so disfigured that when Margaret Stuart later came to bury her husband's corpse, she could identify him only by recognizing her stitching on the socks he was wearing.[55]

Findley did not rest there. In early November, he mobilized his militia for action against the Tory guerrillas of John A. Ashworth, a Dawson County physician and relative of Iley Stuart who had launched a raid of his own. In his official report on the operation, Findley used criminal language to describe Ashworth, "whose thieving, burning, and other depredations had been so extensive in upper counties." The Lumpkin colonel marched his troops over snow-covered Amacalola Mountain and attacked Ashworth's band while they were camped at the house of a Gilmer County Tory named Henry Weaver. After the skirmish, most of Ashworth's men surrendered. Ashworth was sent to a Confederate prisoner-of-war camp in South Carolina, but some of his men were even less fortunate. Findley found papers on the captured men listing Unionist civilians in Dawson County. The militia then marched through Dawsonville, tracked down five of the civilians on the list, including the local sheriff, and imprisoned them for the vague charge of being "engaged in secret negotiations with the enemy." The entire column reached Gainesville on November 7, where Findley separated out twelve Tories whom he branded as "deserters from our army." John Ashworth contradicted this, telling his Union prison mates that only six of the captured Tories he led had ever served in the Confederate forces. Regardless, Findley summarily executed the twelve. For the time being, he was satisfied that Lumpkin County was secure.[56]

Scholars generally define vigilantism as any popular, extralegal violence directed at persons perceived to be lawless. The great vigilante movements in American history—South Carolina, 1767, San Francisco, 1856, Montana 1863-65—all shared a focus on punishing alleged lawbreakers, and all followed a breakdown in the legal system that prodded citizens to spontaneous executions of suspected criminals. Richard Maxwell Brown called American vigilantes "the conservative mob" and argued that such incidents historically occurred on the frontier, where formal legal structures were weak. Elites often led vigilante groups, since they had the most to lose from a situation in which widespread crime threatened property. In the American South, vigilantism was tied inextricably to concepts of honor, and communities sanctioned extralegal violence if they perceived the greater needs of justice and honor were served.[57]

The Lumpkin County execution may not fit the vigilante paradigm precisely. The killers here were not members of a temporary civilian mob but were organized officials of the state. But in a larger sense these killings did exemplify vigilantism. The war had destabilized north Georgia and left its residents feeling fearful and isolated from central authority. Local military authorities, composed of members of the community, acted to fill a vacuum left by the disintegration of the legal system and took matters into their own hands, rounding up enemies of the Confederacy and executing them without due process or formal charges. Although the common citizenry did not directly participate in the spontaneous violence of October and November, Findley's men clearly acted with the approval of at least part of the public. In the wake of the killings, Huldah Fain noted laconically that "Findley caught Ashworth and 26 of his men at Bucktown. They took them to Gainesville and killed 12 of them. I hope they [the militia] secure the country before they sleep."[58]

These killings were illegal—Confederate troops who perpetrated similar activities at Shelton Laurel, North Carolina, faced court marital—but that does not mean that Findley acted without regard to justice. Even though the Tories were given no access to judicial proceedings, the militia did observe certain quasi-legal proprieties. When the Lumpkin troopers captured the Tories, they did not shoot the men on the spot but went through the inconvenience of transporting them to central locations for "judgement" by Colonel Findley. Stansbury, Stuart, and Witt were jailed for at least one day while their fate was deliberated. Only then were they taken out and killed in a formal military ceremony. As scholars of southern lynching observed, ritual was an important element of extralegal violence. Although racial dynamics of lynching were absent in north Georgia, the Dahlonega firing squad shared with the lynch mobs of a later generation a common concern with justice and a common determination to follow formalistic behavior to lend the weight of custom to their activities. In both cases, it was vital for the killers to feel community sanction for their activities, to engage in some of the trappings of legalism. What happened in Lumpkin and Dawson counties in the autumn of 1864 was something between a lynching and an official state execution. The victims did not have the benefit of a trial, but they did experience an informal process of community judgment.[59]

But if some mountain Rebels still clung to legalistic pretense in fighting their enemies, others abandoned all such restraints. By late 1864, a new and even more dangerously violent element arose to plague north Georgia Tories. These were the pro-Confederate guerrillas, unbound by any formal institutional allegiances to the state militia or the Confederate military. Alternately labeled as *scouts, regulators,* or *bandits,* these guerrilla groups were composed of Confederate deserters who had returned home to protect their families from Tories, civilian "home guards," and a few opportunists and criminals.

But even though the guerrillas had indeterminate allegiances, many claimed to defend the Confederate cause by killing deserters and Tories who threatened their communities. Thus, when guerrillas came to Jesse Turner's White County house in 1864, they justified their actions by accusing Turner of being "a Union man" and led him off, saying "we are going to take you to Atlanta." Turner's family discovered his dead body hanging on a sapling in Lumpkin County soon afterward. Pickens County guerrillas targeted the Tory band with whom John Azor Kellogg found refuge, brutally killing and mutilating local dissenters. And some secessionists in Gilmer applauded guerrillas there for "doing a great deal of good" by killing local Tories.[60]

John Gatewood was the emblematic example of the pro-Confederate guerrilla. Born in Fentress County, Tennessee, Gatewood joined a Confederate Cavalry regiment at the war's outbreak and fought until the winter of 1862–63, when he deserted. While "laying out" in the mountains of East Tennessee, he formed a cadre of approximately fifty men, who operated out of a base in northwestern Georgia's rugged McClemore's Cove. From there, Gatewood's band launched raids into Tennessee, Georgia, and Alabama. An imposing figure, Gatewood was six feet tall and wore his red hair long and his rusty beard short. Witnesses reported he had a calm manner that belied a capability for spontaneous, casual brutality. Union citizens feared Gatewood, labeling him the "long-haired, red-bearded beast from Georgia."[61]

Gatewood's loyalty was somewhat vague and malleable. He did not work closely with any organized Confederate units and was reported to have deserters from both armies in his ranks. But highlanders generally perceived him to be "Southern in his sympathies," and so did William Tecumseh Sherman, who proclaimed Gatewood a mortal enemy and urged his soldiers to spare no effort to "get Gatewood disposed of." Some Southern newspapers portrayed "Gatewood the Regulator" as a champion defending pro-Confederate civilians from Unionist guerrillas, and some evidence suggests that Gatewood saw himself as a Confederate avenger protecting citizens from Rebels, deserter bands, and Tory irregulars. In February 1865, Gatewood took a number of Unionist prisoners and promised to "keep them as hostages for the safety of the Rebel citizens." On other occasions he professed to target "only Scouts and Rebel deserters," and in fact he often charged his victims with being deserters from the Confederate army. But other evidence casts doubt upon Gatewood's Confederate loyalties. Many Rebels feared the red-haired terrorist as much as Unionists. When Ambrose Bierce was captured by soldiers in Joseph Johnston's Army of Tennessee, the novelist's captors described Gatewood as "a greater terror to his friends than his foes."[62]

Violence was Gatewood's defining characteristic. Harrowing contemporary accounts of Unionist civilians and U.S. military officials portrayed a ruthless man who killed at a whim in the most brutal fashion. In one raid into northern Alabama in 1864, Gatewood killed an old man and his son-in-law in their yard; then he went inside their cabin and ate dinner. Another witness reported Gatewood executing a Union refugee in front of his family. While the Tory's mother was "begging of the rebels to desist," the Rebel guerrilla "sprang before her, fastened his hand in the hair of the dying man, pulled him over with his face upwards, and placing his revolver near his lips, in spite of this mother's efforts, emptied the contents of it into her son's mouth mangling and blowing away his face in the most shocking manner conceivable." On a single raid into Tennessee in the winter of 1864, Gatewood and his men killed at least twenty-five men in two days, murdering deserters, refugees, and innocent bystanders. Gatewood used his ferocious reputation to intimidate his victims. He threatened citizens of Walker County, Georgia, that he would "come up into the Cove and make them smell hell." The guerrilla also liked to brag about his murders. Jesse Tucker recalled passing a grinning Gatewood on a public road in 1864, when the guerrilla called out casually that "he had just killed two men." Gatewood spared another victim by claiming "he had already killed a lot of men that day" and was tired. Walker County citizens reported Gatewood proclaiming after one bloody raid that he "would kill no more quiet citizens" for the present but would restrict his activities to those in arms against the Confederacy.[63]

In November 1864, a group of north Georgia Tories encountered Gatewood while refugeeing to Tennessee. Peter Parris was one of the Fannin County men whom William Lillard recruited in the Federal 5th Tennessee Mounted Infantry in the summer of 1864. While Parris's brothers and their wives went on to Tennessee, he stayed behind to recruit more enlistees, and by November he had assembled a group of eight north Georgian men—half of them from Fannin, the rest from bordering Towns and Union Counties. Frightened by the recent Findley execution, Parris and his cohorts decided to leave for Tennessee during the last week in November. For safety, the Tories coordinated their refugee plans with another local Union family, which followed close behind on the journey.[64]

Parris's band followed the course of the Ocoee River through northern Fannin County, crossed into Tennessee at Copperhill, and took the rugged wagon road toward Cleveland. Near a creek called Madden Branch, just east of the Polk County seat of Benton, John Gatewood's men surprised the would-be Union recruits. The guerrillas dismounted the captives from their horses, robbed them, and then stood them up against the wall of a cliff, where Gatewood methodically began shooting each of the recruits in the head. Peter Parris watched the Rebel raider execute each of his compatriots, and when sixteen-year-old Elijah Robinson fell dead, Parris "knew he would come next," so he broke and ran. As he recalled almost forty years later, "the only hope was to crawl under the belly of the horses . . . and climb up an almost perpendicular cliff." The guerrillas fired at Parris as he escaped, wounding him in both legs, a shoulder, and one hand, but the Fannin Tory survived the ordeal and crawled to the home of a Union sympathizer where he recovered for some weeks. Another recruit escaped simultaneously by jumping into the Toccoa River. Eventually both men made it Cleveland and enlisted in the 5th Tennessee. But the other six defectors were killed, and their bodies were left in the middle of the road, where they were later discovered and buried by local Unionists, who remembered the incident as the Madden Branch Massacre.[65]

Gatewood's war evinced little of the legal overtones or ethical pretense of the vigilante violence that Findley's militia exhibited. Gatewood killed at random, seemingly without cause or compunction. When he captured the Parris band, Gatewood did not bother to consult superiors or make claims about serving justice. He simply murdered the men on the spot.

Gatewood and other guerrillas did not feel bound by some of the restraints that had limited violence earlier in the war, and they pursued their
brutal combat with little regard for the social sanctions against arbitrary
violence. If the Tories killed to protect their homes and Findley's militia
killed for law and order, Gatewood's men killed because they could, and
because no one could stop them. Some pro-Confederates recognized the
difference and criticized the guerrillas for moving beyond the pale of
legitimate behavior. One Union County Confederate opposed the guerrillas' ruthless impunity, noting sadly the irregulars often showed little
precision regarding whom they killed. They had "killed some of our best
citizens . . . in cold blood," John S. Fain reported, and another mountain
Rebel complained that a group of guerrillas "claiming to be acting under
order from [Confederate] General Johnston . . . shot down a citizen in
Ellijay who is a justice of the Inferior Court and had always been a loyal
man and a zealous supporter of the Southern cause."[66]

In the winter of 1864, Weir Boyd looked with a critical eye at the car-
nage wrought by the region's internal civil war and pleaded for a return
to civility. He decried with equal vigor the "anarchy" wrought by Tories
and guerrillas and the "military despotism" of Findley's militia. Indeed,
Boyd charged Findley's men with "arrogating to themselves the power of
forcible impressment . . . compelling citizens who are not subject to their
will to do military service—and attempting to arrest other who have the
courage to assert their rights." Boyd regretted the war's brutal progression, but perhaps he did not see how the cumulative chain of events had
created the situation that he decried. The progressive escalation of violence bred a situation in which no one could be sure who would be the
next victim.[67]

The defining characteristics of north Georgia's civil war—violence and
localism—remained salient until the end of the conflict. The last few
months of the war were marked by increasing bloodshed and internecine combat. Until the end, north Georgians on both sides maintained
dual commitments to local and national goals, and the end of the war
revealed the prominence of community and the need to balance varying
loyalties.

Tories did not respond meekly to the Confederate atrocities of late
1864. The Unionist press blared with sensational stories of rebel depredations in north Georgia, using them as evidence of the inhumanity of the
enemy and the need for harsher measures to suppress the Southern na-

tion. The *Chattanooga Gazette* reported Findley's Gainesville executions soon after they occurred, magnifying the scale of the atrocity by claiming that the militia had killed over one hundred Tories instead of the actual twelve. The paper referred to Findley's men as "inhuman . . . monsters" and asserted its hope that "these beasts may yet get caught and have their just deserts meted out to them. No quarter should be shown the perpetrators of such an act."[68]

North Georgians in the Federal armies concurred with such analysis and increased their attacks on Rebel guerrillas, skirmishing with John Gatewood's guerrillas throughout the winter of 1864–65 and adopting a "no quarter" battle cry. Many Northern officers sympathized with tribulation of their Appalachian recruits and sanctioned brutal retaliation for Confederate outrages. When one north Georgia Unionist complained of being brutalized by Confederates, his commanding officer promised to punish the men if they were caught. The officer said, "in the mean time, if you should happen to shoot them, there would be no great harm done." And when Colonel Horace Boughton's Ohio regiment caught one of Gatewood's guerrillas, the colonel asserted to superiors that "I think it would have a good effect if we were permitted to send him to the place where the late murders were committed [Madden Branch] and have him shot."[69]

But soon the north Georgians grew too zealous for many in Union command, and army officers in charge of mountain regiments became increasingly critical of the highlanders in their ranks. When soldiers of the 1st Georgia State Troops Volunteers (U.S.) began to retaliate against Rebel civilians, one Union officer demanded that "this robbing houses indiscriminately, [and] tearing bed clothes off women [by] Federal soldiers must be stopped." The 5th Tennessee Mounted Infantry, which contained many north Georgia Tories, earned a particularly infamous reputation for undisciplined violence. Federal officers filed several complaints against the unit for robbery, vandalism, and murder. One Union general warned a subordinate to watch the regiment closely, for "the numerous complaints . . . of outrages committed by both officers and men of this organization makes it necessary that they should be placed under the restraint of discipline, which does not exist in the organization." In one incident, some of the regiment's members summarily killed a "good loyal citizen" whom they assured their commander was "with the [Rebel] guerrillas." When a Union general ordered the regiment's colonel, Stephen Boyd, to send a detachment out to "take prisoner the wife of the Rebel Gatewood," he had to specify that "no depredations of any kind [will be] committed. . . by your officers or men. For any acts of violence or depredations . . . the General Commanding will hold you strictly responsible." Indeed, one of Boyd's officers did ultimately face court-martial for not controlling his vengeful recruits. For the Georgians of the 5th Tennessee, unrestricted violence was the only response to Rebel atrocities.[70]

Another source of friction in Union ranks was the pervasive localism of the Georgia troops. When ordered to fulfill missions that did not directly involve protecting their homes, many of the highlanders refused. Many deserted, as Stansbury and Stuart had. Others simply failed to execute missions for which they saw no clear local purpose. At the Battle of Dalton, in October 1864, members of the 1st Georgia State Troops Volunteers "fled . . . to the mountains" rather than join the defense of the city. Probably the unit's behavior had something to do with the rumors that Confederates were executing any Tories they captured. But it also was related to the highlanders' conceptions of their duties—their mission was not to protect Dalton, but to protect their homes. Because of their narrow definition of their duties, Union general James Steedman found the north Georgia recruits "utterly worthless" and recommended the unit be disbanded, which it was in December 1864.[71]

For mountain Rebels, the approaching defeat only heightened the inner tension between their local and national goals. Many upcountry soldiers, increasingly discouraged by losses on the battlefield and stories of deprivation and lawlessness at home, deserted the ranks. M. C. Briant, sitting in the Richmond trenches in February 1865, excoriated mountaineers who left the army. He wrote that "the fault is our own. The people have grown weak without cause. Our soldiers have . . . disgracefully thrown down their arms and fled for safety at their homes, with those for whom they ought to have been willing to die—among the women and children." But other prominent Confederates, like Elijah Chastain, were more understanding of the conflicting forces acting upon highland warriors. He admitted that many of these deserters were "still loyal men" who had simply returned home "for the protection of their families."[72]

James Findley embodied the inner conflict that mountain Rebels felt as the war drew to a close. In January 1865, he wrote Governor Brown several letters asserting his Confederate patriotism and professing his willingness to do anything necessary to "sustain our independence." Findley defended the loyalty of his militia and his eagerness to lead them against the enemy—"they will follow me anywhere," he said of his troops. But in the same letters, Findley evinced a profound concern with local affairs. He asked Brown to suspend the draft in the mountain counties, even though the Confederacy needed the manpower, because he feared that the draft would weaken his power to fight his "tory enemy" and encourage his men to "flee to the mountains" rather than serve in the Confederate armies. He gave top priority to his local missions, "hunting up property that has been stolen from the citizens," "arresting those who commit depredations upon our citizens," "getting them [the Tories] out of the woods." In this litany of the local, Findley illustrated the parochial sense in which he viewed nationalism. The stress of war had magnified that focus, but it had been present from the beginning. In February, as the lights dimmed for the Confederacy, Findley was ordered out of his mountain fiefdom to help guard supply depots in Washington, Georgia. But within weeks, the colonel had somehow arranged for his unit to return to Lumpkin County for a leave of absence, after which he would continue his former activities, hunting "deserters, stragglers absent without leave from their commands, and men liable to conscription."[73]

For Findley and most north Georgians, the end came when Confederate general William Wofford ordered all Rebel forces in the region to lay down their arms and all stragglers and deserters to return to their homes. John Gatewood ignored the order and continued his attacks through the summer of 1865. Since the guerrilla had always seen his war as something separate from the broader effort, he recognized no official declaration of peace. In the end, with Federal and former Confederate troops bearing down upon him, Gatewood escaped to Texas, where he was lost to history.[74]

As the Confederacy crumbled around them in March 1865, two north Georgia newlyweds commiserated over the fate of Southern arms. Huldah Fain Briant, at home in the mountains of Gilmer County, exchanged letters with her new husband, M. C. (Chris) Briant, who was serving with the Army of Northern Virginia. Throughout the war, the two had kept in close contact, with Huldah keeping Chris informed about events in the community and Chris updating her on his battlefield experiences. Both frequently shared their outrage and shame at the disloyalty in the mountains and urged the suppression of the Tories by whatever means necessary. As the end approached, the couple continued to ruminate about events on the home front but also focused on their shared national vision of an independent Confederacy. Huldah's commitment to the Southern cause still burned bright despite irrefutable military reverses. "I am just what I was when the war first began," she affirmed, "I was a Rebel then and I am yet and my best wishes are with the Rebels." Cautiously optimistic, Huldah wrote, "I hope our armies will be successful another year. I also hope the Lincoln govt may see their former blindness, and know that ours is not a people to be subjugated." Chris responded warmly; "I read with delight your patriotic sentiments. Ah! I was . . . gallantly proud that I was blessed with such a companion." He praised his wife's patriotism and promised to continue the fight regardless of consequence. "The probability is our whole country will be overrun and I may not get to see you for years, for I will never give up this contest as long as we have men to fight." Huldah responded to her husband's bravado with her own. She lionized the Confederate fighting man as the symbol of an unrepentant South: "the Old Veterans, long may they live, for subjugation will be unknown as long as we have Veterans in the field." And she contrasted brave soldiers like her husband with the dissenters, traitors, and malcontents who seemed to pervade the mountain counties:

> It wounds my very heart to see so many men lying about doing nothing, knowing the privations and hardships others are going through . . . and if our independence is ever gained they must share in the honors, but I thank Heaven if they do it will be with many blushes, for it will be thrown into their faces as long as they are men; we all know where the soldiers are and know who does the fighting. Any man that wants to serve their country goes where he can render service, and we know that those who . . . do render service, as some of the Old 11th has, are soldiers, and they are worthy [of] all the praise that can be bestowed upon any people, and they are all that will receive any complements from me.[75]

Huldah Fain Briant committed these thoughts to paper while the Confederacy was alive, and they evinced her desperate hope that the war might still be won. But in many ways her sentiments belonged to the future and not the present. Huldah's rhetoric prefigured that of other Southerners who would spend the postwar years struggling to define the Confederacy's place in history. For the remainder of the nineteenth century, former mountain rebels would seek to enshrine the memory of the indefatigable Confederate soldier, while simultaneously ostracizing those dissenters who in their view had undermined the Southern cause. For the people of north Georgia, history was the new battleground. In the decades to come, they would strive to reconcile their communities with the divisive legacy of the past. Former Tories and former Confederates stared at each other across a chasm of memory in 1865, and each side would try to find its own tortured path across to the future.

5 / *The War They Knew*

RECONSTRUCTING COMMUNITY
AND MEMORY IN NORTH GEORGIA,
1865–1900

In the decades following the Civil War, north Georgians shared in the national experiences of Reconstruction, modernization, and industrialization. They also endured unique problems dealing with the legacy of 1861–65. Former Tories and former Rebels continued their wartime rivalries, engaging in political, legal, and even physical combat. In addition, the opposing factions fought a long struggle over the construction of the past that overlay most postwar social and political conflicts. Ex-Rebels shared the Southern obsession with the Lost Cause and sought to carve out a special niche for mountaineers within Confederate mythology. Erstwhile Unionists opposed this characterization, casting doubt on claims of a unified Confederate Georgia by joining in the myth of national renewal celebrated by the victorious Yankees. Therefore, north Georgia's Civil War did not end in 1865; it simply shifted theaters—from the battlefield to the minds and memories of the participants.

The Union army laid waste to much of Georgia during the Civil War, but it never entered the mountains in force until after the shooting stopped. By 1867, the Freedmen's Bureau and the U.S. military had a presence in Fannin and Lumpkin Counties. In Dahlonega, the Federal troops had taken over the abandoned Mint Building as a barracks, for practical and symbolic reasons. The mint was the largest public building in town suitable for housing troops, and its occupation represented the Union's reclamation of its former property. But the mint was a dubious prize for the conquering Federals. Lieutenant Colonel John Wilkins found the interior of the building a repugnant disappointment compared to its majestic exterior. "When I arrived it was filthy beyond description," he wrote. Old coining machinery lay about unused, and debris littered the floors, the detritus of Confederate troops and militia who had barracked there for four years. When not cleaning up their living quarters, the troops patrolled the town, showing the flag and assisting Unionists and freedpeople.[1]

The first priority for federal officials in north Georgia was caring for the indigent and impoverished. Like the rest of the state, the mountain counties had suffered enormous economic dislocation during the war, and recovery was slow. In Dahlonega, the local business establishment was decimated. A few elites like merchant Archibald Wimpy continued to thrive in the postwar environment, but many others were destroyed by the devastation of the conflict and the liberation of the African American workforce. The R. G. Dun Company's postwar credit reports on the town read like casualty lists—Charles Besser went bankrupt "owing to severe losses during the war, negroes and Confederate bonds"; George Quillian was "broke all to pieces pecuniarily"; James Harris had "accumulated a handsome property . . . but lost much of it in the war"; William Perry was "an old merchant . . . successful before the war," but now he "drank too much" and was forced to abandon his dry goods business.[2]

Mounting environmental and demographic crises exacerbated the economic downturn. Inadequate rainfall, a deadly smallpox epidemic, and the dwindling number of available farm laborers due to emancipation and war casualties all combined to create near-famine throughout Georgia. In response, Freedmen's Bureau agents provided food, medicine, and supplies to the destitute. In the mountain counties, this was a tall order indeed. The need was immense. One north Georgia bureau agent predicted that "unless the government provides aid hundreds of the poor destitute citizens in this portion of the country are bound to die for want of something to eat." Another reported that "fully one half of the inhabitants" in his district were "in a wretched condition." The poorest had "neither corn nor bacon to subsist on," and even many in the middle class "have not tasted meat for months." In Dahlonega, the poor were "very destitute of clothing," and the post commander had to provide emergency food rations to the elderly citizens "to keep them from perishing." Fannin County was one of the most afflicted in the region. Federal officials there begged their superiors for food to distribute to the poor, who lived in "the most deplorable conditions" because of "the failure of their crops . . . due to the drouth which was almost universal in the mountain counties." The Freedmen's Bureau distributed tons of food aid to Fannin and other counties, but the logistical problems involved in transporting the supplies hindered the effort. Federal supply trains were forced to travel along "a very rough and mountainous road," and oftentimes food spoiled or was lost before it could be distributed to the highland families who needed it. As one agent complained, "There is considerable destitution and suffering among the poorer classes, and unlike the Rail Road towns [they] do not receive as many supplies from Aid Societies and other sources, being so far inland."[3]

The Freedmen's Bureau faced a unique series of problems in north Georgia compared to the rest of the state. With so few black people in the mountains, bureau officials focused primarily on the needs of white refugees and Unionists. Indeed, there was something of a debate among the agents as to whether the freedpeople of the region needed assistance at all. The chief bureau agent in north Georgia claimed that "the condition of the Freedmen in Dawson, Lumpkin, White, Fannin, Murray, and Union county is excellent," but worried that "the destitution in the above named counties is principally confined to the whites." Another agent conceded "there may be . . . at Dahlonega and vicinity a few blacks that require some attention," but he insisted that overall "the Freedmen . . . are doing well and I think even better than the poorer class of whites." But other bureau personnel disagreed. The agent in Fannin County wrote sympathetically of the plight of the county's small black population and demanded more aid for the jobless, homeless, and hungry former slaves in his charge. And in Lumpkin County, some agents asserted, the black population "very much needed someone to look after their interests." These internal divisions evinced the well-documented complexity of racial attitudes among Freedmen's Bureau staff. Some of the agency's personnel likely turned a blind eye to black poverty, since that was the condition they expected of the race, but they were shocked to see the whites of the region living in similar conditions. The indifference of some bureau agents to mountain blacks also stemmed from their philosophical preconceptions about race and poverty. Many agents saw direct assistance as a "handout" to the freedpeople that sapped the work ethic and weakened the crusade to transform African Americans into the self-sufficient exemplars of free labor ideology that Northern reformers dreamed of.[4]

But the African Americans of north Georgia were not passive participants in these debates. From almost the moment federal officials occupied the mountain counties, local black men and women campaigned actively for the authorities to fulfill the full promise of freedom. In the aftermath of emancipation, whites faced not the "servile insurrection" they feared but the persistent assertion of African American rights. Upcountry blacks affirmed their citizenship in much the same ways as former slaves throughout the South, agitating for federal intervention to provide physical protection, economic independence, and social autonomy.

Throughout the Georgia high country, freedpeople faced constant intimidation from local whites and responded by seeking federal aid. A black man who worked for William P. Price, the U.S. congressman from Dahlonega, complained to the bureau he had been fired because he voted against his employer in the congressional election. Hannah Powell reported being "knocked down" by a white man who claimed she had been "swearing a lie out against him." Unknown white men gunned down McLean Jones in his yard, and his aged widow suffered several burglaries at the hands of white assailants who stole or destroyed virtually everything she owned. Other blacks reported being shot at, beaten, arrested, and robbed. They appealed to the Freedmen's Bureau because "the civil court will seldom take any notice of a request of a freedman, and when they do . . . the courts will give them no justice." Sometimes black people had the support of local white Unionists who had fought for the Federals during the war. James G. Brown, the Murray County native who had helped form the 1st Georgia State Troops Volunteers (U.S.), stayed in the mountains after the war and served as an advocate for the freedmen. Brown was outraged when a local justice of the peace threw out the complaint of a black man named Allen because the plaintiff was "a negro and . . . should not be allowed to testify against a white man." Brown upbraided the justice, telling him "he was not only acting against the proclamations of the president but also in direct opposition to the existing laws of Georgia." Another discharged Federal soldier wrote his former commanding officer asking for justice for a north Georgia freedman being tried unfairly in "a Rebel court." He pleaded, "in the name of God and all that is just the loyal freedmen should be protected." But the alliance between freedpeople and Unionists was far from immutable. A black farmer named George Davis said he was "wrongfully removed or driven off from a certain piece of land he had leased for two years" by William Wehunt of Dawson County. Wehunt was a Union army veteran, but his Tory past clearly did not dispose him to defend the economic interests of black mountaineers.[5]

Despite ruthless enemies and mercurial friends, African Americans in north Georgia refused to concede their rights. Black farm laborers filed complaint after complaint against white landowners for poor treatment, summary firing, confiscation of private property, and refusal to pay wages. Blacks clamored for assistance so vociferously that the Freedmen's Bureau agent in Dahlonega finally admitted that action must be taken to "protect these people against their employers." "These people" were especially strident when it came to defending their children. In north Georgia as throughout the Reconstruction Era South, black minors were often held in service to white landowners in a state of quasi-slavery against the will of their parents. This system of apprenticeship was one of the most onerous of the Black Codes, and freedpeople resisted the arrangement as much as possible. They flocked into the Freedmen's Bureau post at Dahlonega to demand the release of their children. A black mother named Jenny complained that "John Hockenhull of Dawson County now holds without consent her two sons . . . and refuses to let her have or see them"; Thomas Riley insisted the bureau help him retrieve his "stolen child"; Charity Ramsey asked for the return of her three children "held without consent and without compensation"; George Davis requested "that his son now withheld from him by Edmund Davis be put in his possession." These parents had varying degrees of success in enlisting aid from the Freedmen's Bureau. Some agents tried to secure the release of apprentices, while others ignored the problem and insisted that the freedpeople were "well treated by the whites." But whatever the results, black fathers and mothers persistently asserted their familial rights, and in the process they played an active part in defending citizenship rights for former slaves.[6]

Like black Southerners generally, north Georgia's freedpeople strove single-mindedly to seize educational opportunities and build up the institutional foundations of African American Christianity. Freedmen's Bureau officials noted almost immediately that local blacks "seem to take an interest in the subject of education," but the federal government initially offered little assistance beyond encouragement. So Dahlonega's blacks took it upon themselves to organize their own school, one of the only ones in the mountain counties. With the help of a few local whites, freedpeople raised money, hired teachers, and arranged for a land grant to build a schoolhouse. A sympathetic white minister named Wootten agreed to teach the school, sometimes assisted by his more accomplished black pupils. Between eighty and one hundred black students attended regularly in 1867–68, defying the opposition of the majority of the white community, whose attitude toward black education was "bad indeed." Finally, the Freedmen's Bureau agreed to provide funds for the construction of a new school building, but only after the African Americans of Dahlonega had "proved" their self-sufficiency and desire for education. Such paternalism was characteristic of the bureau's education policy in Georgia, but the former slaves used the system to their best advantage. This was also the case when it came to religion. Almost as soon as the war ended, freedpeople tried to break away from the religious control of their former masters by establishing their own churches. This drew opposition from the whites at Dahlonega's First Baptist Church, who resented the fact that their former black congregants seemed to feel "no sort of bond or tie" to their former masters and "no longer owed allegiance of any sort to the white people." Ultimately, the black congregation had to sue for the right to possess their own church lands, and remarkably, the Lumpkin County Superior Court ruled in their favor. Throughout the Reconstruction period in north Georgia, the former slaves of the region fought hard to establish a community and defend cultural autonomy.[7]

Race played a major but not overriding role in Reconstruction Era politics in north Georgia. In the immediate aftermath of Confederate defeat, white conservatives in the mountains joined their compatriots throughout the state to take advantage of President Andrew Johnson's lenient terms for reconstructing the South. Weir Boyd marshaled the forces of reaction in Lumpkin County. Still wielding considerable political influence in the mountains, Boyd gained a seat in the constitutional convention of 1865. He helped craft the first postwar constitution and played a role in the state regime that enacted the repressive Black Codes, rejected the Fourteenth Amendment to the U.S. Constitution, and elected former Confederate vice president Alexander Stephens to the U.S. Senate. But with the advent of congressional Reconstruction in 1867, a new political reality emerged. Boyd and many of his allies were temporarily disenfranchised and barred from office. Black suffrage was now encouraged and protected by the federal government, and a new, more liberal state constitution was approved in 1868. Political clubs known as Union Leagues sprang up throughout northern Georgia, creating a grassroots base for the Republican Party. The GOP quickly gained a foothold in the mountain counties, aided by the conversion of the popular former governor Joseph E. Brown, who joined the Republicans in 1868, claiming, "I still preferred the government of the Unites States to any other recognized government."[8]

Blacks composed a significant component of the region's GOP organization, especially in counties like Lumpkin, where freedpeople lived in some numbers. But even here, African Americans probably composed only one-third of the county's two to three hundred Republican voters by 1868. With the comparatively small African American population in the mountains generally, political divisions chiefly involved white opponents. North Georgia's white Tories were the real winners arising from congressional Reconstruction, and they dominated Republican voter rolls. And just as in wartime, their motivations were complex. Many likely supported the GOP as the party of Union. Others acted out of antipathy for the ruling pro-Confederate establishment that had victimized dissenters during the war. John Woody, who was tried for treason against the Confederacy in 1863, became a leading Republican after the war and won a federal appointment as county postmaster in 1874. Still others joined the Republicans out of sheer opportunism, as a way to advance politically or economically in the new order wrought by congressional Reconstruction. James J. Findley was a prime example of this phenomenon. The former Lumpkin County militia commander, who brutally suppressed Tory dissent during the latter stages of the war, was a Republican by the early 1870s and even ran for the U.S. Congress on the GOP ticket. Findley eventually converted his Republican allegiances into political patronage, becoming a deputy U.S. marshal for north Georgia. But whatever their motivations, Lumpkin County Republicans consistently mustered 30 to 40 percent at the polls during the Reconstruction Era. They secured some positions in local government and came close to frustrating Democratic initiatives. When Georgia conservatives called for another constitutional convention in 1877 to rewrite the liberal document of 1868, the measure passed in Lumpkin by a scant 69 votes.[9]

But Lumpkin Republicans had limited success. They never won a major elective office between 1865 and 1877. Voters there rejected Republican governor Rufus Bullock in 1868, defeated Ulysses S. Grant in both his presidential bids, and awarded Democrats every election for the state legislature during Reconstruction. As they had during wartime, Lumpkin dissenters lacked leadership and faced formidable opponents, for most of Dahlonega's elite mobilized against the Republicans, including Weir Boyd, Archibald Wimpy, and Harrison Riley. And former Confederate officers, such as Congressman William P. Price, used the legacy of their military service for political gain. The editors of the *Dahlonega Mountain Signal* were also solidly Democratic, using their pages to decry "radical abuses" and African American civil rights. These conservatives had the last word on Reconstruction in Lumpkin County. In 1877, a reinvigorated Weir Boyd tirelessly stumped for the constitutional convention. Drawing on his reputation as a Confederate soldier and wartime community leader, Boyd told his Lumpkin constituents that the Republican Party had "openly robbed the people" with high taxes and needless expenditures for too long, and he called for dramatic government retrenchment, the abolishment of the common schools, and the end to the Homestead Act of 1868 providing debt protection for small farmers. Although Boyd affirmed that "the colored people of our state should be allowed all the rights and privileges they are now entitled under the Constitution of the laws," and he urged whites to give blacks their "sympathy and protection," he denounced the Constitution of 1868, which protected black rights as "dictated by military coercion by men . . . who had no interest in common with you." Trumpeting this Bourbon rhetoric, Boyd won election to the convention and assisted in writing what one historian called "the most profoundly conservative constitution in Georgia history."[10]

Fannin County's experience with Reconstruction offered a striking political contrast. The formerly Democratic county shifted into a Re-

Weir Boyd when he served in the Georgia State Senate in the 1880s. A prominent Lumpkin County lawyer, soldier, and politician, Boyd was a key leader of the pro-Confederate forces in north Georgia. (Georgia Division of Archives and History, sc1888-89)

publican stronghold during Reconstruction. In the election of 1868, Fannin voters resoundingly supported Governor Rufus Bullock and Ulysses Grant by margins of over 60 percent and overwhelmingly affirmed Grant again in 1872. Fannin sent Republicans to the state legislature consistently, where its representatives voted for the approval of the Fourteenth and Fifteenth amendments to the U.S. Constitution (Lumpkin's representatives opposed these amendments). Even after the unpopular Civil Rights Act of 1875 had weakened the GOP in the mountains, Republicans occupied the county's seats in the legislature. And Fannin decisively rejected the Bourbons' call for a new state constitution in 1877, casting a stunning 86 percent of its votes against convening the convention so dearly supported by Weir Boyd.[11]

There were a number of reasons for the political dichotomy between Lumpkin and Fannin Counties. Fannin had always been firmly connected to events in nearby East Tennessee, where Republicans were a powerful political force after the Civil War. Where Lumpkin's Unionists were under the thumb of pro-Confederate elites, Fannin's residents looked across the border for Republican leadership and support. Also, with a larger African American population to deal with, Lumpkin whites probably found Democratic racial rhetoric more appealing and were more resentful of the federal policies that threatened the racial caste system. Indeed, Lumpkin's former slaveholders deeply feared the potential for a new racial order after emancipation—one of the inferior court's first postwar acts urged measures to "restrain the negro population." Thus motivated, Lumpkin's elite resolutely opposed radical rule and successfully used the reins of power to advance their goals. In Fannin, which had one of the smallest black populations in the state, fears of racial upheaval found less resonance. Certainly, Fannin's Republicans held no uniquely liberal racial attitudes, but residents found other reasons to support the party of Lincoln. The county's extreme poverty made it more dependent upon federal aid and support and therefore more beholden to the Republican Party. In 1870, Fannin and Towns Counties were the two poorest counties in the state, as measured by per capita property valuation. And the economy only plummeted further during the next decade. Fannin was more reliant upon food aid from the Freedmen's Bureau than Lumpkin was. And the Homestead Exemption clause of the Constitution of 1868 was a particular benefit to Fannin's numerous poor white farmers. In addition, the fact that the wildly popular Joseph E. Brown shifted (temporarily) to the GOP probably influenced many voters in a county that had consistently supported Brown throughout his career. And looming always was the legacy of the Civil War. Fannin had been more thoroughly disaffected from the Confederacy, more of its young men had enlisted in the Union military, and many of its leading citizens opposed the Rebellion. While historians have warned against making a simplistic correlation between wartime Unionism and mountain Republicanism, it does seem that the war experience provided the crucial difference between the postwar political history of these two north Georgia counties. And the split between the two counties symbolized the enduring divisions between Tories and Confederates in the region.[12]

But in north Georgia, Reconstruction was more than a series of political debates about race, poverty, and state sovereignty. It was also a struggle to define the meaning of the Civil War and to establish the role of mountain people in that conflict. During Reconstruction and after, highland Georgians struggled to reconcile their present lives with their past experiences. The specter of the war influenced virtually everything they did in the decades that followed, and for each faction, recollections had different resonance. The conflicting memories of the war years affected the way former Tories and former Rebels interpreted contemporary events. This bifurcated public memory makes the mountain counties of Georgia an interesting variation on the history of the South during the latter third of the nineteenth century.

From almost the moment the guns ceased in 1865, Tories and Rebels sought to stamp their own version of the conflict on the region's memory and to use that memory as a weapon against their enemies within the community. As soon as Federal occupation troops arrived in Dahlonega, anti-Confederates flocked into the post headquarters asking for assistance in avenging the wartime atrocities committed by their opponents. Often these plaintiffs were turned away, because government orders insisted that "military authorities will not interfere with matters which transpired during the Rebellion." But despite such official claims of disinterest, the Freedmen's Bureau could not avoid entanglement in the war's legacy of recrimination. Agents repeatedly found themselves caught in the middle of factional disputes, and they often found it difficult to remain neutral.[13]

Unlike East Tennessee, where Unionists carried out a thorough purging of former Confederates from public life, the postwar struggle in north Georgia was more evenly contested. Neither faction was willing to let the other forget the grievances of the war period. For pro-Confederates, their Tory neighbors served as raw reminders of defeat and treason, living evidence of the disloyal stereotype that had plagued the moutain counties during wartime. Accordingly, when dissenters who had fled Fannin County for Tennessee during the war began to return to their former homesteads in 1866 and 1867, they found no pleasant homecoming. Impoverished, hungry, and rootless, these refugees faced a "bitter spirit of opposition manifested . . . by the disloyal portion of their fellow citizens," according to a Freedmen's Bureau official, who excoriated "the evil machinations of traitors" for continually harassing the returning Tories. Another agent assigned to north Georgia found a well-organized pro-Confederate establishment steadfastly determined to undermine the bureau and its local allies. "I have some very bitter enemies in this place," he wrote, "who are enemies to all Northern men, in fact enemies to all who are Loyal to the Federal Government." Another bureau official concurred, complaining "their exists such a great prejudice against the loyal class in this country." Local anti-Confederates found this prejudice often resulted in violence and intimidation. Nancy Bowman was branded "a dirty Yankee woman" by her neighbors and was told, "if I did not quit speaking of the ex-Confederates lightly that some of them would throw a load of lead into me." [14]

Tories fought back against these attacks in a variety of ways. Like African Americans, they tried to enlist a sometimes-reluctant Freedmen's Bureau as their ally. They appealed to U.S. military officers by calling on memories of shared struggle against the secessionists during the war. When Nancy Bowman issued her complaint against local pro-Confederates in 1867, she conjured memories of the war by portraying herself as a fellow soldier who had sacrificed for the Union. "The Rebel Army burnt my house at Ringold . . . [and] the Mayor of this city ordered me out of the streets," she reminded the Union officers, but despite this persecution she claimed to have served loyally, caring for "the sick and wounded soldiers of the U.S. Army." When bureau agents refused to assist Bowman to her satisfaction, she accused them of disloyalty to the Union. The local bureau superintendent, she reported, "was a Rebel and only pretended Unionism to keep his situation under the Government. He is also a minister and I have heard him pray for the overthrow of the Government and success of the Confederacy." Other Tories echoed these complaints of traitors within the Freedmen's Bureau. Several of them testified against a north Georgia bureau agent named George Selvidge, who was charged with corruption in 1867, asserting in their depositions that the man had been a vocal Rebel during and the war and afterward continued to harass loyal Unionists from his post in the bureau. [15]

Anti-Confederate mountaineers used other tools of authority as weapons in their postwar battles for status and revenge. In the years immediately following the war, former victims of the Confederacy sought to redress old wrongs by turning to the judicial system. In Lumpkin County, Tories often filed suits against their wartime tormentors for alleged crimes and misdemeanors committed during the hostilities. Former Confederates found themselves brought before the Lumpkin County Superior Court to answer charges such as trespassing, robbery, and kidnapping. Samuel Lovingood sued two ex-Rebels for stealing his cattle on an impressment raid in November 1864. Elisha Hunt charged James Findley and Moses Whelchel with "carrying away one hundred hides of leather, at a value of five-hundred dollars," on one of the Lumpkin colonel's missions in to Fannin County in February 1865. James Payne filed multiple suits against the sheriff of Lumpkin County for trespassing, false imprisonment, and assault—charges stemming from Payne's 1863 arrest for treason. Payne vividly remembered the shame of his wartime arrest and claimed in court that the sheriff and his deputies had "seized and laid hold of said plaintiff and with great force and violence . . . dragged [him] about in the streets of the town of Dahlonega." Payne recalled for the judge how he was "handcuffed and tied hand and foot with chains and [forced] to march through . . . branches and creeks [in] the extreme cold to the city of Atlanta." While imprisoned, Payne claimed, he had been "beat, bruised, and ill-treated" for three months. He demanded $30,000 in damages.[16]

Former Confederates usually answered charges like these with the venerable defense that they were only following orders. When some ex-Rebels faced charges of stealing a citizen's goods during the war, their lawyer responded that his clients acted legitimately under the Impressment Act of 1863—"these defendants acted according to the provisions of the Act of the Confederate Congress. . . . They are not responsible." In this, Confederates had the support of the law. The Georgia General Assembly passed a statute in 1866 absolving Confederate soldiers for any actions they had committed under orders from a superior officer. But this did not stop Tories from filing suits. Many Unionist plaintiffs asserted that the legislature's amnesty did not apply to "roving, irregular bands of persons assuming to be Confederate soldiers," such as John Gatewood, and armed with this rationale they managed to secure convictions against former pro-Confederate guerrillas. The irregulars who murdered Jesse Turner in 1864 received jail terms in 1867. But this justification could be used both ways. The same year, pro-Confederates responded by filing charges of their own. They convinced local and federal authorities to investigate the murder and mutilation of Bird McKinney by Union recruits in 1864.[17]

Overall, Lumpkin juries proved unwilling to convict those whom they perceived as having acted under the legitimate authority to keep law and order during the war. In February 1866, the courts took up one of the most divisive incidents of the county's recent past when prosecutors brought murder charges against the seven members of the firing squad who executed Solomon Stansbury, Iley Stuart, and William Witt in October 1864. Significantly, James Findley was not among the accused, even though most witnesses concurred that he ordered the shootings that day on Bearden's Bridge Hill. No written order explicitly linked Findley to the killings, and the former militia colonel still possessed formidable influence within the community that probably insulated him from the legal proceedings. Moreover, many Lumpkin citizens approved of Findley's wartime activities and valued his reputation as a defender of law and order. Long after the war was over, the *Dahlonega Mountain Signal* referred wistfully to Findley's service, noting that he had been "the best Sheriff on his circuit" and urging his appointment to the U.S. marshal's office of the region. Findley's wartime subordinates proved similarly untouchable when brought to trial for the executions of 1864. In the case of *The State v. William Crisson, Macy Crisson, Benjamin Van Dyke, Hardy Forrester, J. A. Hollifield, Ferdinand McDonald, J. R. Pruitt, and W. H. Worley*, the grand jury refused to indict the erstwhile Georgia militiamen. No record of the jury's rationale exists, but their general perspective on war crimes is evident in the language of another ruling they issued that summer. When another Tory charged a former Confederate with wartime atrocities, the jury dismissed the charge, stating that "we . . . recommend the solicitor general to enter a 'nol. pros.' on all old war prosecutions." Dahlonega's pro-Confederate community sent a clear message in these verdicts—Findley's militia had acted in defense of law and order, and the killings, though perhaps beyond the formal limits of the law, had been necessary in order to serve the greater good. None of the militia ever faced an accounting for their role in the mass killings of 1864.[18]

When not battling in the political or legal arena, north Georgians fought with more lethal weapons. As Reconstruction waned, north Georgians occasionally resorted to the violent methods they had employed during the Civil War to resolve community disputes. For some highlanders, violent retribution followed them even after leaving the region.

William A. Twiggs, the Fannin County Tory who launched the bloody mountain uprising of 1864, died in Arkansas thirty years later, when an "irresponsible mob" surrounded his house and shot him. A witness said the mob's "hatred of the deceased was . . . purely political, and as Twiggs had been a Federal soldier his murderers could not tolerate his presence." The most sustained violent outbreak in the region's postwar period was the Moonshine War, which raged across the mountains from the 1870s to the 1890s. During that period, federal revenue agents cracked down on illegal whisky distilleries throughout Appalachia, focusing the lion's share of enforcement efforts in the Georgia high country. Federal troops and marshals invaded the region several times, often using Dahlonega as a staging area for raids into the rugged mountains of Fannin, Union, and Towns counties, just as state militia had done during the war. Bloody battles often resulted between the revenue agents and the "blockaders," as illegal still operators were known.[19]

The Moonshine War was not a direct extension of Civil War rivalries, but certain features overlapped. The conflict over liquor taxes evinced the same tension between local autonomy and central authority that had been so fundamental in north Georgia's Civil War experience. Revenuers and blockaders were essentially refighting the battles between dissenters and state militia from an earlier era. But ironically, the warriors had switched causes. Tories and Unionists, represented institutionally by the Republican Party, were now agents of a federal government that was trying to force local people to conform to the dictates of central authority. And former Confederates, who had embraced stern state powers in defense of secession, later opposed the regulatory power of the U.S. Bureau of Internal Revenue. Sion Darnell was a Pickens County native who had enlisted in the Union army during the war to fight against the "domineeringly exerted" power of the Confederacy to invade mountain homes in search of manpower and supplies. But in the 1880s, Darnell, now a prominent Republican, was appointed assistant attorney general for north Georgia and charged with enforcing federal liquor laws. From this post, Darnell claimed that the poor mountaineers who operated illegal stills were "engaged in an organized and armed rebellion against the lawful constituents of authority of the United States." For this former Unionist, moonshining was part of a very old conflict, and the blockaders represented the "pernicious" doctrine that "the United States is yet a foreign government, and that its officers and agents are intruders upon their 'natural rights.'" For their part, former Rebels decried centralization in the name of the federal government and argued that "the brutal enforcement of the revenue laws" was destructive of local autonomy. Just as the wartime Tories had revolted against the draft and impressments, postwar Rebels claimed that the Republicans were "the party of oppression" that victimized farmers with "the infamous machinery of the internal revenue laws," preventing them from "distill[ing] the fruits of their farms unmolested by armed bands."[20]

The legacy of the Civil War clearly helped determine the way mountaineers perceived and interpreted the moonshine issue. Many poor highland farmers who had supported the Union during the war now felt betrayed by the federal government's attempts to prevent them from engaging in a time-honored economic and cultural activity—making corn liquor. As one blockader put it, "it nattally gits up our boys' dander to hev our liberties took away from us by our own Guvment what we fought to keep up agin the Secesh." Aaron Woody of Lumpkin County felt his wartime service to the United States should mitigate his infringements upon internal revenue laws. When arrested for resisting a revenue officer in 1882, Woody wrote the U.S. attorney general asking for clemency, urging him to consider his wartime loyalty and that of his father, the prominent Lumpkin Unionist John Woody. "I was convinced," the younger Woody wrote to the head of the Justice Department, "that you was not only a friend to the government, but a friend to those who fought thur battles." After the inevitable assertions of innocence, Woody offered, "as to my loyalty I refer you to Rolls of the Co. A 10th Reg Tenn Cavelry. There you will see that I am an Ex-Federal Soldier, my father also." Woody claimed that he was being persecuted by a vengeful former Confederate who was the deputy federal marshal in his district. "The men who is now howning after me is Ex-Rebel gurillas," Woody argued.[21]

But many north Georgians claimed the opposite was true. Blockaders often resisted the federal marshals because they believed the revenue system was being used by former Tories to take vengeance upon former Rebels. For these people, revenue collection represented an institutionalized license to oppress pro-Confederates, and the marshals and troops who hunted down still operators were reenacting the destructive raids by pro-Union bushwhackers during the war. When an angry mob attacked the home of a revenue official in Fannin County, the vigilantes justified their actions by claiming that the federal agent had been a Tory during the war, a man who had deserted his "stricken country" (the Confederacy) and "stole hogs for an amusement and robbed the houses of soldiers who were bleeding on the fields of the Old Dominion." Clearly, the Moonshine War involved complex loyalties and allegiances. There was no ironclad continuity between wartime Unionism and support for the revenuers; neither was there always a strict correlation between former Rebels and the blockaders. Many north Georgia Republicans opposed strict revenue enforcement, and many Democratic elites were temperance men, guardians of middle-class morality who sought to prohibit alcohol consumption at the same time they criticized the U.S. marshals for oppressing blockaders. But what is interesting is the way the parties couched their rhetoric in terms of wartime loyalties and sought to identify their cause with the Union or the Confederacy.[22]

Civil War loyalties intersected with the distillery issue in a remarkable series of events in Fannin County in the early 1880s. On the night of April 6, 1880, a crowd of twenty men massed at the house of John A. Stuart, a federal revenue officer in Fannin County. Stuart was a native north Georgian who had served in the Union army during the Civil War and who was rumored to have targeted former Confederates in his campaign against local whisky distillers. In the crowd that night was Walter Webster Findley, a brother of James Jefferson Findley and a pro-Confederate during the war. (As further proof that Civil War allegiances did not always determine loyalties in the whiskey wars, James Findley himself was by this time a U.S. deputy marshal, known for both his corruption and his enthusiasm for arresting distillers.) The mob attacked Stuart's cabin, as the victim later reported, "and set fire to my house and stable and burnt both to ashes. . . . Also fifteen or twenty shot at me and my son alternately, wounding my son. I opened fire on them as soon as I could get my arms when they all break to run."[23]

Walter Findley was captured, tried, and found guilty for the assault, but at the sentencing he drew a pistol and shot his way out of the Atlanta courtroom. He was soon recaptured and sentenced to federal prison. After six months, Findley applied for a presidential pardon. But a group of north Georgians petitioned President Chester Arthur not to let Findley out of jail. One of the leaders of the petition drive was Robert Woody, a Fannin County Tory and Union army veteran. Woody insisted that Findley was part of a band of neo-Confederate "brigands and vagabonds" who were "allied with any and all who would resist the U.S. law." Findley got his pardon, but soon after his release he attacked Robert Woody in front of a Fannin County church. In the gunfight that ensued, Findley shot Woody several times and killed an innocent bystander who strayed into the line of fire. Woody survived, Findley was acquitted of attempted murder charges, and the feud between them continued for many years.[24]

Tories and Confederates thus continued their wartime rivalries in a variety of ways. The legacy of the Civil War subtly influenced the way north Georgians perceived and reacted to social and political struggles in their communities. And as the generation of 1861 aged, the battles over memory became even more direct. In the 1880s and 1890s, the nation became obsessed with commemorating and memorializing the Civil War and its participants. Nationally, the new remembering of the war pitted three myths against each other—the pro-Confederate Lost Cause that white Southerners championed, the reconciliationist vision of most northern whites, and the emancipationist interpretation of African Americans and white abolitionists. North Georgians found themselves swept up in the phenomenon. But for them, constructing a public memory of the war held special hazards, because it required them to face up to the harsh realities of the region's divisive heritage. In the Georgia upcountry, Tories and Rebels struggled over the construction of their unique wartime history, seeking to enshrine all they thought noble about their respective causes and to conceal the darker aspects of the conflict. In countless social gestures, community ceremonies, and personal memoirs, the two factions told different stories about the war, stories that evinced the personal psychic needs of the individuals involved. Each north Georgian remembered the war in the manner he or she required, and these different ways of reminiscing about the war period revealed different concepts of community.[25]

Soon after the cessation of hostilities, Lumpkin County's pro-Confederates sought to codify their interpretation of the war in the region's historical record. Their vision of the recent past saw a unified community in which men and women had come together in brave Confederate solidarity, fighting gallantly in a justified, holy, though sadly losing, cause. This public myth was constructed and defended by local institutions, including the churches, municipal authorities, and the county chapter of the United Daughters of the Confederacy. A new military school, North Georgia Agricultural College, also played an important role. Founded in 1871, NGAC was a virtual monument to the Confederacy. Professors and administrators vaunted Christian virtue and manhood, organized the male students into a corps of cadets, and made military drill a key part of the curriculum. The college also played a major role in enshrining the memory of the Lost Cause. Much of the administration was composed of Confederate veterans, and the cadets took a leading role in the yearly ceremonies surrounding Decoration Day, which later became known as Confederate Memorial Day.[26]

The memorialization of the Confederate war dead was the earliest manifestation of the Lost Cause in the county. Beginning in the spring of 1866, Dahlonega's citizens made yearly pilgrimages to Mount Hope Cemetery to decorate the graves of Rebel soldiers. By the early 1870s, the ceremony had become a large, organized, semi-official community event. "Dahlonega's earnest, true-hearted Southern women" orchestrated mass observances every April on Decoration Day. The day began with throngs of citizens gathering in the town square and then marching in procession to the college chapel, where town leaders gave speeches and led the assemblage in hymns and prayers. The ceremony culminated with the college corps of cadets and uniformed Confederate veterans leading a solemn march to the cemetery. Once there, the women strewed the graves of the Rebel dead with "garlands of the loveliest flowers of spring," and

The Corps of Cadets posing in front of North Georgia Agricultural College in 1900. Founded in Dahlonega in the 1870s, the college would serve as a physical and spiritual symbol of the Lost Cause in the Georgia mountains. (*Vanishing Georgia*, lum076, Georgia Division of Archives and History, Office of Secretary of State)

afterward the cadets fired a salutary volley of musketry to end the day's observance.[27]

While Lumpkin County took care to honor its Confederate dead, the living veterans of the Civil War also played a central role in the making of the Lost Cause myth. Beginning in the mid-1880s, Lumpkin's Confederate veterans held annual regimental reunions. These gatherings provided a forum for veterans to bond and reminisce, as well as a venue for the community to recognize and show respect for the living symbols of Southern honor and Confederate pride. The reunions of the 52nd Georgia Volunteers were emblematic of this trend. The Lumpkin regiment was among the most famous in the mountains. Weir Boyd, James Findley, and other Dahlonega elites formed its leadership, and the unit had seen heavy action in the Western Theater. The reunions were solemn, formalized, sentimental affairs, involving both the veterans and the general public, who were invited to share in the ceremonies and offer public deference to the veterans. Reunions usually began with a presentation of the colors, as the bullet-riddled battle flag of the regiment was paraded down the aisle for all to see. Then followed emotional speeches by Boyd and the other living officers, who recounted in great detail the history of the regiment, including each engagement it fought and each casualty it incurred. The most moving stories often depicted the fate of Boyd's own son, Augustus, who was killed at the Battle of Baker's Creek in 1863. Soon the reunion of the 52nd rivaled Decoration Day as an expression of mass fealty to the Confederacy. In 1896, the ceremony drew almost three thousand people and had to be held outdoors.[28]

The rhetoric that Dahlonega's elites offered up on Decoration Day and at the soldier reunions echoed much of the general Southern opinion of the Lost Cause. Speakers eulogized the "celebrated Stonewall Jackson, that noble Christian hero," and "our renowned chieftain, General Lee." They assured the listeners of the nobility of the dead soldiers, asserting that "notwithstanding the cause for which our brave heroes fought, bled, and died, was lost . . . the stricken Southern people . . . can never yield the pride they feel in the chivalrous gallantry of their departed sons." Of the Confederate effort itself, they said, "A lost cause! If lost, it was false; if true, it was not lost. We may confidently look forward to the time when the immortal principles of our father shall again be recognized." Lost Cause mythology downplayed slavery as a central cause of the war at the same time the institution's apologists portrayed it as a benign, even beneficent system for managing the races. The editor of the *Dahlonega*

Mountain Signal, a principal organ of neo-Confederate propaganda, related proudly the story of William Hampton, a local planter who had lost
everything during the Civil War. According to the paper, Hampton was
"old, broken down, and penniless" when he was rescued by one of his
former slaves, Julia Hampton. "She said she was tired of seeing her old
'marster' without a home and at once deeded him a lot of land on her
place and had a cozy house built for him." This sentimental recasting of
racism and slavery was a common thread in white Southern remembering
of the war. The makers of the Confederate myth emphasized the importance of celebrating a proper version of the past and urged the youth
to value the official perspective of the generation of 1861. Decoration
Day was vital in "perpetuating the heroism of our race, and inciting our
young people to emulate the great deeds of their fathers and mothers."
This was no small issue: remembering the past "correctly" was the key to
the future of the South.[29]

This rhetoric of glorious Christian martyrdom echoed through the
South at this time, but in Dahlonega, the language had a unique ring.
In their crusade to glorify their people's loyalty to the South and elevate
mountain Rebels in memory, pro-Confederates also had to write the dissenters and Tories out of recent history. When Weir Boyd remembered
the war, he recalled that "when the struggle for southern independence
was made . . . the mountaineers of my section rallied to their country's
standard, and the cemetery at Dahlonega and many of the battlefields
in Virginia and in the west attest their valor and patriotism." There was,
of course, no mention of the region's dissent or of Union veterans in
Boyd's speech, and perhaps his was an attempt to erase "the stain upon
our name" that some Dahlonegans still felt. The Dahlonega chapter of
the United Daughters of the Confederacy certainly felt the burden of the
disloyal stereotype, and the leadership felt defensive about their relatively
late entrance into the Lost Cause fad (the chapter did not convene until
1905, a decade after its national founding). Local UDC chapter president
Mattie Gaillard defended the women of Dahlonega and insisted that their
late arrival at the business of Confederate commemoration did not mean
the women of the town were negligent in their duty. "The people of this
place had [not] been laggards in looking after and caring for the graves of
those who fell in defense of the South," Gaillard wrote, "for it is a matter
of fact that this dear old mountain town was among the first, if not the
first, in the South to perform the duty of decorating the soldiers graves,
a number of whom were buried in our cemetery." William McAfee, an-

other Lumpkin veteran of the Confederate armies, made explicit mention of this regional inferiority complex in his 1873 Decoration Day speech, stating, "it is a notorious fact, and yet true, that middle and lower Georgia looks upon us as a kind of ignoramus people, and have no minds susceptible of culture." In the face of these prejudices, McAfee erected a counter-stereotype, claiming, "it is a known fact that owing to the excess of the pure oxygen we breathe, we possess an advantage over middle and lower Georgia, causing a quick and shrewd perception." (This strategy was a throwback to the Civil War, when highlanders had capitalized upon their region's violent reputation to claim superior fighting skills for their soldiers.) For mountain Rebels, therefore, the Lost Cause had a particular resonance. By embracing it, they once again asserted their loyalty to the Confederacy, which they feared other Southerners still doubted.[30]

Dahlonega's elites needed to sanitize the history of Lumpkin County's war. They not only excised the Tories from the official tale, but they also hid from public view their brutal repression of dissenters during wartime. No Decoration Day speech hinted at the county's inner guerrilla conflict, the abuses by impressment and conscription officers, or the summary executions of Unionists. Instead, they focused on the noble sacrifice of civilians, the selfless bravery of the soldiers, and the vital role mountaineers played in major combat operations. When James Jefferson Findley spoke before an 1885 reunion of the 52nd Georgia Volunteers, he discussed at length the regiment's origins and shared memories of those who had been killed in action. But he failed to mention his decision to leave the regiment in 1862 in order to suppress dissent on the home front. Neither did he explain or justify his summary execution of Tories in the fall of 1864. And when Findley died in 1888, his obituary glossed over his wartime record and remembered him mainly as "a genial, liberal, wholesale gentleman." In north Georgia, Walt Whitman's famous prediction came true; the real war never got into the books.[31]

In peace as in war, there were telling differences between Lumpkin and Fannin Counties. The struggle over Civil War memory further highlighted the contrast. While Lumpkin became a focus of Lost Cause mythology, Fannin residents erected an alternate edifice of recollection. Public expressions of neo-Confederate ideology were rare in the mountains north of Dahlonega. Decoration Day, if it was observed at all, was substantially more muted. The newspapers did not announce, cover, or even mention the ceremonies commemorating the Confederate dead. Reunions of Confederate soldiers were also less common and celebrated, perhaps because of the rather checkered history of most Fannin units. In the absence of an organized crusade to establish the Lost Cause, mountain Tories were free to build a counter-myth, one that found deep resonance among north Georgians who had dissented during the Civil War.[32]

Tories had no formalized expression of collective memory to rival the Lost Cause. But in various ways they did attempt to offer a history of the Civil War that countered the "official" Southern perspective. Mountain Unionists held their own gravesite ceremonies on Memorial Day, which the U.S. government formalized in 1868 as an official day of mourning and commemoration of the Federal dead. (Union Memorial Day was in late May, while in Georgia, Confederate Decoration Day came in late April for most of the nineteenth century). At first, these activities in the Georgia mountains were rather small, nothing to rival the size and scope of Confederate Decoration Day. There were many reasons for this. Some of the Tory dead had never officially enlisted in the U.S. military. Their graves were probably scattered in small family plots throughout the region, not congregated in a central park like Dahlonega's Mount Hope Cemetery. North Georgians who had actually joined the Union army were often buried in far-away Federal cemeteries, inaccessible to most impoverished north Georgia families. But by the 1880s, upcountry Unionists were playing a vital part in the Memorial Day services. With logistical help from the Georgia chapter of the Grand Army of the Republic (GAR), trainloads of Tories made the trip each year to the Federal military cemetery in Marietta, Georgia, to participate in the decoration of Union graves. They joined in processions of five to six thousand people marching from the train depot to the burial grounds, accompanied by both civilian brass bands and active army units from nearby Fort McPherson. At the graveyard, there were speeches and prayers and music, followed by the decoration activities, which turned each soldier's grave into a mound of spring flora and miniature American flags. Some mourners brought bouquets of native mountain flowers all the way from their homes in the highlands to place on the graves of relatives. In their presence at the Marietta ceremonies, mountain dissenters committed themselves to an alternate remembering of the Civil War.[33]

The Grand Army of the Republic served as the institutional vanguard of Union memorialization. Formed in 1866 in Illinois, the Union veteran's organization was one of the most influential interest groups of the nineteenth century. Although most powerful in the North, the GAR also existed in the South, where it served as a counterpoint to the United

Daughters of the Confederacy and other local instruments of Lost Cause propaganda. The first Georgia post of the GAR mustered in September 1884. Within five years, there were over two hundred members concentrated in six organization posts statewide, consisting both of northern veterans who had resettled in Georgia and native-born Georgians who had served in the U.S. military during the war. These former Union soldiers joined the battle with the Lost Cause directly during the 1880s and 1890s. They mobilized their members to organize Memorial Day observances at Federal military cemeteries, which they claimed was "a holier duty" than the Confederate Decoration Day ceremonies that other Georgians attended. The Georgia GAR also collected funds to buy the property surrounding the notorious Andersonville prison, with hopes of erecting a memorial to the thousands of Union POWs who "elected to starve to death rather than accept life and enlistment under the rebel flag." That flag itself was another target for the organization. In 1892 the members resolved to oppose display of the Confederate banner in public, arguing that "The day for flaunting the flag that went down in blood and defeat at Appomattox was long since past; that the place for that flag, if it had any at all, was on the walls of a camp of Confederate survivors. The old banner . . . might be well honored and revered as a sacred relic by those who followed it; but the principles which the banner represented had been decided by the God of Battles to be wrong, and to-day, in a united country, there is room for but one flag, and that flag [is] our grand and beautiful, God-given and God-blessed 'Old Glory.'" Fighting against the Confederate flag in the heart of the deep South was a bold, if not foolhardy, tactic for the GAR, but it reflected the members' conception of themselves as an embattled minority determined to resist the pro-Confederate version of history. The Georgia membership felt they were manning the hostile frontier of Unionism in the South, or, as they put it, "we ex-Union soldiers in the South . . . are the advance guard of the Grand Army of the Republic and we hold the picket line."[34]

The GAR formed two units in the mountains. Veterans established the Blue Ridge Post in Pickens County in 1888 and ten years later the William T. Sherman Post in Fannin County. Naming the Fannin unit after the Union general who had made Georgia howl during the march to the sea evinced a combative spirit of resistance among mountain Tories, as well as the historic disconnect between their communities and the rest of the state. Prominent dissenters from throughout the region joined these posts, and few of them were carpetbaggers. A GAR official said that the mountain units were composed "almost entirely of natives of that section." A glance at the membership rolls reveals a host of common Tory family names such as Woody, Wehunt, and Long. Throughout the 1880s and 1890s these men paid their dues, held regular meetings, and participated in the Memorial Day observances. But it was difficult to maintain GAR units in the mountains. As always, regional geography was a challenge to any central organization, and groups of veterans were often too divided in isolated hollows to organize. "In North Georgia," the department commander noted, "there are hundreds of ex-Union soldiers unconnected with the Grand Army, but they are so widely scattered that it is, as yet, almost impossible to gather them into posts." The hostility of Rebel highlanders also stymied the GAR. The temerity of the Unionists rankled their pro-Confederate neighbors, who opposed any rival to the holy Lost Cause. They harassed GAR members and dissuaded many others from joining. One officer complained that many "who wore blue during the war . . . have hesitated to face the difficulties which association with the G.A.R. might bring upon them." By the turn of the century, the William T. Sherman Post had disbanded for lack of participation.[35]

Union veterans of the First Regiment, Georgia Infantry (U.S.) in 1898. Reunions like these were intended to preserve a Unionist heritage in north Georgia and were part of a continuing struggle to interpret and possess the past in the decades following the Civil War. (*Vanishing Georgia*, ben077a, Georgia Division of Archives and History, Office of Secretary of State)

But Union veterans soldiered on in north Georgia, fueled by the commitment and leadership of one man—Sion A. Darnell. The Pickens County native had impeccable Unionist credentials. He "was a union man in 1860, during the war fought in the Union army, [and] has uniformly sustained all legislation looking to the . . . protection of the political rights of all citizens." Darnell had shared in the experiences of so many mountain Tories—he and his family had suffered from impressments and conscription, refugeed across the dangerous Tennessee border, and ultimately enlisted in the 5th Tennessee Mounted Infantry to fight against the Confederacy. A prominent Republican after the war, he served as assistant U.S. attorney for north Georgia and even ran for Congress in 1890. That campaign was largely a referendum on north Georgia's Civil War. Darnell blatantly used the tool of memory to garner support among the Tory populace of the Ninth Congressional District, which included both Fannin and Lumpkin counties. In debates and stump speeches throughout the mountains, Darnell invoked his Union military service constantly, telling old war stories and affirming to the crowds that "he never expected to see the day when he would not rejoice in his having worn the blue, and fighting for the union." For their part, Darnell's Democratic opponents used the legacy of the war against the GOP candidate. One pro-rebel politico charged: "Darnell went across the lines and fought against us . . . and if he was not with Sherman on his march through Georgia, and did not assist in leaving a black streak forty miles wide by which thousands of women and children were left without shelter or clothing, it was not Darnell's fault, he was there and would have done so if he had been called on." Darnell lost the race, but his vote distribution revealed much about continuing regional divisions among north Georgians. In Lumpkin County, the font of the Lost Cause in the mountains, Darnell won only 38 percent of the vote, while in Fannin the Unionist won 65 percent of all ballots cast.[36]

Darnell was also one of the founding members of the Grand Army of the Republic, Department of Georgia. He led the Blue Ridge Post for years, and in 1900, after over a decade of working his way up in the leadership, he was elected department commander of the organization. As commander of the Georgia GAR, Darnell was a principal leader in the struggle to possess the battleground of memory. He also proved that Tories were as willing as Confederates to distort and reshape the facts of the war to create a usable past for their adherents. In his address to the annual GAR encampment in 1901, Darnell sketched out a history of the Civil War in the Georgia mountains, perhaps the first ever written. His account detailed the experiences of thousands of mountaineers like himself who had endured the brutalities of north Georgia's conflict, a lurid tale complete with trials, tribulations, and atrocities of almost biblical intensity. The story also did much to amplify the myth of mountain Unionism and conceal the true nature of Tory motivations and behavior. In his retelling of the war, Darnell transformed mountain dissenters from apolitical guerrillas into principled apostles of freedom and national unity. Darnell's brave soldiers were devoted to a Lincolnian ideal of Union and a nearly religious commitment to the United States that drove them to fight against the heresy of secession. He said of the mountaineers:

> Descended from Revolutionary heroes . . . they cherished, with a priceless devotion, that heritage of liberty, so rich in its common blessings, and so worthy, as they believed and still believe, of their highest and best efforts for its preservation. They venerated the Constitution of the United States and all the institutions under it, except slavery; and they loved the flag, which had never cast a shadow upon any land, as the emblem of National authority and glory. Through all the vicissitudes of the years that have come and gone since the struggle of arms was ended, they love that flag still."

Darnell downplayed abolition and emancipation as war goals (as indeed most white Northerners did), but he did claim that highlanders were uniformly hostile to slavery, and criticized the Confederacy as an "oligarchy, founded upon . . . the slavery of human beings and the enslavement of human minds." For Sion Darnell, the official history of the war was glorious, patriotic, and, unlike the Lost Cause, victorious. But the opportunism, localism, and non-ideological character of wartime dissent in north Georgia had to be erased in favor of a romantic version more commensurate with Northern notions of a crusade for national unification.[37]

Like his pro-Confederate neighbors, Darnell also felt impelled to defend the reputation of his fighters to a broader audience. He needed to prove to the Northern veterans of the GAR that highlanders had been loyal beyond reproach. He deflected Yankee criticism of those highlanders who had served in both Confederate and Union armies, arguing that many loyal men had been "compelled by actual physical force, or duress . . . to perform any military service for the Confederacy." These men had deserted at the first opportunity to the Federal forces, Darnell said, eagerly accepting "the first musket offered them, to fight for the Union and the flag they had been taught from their youth to love." Darnell also insisted on the unwavering loyalty of Tory women. He claimed, in direct contravention of fact, that not a single mountain woman had taken advantage of the 1864 Georgia statue that granted divorces to wives of Unionists. Rather, mountain wives had been "heroines" who were "faithful to their husbands' cause, and imbued with the same spirit of devotion which animated them." Darnell also ignored the questionable battle record of Federal regiments from north Georgia. He claimed that the highlanders in blue "were always ready to march at the 'head of the column,' and to fight in the foremost lines of battle." And, like mountain Confederates, Darnell muted memories of the wartime atrocities that Tories had meted out in the name of their cause. Ignoring incidents like the murder and mutilation of Bird McKinney, Darnell insisted that Tory soldiers "notwithstanding their many provocations . . . were always humane and generous to the vanquished." Even so, any "reprisals" the Tories might have committed were excusable because "the limits of human nature had been reached and passed."[38]

Few north Georgia Tories were as articulate as Darnell. But even common people found ways to write their versions of the past. During the 1880s and 1890s, ordinary north Georgians created a grassroots memorialization movement of their own, paralleling the larger culture war waged by elites in the UDC and the GAR. The construction of this folk memory took many forms. Tories commemorated their dead in other ways besides formal Memorial Day observances. The family of one highlander took offense to the quartermaster general of the U.S. Army authorizing a Confederate headstone for the gravesite of John Pack, who briefly served with the 54th North Carolina Infantry (CSA). Later, Pack's family added an inscription of their own to the stone asserting their own version of events, which read: "The Quartermaster General is Nuts. John Pack was never in the 54th N.C. Regiment. He was conscripted into the 59th Tennessee. Deserted after 17 days, lay out and then joined the Yankees." Tories also created living memorials to their cause in the names they gave their children. In dissenter families, children born during or after the war frequently bore Christian names that testified to their parents' loyalties—thus, the postwar census rolls in north Georgia are sprinkled with entries such as Lincoln Wehunt, U.S. Grant Woody, and even McClellan Rickles. Sherman was one of the most popular Unionist names in the mountains. A few pro-Confederate families christened children with names such as Robert Lee Burns or Stonewall J. Green. But this was more common in Lumpkin County than in Fannin, where Union names were especially prevalent.[39]

Tories also "wrote" their own histories by filing requests for compensation from the federal government. After the war, the Southern Claims Commission researched the claims of Unionist Southerners who had suffered material losses during the war, while the U.S. Army's Bureau of Pensions investigated the war records of each man who claimed to have fought in the Union armies. These agencies sent agents scouring the South to collect data on those seeking federal monetary assistance and in the process compiled the wartime recollections of ordinary people and their communities. In thousands of pages of testimony before federal officials, north Georgians asked for compensation. And in the process, upcountry Georgians also told their stories of dissent, endurance, and wartime valor. Certainly, these depositions were not coherent expressions of the past—they were fragmentary, disjointed, often unrealistic re-creations, recounted years or even decades after the fact. Pension Bureau and Southern Claims officials often caught their deponents in blatant fabrications, as Unionists embellished the stories of wartime heroism to enhance the chances of their claim. Peter Parris, the Fannin County refugee who barely survived his encounter with John Gatewood in 1864, claimed in his pension deposition that he and his recruits had been "on a Scout" in north Georgia under orders from Union high command when they were captured. In fact, Parris's men had not even been mustered into Federal service when they encountered Gatewood. Other Fannin Tories claimed to have been engaged in glorious battles for the Union cause, belying their real service as guerrillas and terrorists. But despite these distortions, the act of bearing witness before the busy bureaucrats sent out from Washington allowed Tories to assert their pasts and dispute the myth of a Confederate mountain Georgia.[40]

These testimonies offered the stories of both individuals and entire communities. Pension Bureau investigators and especially Southern Claims Commissioners sought to substantiate claimants' stories by interviewing family members and people from the locality. Part of the standard Southern Claims questionnaire asked the claimant to provide the names of other Unionists in the area. What resulted was a network of individuals and families who offered miniature histories of Tory communities in the mountains. Stansburys, Parrises, Woodys, and Fains all testified for each other's claims. These collective expressions of history were just as real, if less grand, than the ceremonies and speeches of Confederate Memorial Day or the Grand Army of the Republic encampments. Indeed, the Pension Bureau and Southern Claims files often revealed the vivid internal dissension within communities, as individuals offered contradictory versions of the same events. When Solomon Stansbury's widow applied for a pension from the U.S. Army, she and some other supporting deponents claimed that the Fannin Tory had been a consistent Union man during the war. But other witnesses stated that Stansbury "was not a Union man at the start" and had campaigned vigorously for Breckenridge in the presidential election of 1860. Robert Woody also found his army pension jeopardized by community testimony. In 1887, Woody's old nemesis, Walter Webster Findley, successfully campaigned to have Woody's U.S. Army pension revoked by informing federal agents that the wounds that Woody alleged to have occurred in battle with Confederates were actually sustained before the war. Similarly, Thomas R. Trammell, a Fannin Confederate, spent much of his postwar career disrupting the pension claims of fellow highlanders by exposing the Confederate military records of the claimants. (Until the 1890s, U.S. Army pensions were forbidden to anyone with previous service in the Rebel armies). Tories also proved willing to sabotage pension claims of individuals they thought less than honest. One Unionist group petitioned the U.S. Army in 1890, claiming, "In defense of truth and justice to the United States government" they had to inform the Pension Bureau that one of their claimants "was a rebel . . . he cried secession loud."[41]

These continuing disputes about the memory of the war illustrate the limits of reconciliation in north Georgia. In the late nineteenth century, historians have shown, Americans in general began to downplay the sectional divisions of the war and focus on mutually ennobling memories of sacrifice and valor on both sides. This "romance of reunion" sought to mollify diverseness by mitigating or concealing the intractable issues of race and regionalism that had caused the war. The resulting spirit of sectional rapprochement reached its apogee when Union and Confederate veterans gathered for a joint observance of the fiftieth anniversary of the Battle of Gettysburg in 1915. To a degree, highland Georgians also adopted the language of reconciliation with wartime foes. The commander of the Georgia GAR noted proudly in 1893 that "those who wore the blue and gray mingle freely as citizens. The warmest social relations exist between those who were once champions of extreme views on either side." The editors of the *Dahlonega Mountain Signal* were relieved to proclaim that "only a few years ago two hemispheres were shaken by our tremendous and fratricidal cannonades, but now it has all died away and we all abide by the same constitution and obey the same laws." The paper frequently reprinted sentimental pieces about postwar accord between erstwhile enemies, such as the story of two old veterans, one

Union and one Confederate, who meet on the Shiloh battlefield years after the conflict to jointly reminisce about their experiences. Their conversation ends with the Southerner saying "stranger, we fought each other like devils that day and we fought to kill. But the war's over now and we ain't soldiers any longer—gimme your hand!" These feelings went beyond mere platitudes. Some north Georgians even tried to adjust their commemoration activities to include the new reconciliation theme. On Confederate Decoration Day in 1891, Dahlonegans made a point of decorating the graves of both Unionists and Confederates at Mount Hope Cemetery, proclaiming that "the issues involved in the struggle between the states are set aside forever by the blood of the noble and brave of the country."[42]

But in the mountains of Georgia, not all former enemies were willing to forgive and forget. Despite the national trend toward sectional comity, many in the region refused to engage in the historical amnesia required to silence wartime differences and embrace the enemy. They actively fought attempts to recast memory in favor of reconciliation and insisted on aggressively partisan histories as a way of asserting local identity. These disputes often focused on the status of military veterans of both sides—how they should be treated and celebrated, and how their loyalty and commitment should be judged. In arguing about which soldiers to honor and how to honor them, north Georgians defied the accommodating notion of shared martial sacrifice and valor, a hallmark of the romanticized vision of reunion prevalent throughout much of the country. Once again, the mountains proved an exception to the national experience of the Civil War.

As the chief guardians of the war's legacy, military veterans felt a particular duty to maintain a correct public interpretation of their respective causes. They were also sensitive to any charges that might besmirch the reputation of them or their compatriots. And so, when doubts began to arise about the procedure for conducting soldier reunions, disagreements among former combatants energized the entire community in a struggle for the past. In Dahlonega, a firestorm of controversy erupted in the 1880s when one J. R. Dowdy had the temerity to challenge the public memory of the Confederate 52nd Georgia Volunteers. Dowdy had served in the 52nd briefly during the war, but he was also an obstreperous sort who had no compunctions about tweaking the proponents of the Lost Cause in Lumpkin County. In 1885 he roiled the community by insisting on attending the regiment's annual reunion in Dahlonega. For many veterans, Dowdy's presence was an affront, because the man was an open dissenter during the war and had felt no need to apologize for his behavior since. Dowdy did not hide the fact that he had deserted the regiment and refugeed to Union lines in Tennessee later in the war. Worse, he openly disparaged the reputation of his former comrades in the 52nd, claiming that "half of the members were disloyal to the cause for which they were battling" and had deserted during the war just as Dowdy had. Still, he sat and ate chicken with the other veterans at the regimental reunion, refusing to take hints that the gathering was intended only for those who were "friendly to the cause."[43]

Soon the whole community was weighing in on the issue. One veteran wrote the *Mountain Signal* to assert that men like Dowdy were unwelcome at the reunion, stating "those who deserted and went to the other side do not claim to be Confederates." Another correspondent, who called himself Drummer Boy, also supported excluding dissenters from the reunion: "None but those in good standing and who stood brave to the 'lost cause' need apply. Those who deserted their respective commands and all 'Hogbacks' as they are termed are earnestly requested not to be present. A word to the wise is sufficient." To preempt more embarrassing incidents, the 52nd leadership formed a committee to identify and contact veterans whose wartime behavior was deemed dishonorable to the cause. These men were then warned "not to attempt participation in the reunion."[44]

For Dahlonega's pro-Confederate establishment, veterans like Dowdy threatened not only the honor of former soldiers but the entire structure of memory they had painstakingly built to shut the Tories out of the past. The Lost Cause depended upon the unquestioned fidelity of those who had worn the gray. The veterans were the shock troops of Confederate myth, the spearhead of the campaign to forge and maintain the correct view of the war's meaning for the South. For a former soldier like Dowdy to turn upon the cause might expose the reality of the fractious war years and cast doubt on north Georgia's claims to Southern patriotism during the war. So J. R. Dowdy was barred from attending future reunions, and local elites attempted to discredit his alternate version of the regimental history. Interestingly, Confederates ostracized Tories while maintaining the facade of sectional goodwill. They did so by segregating native north Georgian dissenters from the honorable Northern veterans of the Union army. Yankees who had resettled in north Georgia since the end of hostilities were actually welcomed at Confederate reunions in the best traditions of reconciliation. In 1887, Lumpkin's Confederate veterans invited a Northerner and former Federal soldier named Howe to the 52nd's reunion. Mr. Howe was even allowed to give "a brief speech, in which he referred to the restored concord and harmony now existing." But Northern soldiers who had "worn the blue with honor to the end" were put in a different category from north Georgians who had defected to the Federals. As one former rebel wrote, "we are going to invite all the Union soldiers who were living in the north at the time of the war to our reunion; we love brave soldiers. But the men what was born here and deserted us and gined 'tother side, cause they thought we would be licked, can have a reunion of their own if they want it. We don't want 'em to come to ourn." In making this distinction, mountain Confederates kept up the romance of reunion with the North while stocking a reservoir of venom for their local enemies.[45]

Anti-Confederates fought back. One lambasted the entire process of regimental reunions, sniping that the old soldiers of the 52nd were only "commemorat[ing] the death and suffering of the Confederacy." These critics swore that the aging Confederate veterans would soon join the likes of Jefferson Davis and General Joseph Johnston in the fires of hell. J. R. Dowdy, the man who had started the imbroglio, decided to take the advice of his opponents and hold his own separate reunion for dissenters and Tories. On August 26, 1887, Dowdy convened a meeting of "a large number of citizens both ladies and gentlemen." The group marched in procession through the streets of Dahlonega under a large American flag until they reached the schoolhouse, where they shared a meal and listened to Dowdy give an hour-long speech describing the wartime experiences of the dissenting mountaineers of north Georgia. Dowdy defended his desertion from the 52nd steadfastly and reminded his audience that many of their friends and neighbors had done the same, even those who claimed to be un-Reconstructed Rebels now: "I know of 13,000 rebel soldiers from Georgia who deserted their ranks and went to Tennessee and now Dick Dowdy is the only man that can be found who went to Tennessee." Like Sion Darnell, Dowdy initially cast his opposition to the Confederacy in ideological, even moral terms. He proclaimed, "I left the rebel army and went to Tennessee because I thought the yankies were right and the rebels were wrong. . . . I believe in a free republican government where every man is free and has the same privileges." But Dowdy dwelled even more on the more proximate causes of mountaineer dissent, namely the privileges of local rights against outside authority. This was the issue that resonated most strongly with the highland audience. The former Tory said that he fought the Rebels because they represented the coerced conformity of the town elite. "They rode me on a rail once and threatened to do it again, but I have never deviated nor faltered from my principals or opinion." In a reference to the jailings of dissenters during the war, Dowdy thundered, "I do not believe in monopoly or town rule . . . I consider that I can attend to my own business. . . . When a man gets so he cannot attend his business he is then considered a lunatic and they want him down at Atlanta or Milledgeville." He hearkened back to the class resentments that had fueled dissent during the war, comparing his exclusion from the 52nd reunion to the persecution of poor country folk by the pro-Confederate town establishment: "The big side is always wrong, this is clearly shown in the case of Noe and Lot of old" (and in the case of mountain Tories, he might have added). Dowdy urged his listeners to relish their outsider status and ignore the barbs of their misguided rebel neighbors. He promised that they would survive the hostility of the pro-Confederates, just as they had survived being ostracized during the war, when the state legislature had stripped them of their very citizenship. "The broad cloth and aristocracy of Dahlonega has uncitizenized me. But this does not alter my opinion in the least," he affirmed.[46]

Dowdy continued to hold his counter-reunions for many years, struggling to maintain the honor and cohesion of the dissenters, deserters, and Unionists who craved an alternate remembering of the war years. In the meantime, controversy flared even higher when Tories began to apply for federal pensions for their military service to the Union. Congressman Allan D. Candler, who represented north Georgia in Washington, triggered a community conflict in 1886 when he proposed a piece of legislation on behalf of some of his mountain constituents. The law would set aside federal pension funds "for the relief of the First Georgia State Troops," the regiment organized by Union officer James G. Brown in 1864. Many north Georgians were already collecting federal pensions for their service in various Tennessee and Kentucky regiments, but the proposal to provide for the 1st Georgia touched a raw nerve with pro-Confederates. For mountain Rebels, channeling federal funds to the veterans of the only official Union unit raised entirely from Georgia was an intolerable shame. Pensions for the 1st Georgia would equate the wartime actions of the Northern Union soldier with the resistance of north Georgia Tories. The former could be respected; the latter could not. Almost immediately after Congressman Candler offered his pension bill, north Georgia Rebels burst into angry protest. They lambasted Candler and Georgia's Union veterans in enraged letters to the *Mountain Signal,* which soon became a platform for anti-pension agitation in the region.[47]

Rebels opposed the Candler bill because they felt the veterans of the 1st Georgia were traitors to the South whose wartime conduct was illegal and dishonorable. Unlike Northern soldiers, whom Southerners conceded had fought out of conscience and commitment (however misguided), the Tories were treacherous enemies who were beyond all hope of redemption. These "first Georgia hogback yankey fellers," one rebel wrote, were "traitors to their own harth and fireside that give 'em birth." The fact that many 1st Georgia soldiers had initially joined Confederate regiments, only to defect to the North later in the war, signaled to pro-Rebels that they were perfidious, cynical opportunists rather than principled opponents. "The great bulk of them were deserters from the Confederate ranks, mossybacks, and renegades and traitors to the South," one Dahlonegan insisted, while another charged that the Tories were "a gang of deserters, who sought, by their acts, to overthrow their country . . . [and] to keep from doing their duty as citizens of the seceded states." Other outraged pro-Confederates decried the pension bill as "a scheme to defraud the government" by diverting public funds to the most contemptible individuals in the community and swore that "not a man of that regiment will ever enjoy the benefit of one cent as a reward for acting as traitors to their native country." Ultimately, highland Confederates believed that Tories were a uniquely dastardly kind of enemy because they had turned against their own kin and country. It was illegitimate to recognize their service in the same way as enemy soldiers from Illinois, Pennsylvania, or New York, who could be safely integrated into the Lost Cause myth. Thus, one critic raged, "all honor to the Union soldiers from Northern States, but the brand of Cain and the stigma of Ishmael upon every Georgian who deserted Georgia in the hour of her peril. Who are these Georgia Union soldiers who ask Congress to pay them the price of betrayal?"[48]

For mountain rebels, a key differentiation between Tories and northern Union soldiers was that the latter had fought in conventional combat against organized Confederate armies, and the former had fought a guerrilla conflict against local targets. Of the 1st Georgia, one Confederate sympathizer scoffed, "we never heard of that regiment before. Where was it made up, and who were its officers? They are not recognized by the true Union soldier—they are not recognized by the true confederate soldier, and they are not recognized by the Secretary of War." Another opponent of Candler's bill mocked the regiment as "a mythical military organization," chiding that "we have read some of the campaigns in Georgia, but we have never read . . . of anything concerning the exploits of the now celebrated 'First Georgia Federal Regiment.' Were they at Kennesaw, at New Hope, Atlanta, Jonesboro, Franklin, Columbus, Bentonville?" The fact that the Tories fought in irregular fashion against their opponents in the community—conscription officers, tax collectors, and pro-Rebel civilians—placed them beyond the protection of the gallant battlefield myths that surrounded all other military veterans in the postwar age of reconciliation. The sparsely recorded subwar that the Tories fought had actually injured the community far more that the distant battles of the great Civil War armies. Pro-Confederates could embrace regular Union soldiers, who had done them little direct harm, but they castigated the Tory guerrillas as brigands unworthy of pensions or respect by either side.[49]

The controversy over Candler's bill revived all the old passions over wartime atrocities and brought into sharp relief simmering recriminations over the bloody incidents in north Georgia's Civil War. For mountain Rebels, the Tories' treason was compounded by the brutality they had shown in combat. In an effort to mobilize public opinion against the pension bill, Lumpkin elites branded the former Tories as criminals and savages, just as Confederate mountaineers had done during the war. One upcountry Confederate veteran gossiped about several of his neighbors who had joined the 1st Georgia, saying that these men were well known even before the war as horse thieves, gold robbers, and cads. "We go in for pensioning the honest soldier," another Dahlonega Confederate wrote, "but any attempt to foist thieves and bushwhackers on the country should meet with proper rebuke." This public image of the 1st Georgia as a pack of gangsters found trenchant expression in one scorching editorial in the *Mountain Signal:* "They were . . . a band of thieves and cutthroats, who recognized fealty to no government, and had regard to neither age nor sex. If there was a single exception among them to the general rule, we never heard of it at the time. And if there was a single mean or cruel thing on the criminal calendar that they didn't do, it must have been something they forgot. The government might just as well go to Sing-Sing for objects of its maintenance." When a Unionist in neighboring Dawson County tried to defend the veterans of the 1st Georgia as conscientious soldiers who had done their duty, the editor of the *Mountain Signal* countered that the Tories were "men whose only deeds of valor consisted of warring against women and children."[50]

In portraying former Unionists as mere outlaws, mountain Confederates also justified their own brutal measures to suppress dissent during the war. One critic of the pension bill claimed that the soldiers of the 1st Georgia were "nothing more than a gang of robbers and bushwhackers" whose dishonorable conduct earned them the harshest possible treatment. "Several of them came back to their homes and whenever one of them were caught he was either hanged or shot," the former Rebel noted with satisfaction. The agitation over the pension even caused upcountry Confederates to revisit one of the most painful incidents in Lumpkin County history, one that they had taken great pains to hide or ignore in the years since the war. Referring to Colonel Findley's 1864 execution of the Unionists Stansbury, Stuart, and Witt, one Rebel apologist recollected: "We know of three men who belonged to a confederate command, that went from this county, that deserted and went hence, and when they came home on a visit, or to get information for the enemy, they were arrested and shot. These men were no more entitled to the benefits of the pension acts than any other gang of deserters." Of course, Tories remembered the story differently. They insisted that Findley's militia had been mere "bushwhackers" whose idea of duty was to seize a group of "poor ragged boys, condemn them to death, take them out . . . and shoot them down like dogs." But Lumpkin Confederates endorsed any means necessary to destroy dissent and secure the Confederacy, in memory if not in reality.[51]

The campaign to stop passage of Candler's pension bill was not merely an act of Confederate revenge or an attempt by the bitter vanquished to deny their Unionist neighbors a few dollars a month in federal assistance. For north Georgians, the stakes in the pension controversy were considerably higher. At issue was the memory of the Civil War, and the way the conflict would be remembered would illustrate the community's values and self-perception. By giving the veterans of the 1st Georgia the imprimatur of legitimacy through the federal government pensions, mountain rebels felt that the Lost Cause would be violated and their soothing memories of noble Southern struggle destroyed. For Tories, a federal pension offered not only financial assistance but also formal recognition that they had been in the right during the war, that mountain dissenters had played a valued part in the victorious, nationally celebrated cause of the Union. In the battle over memory, north Georgia's factions refought the Civil War to a draw, with neither side willing to concede to their opponent's version of the story. To be sure, as time passed and the generation of 1861 passed away, the struggle to define the war's place in regional history faded somewhat. Even in the midst of the memory wars, new issues were coming to the fore in north Georgia. Throughout Appalachia, forces of industrialization and development made a concerted assault on the Southern mountains in the last decade of the nineteenth century. Struggles over logging rights, railroad access, mining operations, and fence laws largely replaced the Civil War as a continuing issue. As for the pension bill, it languished in Congress for years. Allen Candler, the bill's sponsor, spoke out against it on the floor of the House of Representatives. Over a decade later, north Georgia Unionists were still crying for recognition and relief. As the twentieth century dawned, Sion Darnell reiterated the call for pensioning the 1st Georgia veterans, expressing his hope "that long delayed justice may be done to this worthy and neglected class of claimants."[52]

For some north Georgians, silence was the best way to deal with the disturbing memories of the war. In 1894, the *Dahlonega Mountain Signal* printed a series of memoirs written by William R. Crisson, then one of the oldest living residents of Lumpkin County. One of the original "twenty-niners," Crisson had lived the county's history from the beginning. He entertained the *Signal's* readers with lively tales of the gold rush days, filled with humorous anecdotes and exciting adventures from Lumpkin's frontier past. Savage Cherokees, hard-drinking miners, and violent mountain men populated this colorful history. But when he came to the Civil War period, Crisson was curiously quiet. It was not for lack of direct knowledge. He had witnessed the key moments in Lumpkin County's war. He had taken testimony in the treason trials of 1863, had watched George Lee's troops invade Dahlonega, and had served in James Findley's militia. He commanded the firing squad that executed Solomon Stansbury, Iley Stuart, and William Witt on the banks of the Chestatee River in October 1864. But virtually all he had to say about the war was that "it was a sad misfortune to the whole South," only lightened by the "noble, untiring efforts of our patriotic southern ladies to vindicate and uphold our just cause." It is impossible to tell whether his silence evinced guilt about his actions or a conviction that he needed no justification for them. Perhaps William Crisson simply felt that what the war had done to him was best forgotten.[53]

Epilogue

Near the end of Charles Frazier's novel *Cold Mountain,* a cadre of Appalachian fugitives plots their escape. The Civil War is coming to a close, but the mountains are still full of uncertainty, ravaged by rival bands of pro-Confederates, Tories, and non-aligned outlaws. The leader of the group, named Inman, is a deserter from the Confederate army, and he ponders his chances for survival in this dangerous environment:

The choices were these. Inman could return to the army. Short-handed as they were, he would be received with open arms and then immediately be put back in the muddy trenches of Petersburg, where he would try to keep his head down and hope for an early end. Or he could stay hidden in the mountains or in Black Cove as an outlier and be hunted like a bear, wolf, or catamount. Or he could cross the mountains north and put himself in the hands of the Federals, the very bastards who had spent four years shooting at him. They would make him sign his name to their oath of allegiance, but then he could wait out the fighting and come home.

Ultimately, Inman decides on the third option, for reasons that go the heart of the character's worldview. He chooses to defect to the Union, not out of ideological commitment, but because that path promises to lead him back to his community and "whatever new world the war left behind." It represents his best chance to "come home." Indeed, throughout Charles Frazier's novel, the main characters remain focused on home above all. Inman lays down his rifle and risks innumerable obstacles in order to return to his mountains and his beloved Ada. For her part, Ada spends nearly half the novel striving to maintain her homestead. With the help of her companion Ruby, Ada plants and harvests, builds and restores, all while dodging local pro-Confederate militia. For the women of Cold Mountain no less than the men, the war is something to be endured, escaped, so that the normal life of the community can be restored. It is fitting that the novel ends with a communal meal, as the survivors take refuge in an odd kind of extended family rebuilt from the war's ashes. Historians have found much about which to criticize Frazier's novel, but in his insistence on the primacy of local motivations, the author is correct. For the people of north Georgia, no less than with the western North Carolinians of *Cold Mountain*, the Civil War was refracted through the prism of local perceptions.[1]

In the vast historiography of the Civil War, and in the slightly less voluminous historiography of Appalachia, north Georgia has remained a neglected region. There is still no comprehensive history of the region. But by examining the history of two north Georgia counties, I have tried to illuminate several issues of importance to scholars of the Civil War, the Appalachians, and the South as a whole. By looking at the war period in Fannin and Lumpkin counties, we can gain a more complex perspective on why Civil War soldiers fought and how their concepts of community affected and were affected by the course of the conflict. We also gain new evidence in the still-developing picture of life in the nineteenth-century Southern mountains.

Fannin and Lumpkin may not be strictly representative of north Georgia, but they embody many of Appalachia's contrasting characteristics. From their founding, the two counties followed different social, economic, and political paths. Lumpkin was founded in the midst of Georgia's gold rush and was integrated early into the state's commercial network. For a mountain county, Lumpkin possessed a relatively large slave population, and the bustling town of Dahlonega, with its branch federal mint, served as an important link between Lumpkin and the rest of the state. Fannin County was less developed, more of a frontier area, and less connected to the rest of the state. There were no important towns, few slaves, and fewer transportation routes to the south. Many of Fannin's residents migrated to Georgia from North Carolina or Tennessee, and many of them were oriented economically and socially to the north.

When the secession crisis struck, heavy cooperationist sentiment existed in both counties. However, belying the myth of a solidly Unionist

Appalachia, both counties generally supported the Confederacy after the war began. Hundreds of Fannin and Lumpkin men enlisted in the Confederate armies, and civilians mobilized to support the war effort. Some dissent did continue, however, and the stigma of Unionism remained, causing mountain secessionists to be increasingly sensitive to charges of disloyalty. This sensitivity would become a powerful motivator for some of the mountain Rebels' later actions.

As the war dragged on, the situation in north Georgia became more divisive. The Confederate Conscription Act of 1862 incited widespread disaffection, especially in Fannin County, where large numbers of Confederate soldiers deserted and returned home. By 1863, the north Georgia mountains hid thousands of deserters and anti-Confederate dissenters, who were alienated from the Confederacy due to conscription and impressment. Lumpkin's soldiers were less likely to desert, and its civilians tried aggressively to assert their Confederate loyalty. Their efforts contributed to a crisis of fear that had bloody consequences later in the war.

Local interests dominated north Georgian's reactions to the conflict. For Tories, the Confederacy was a threat to community and family, and therefore they resisted. Confederates may have had a stronger sense of nationalism to the Confederacy, but even their allegiances were built upon local foundations. Throughout the war, mountain Rebels tried to balance the sometimes competing forces of nationalism and localism.

In 1864, guerrilla war burst upon north Georgia with full fury. Tories gained new allies with the approach of the Union army, and highlanders flooded into Union lines. Several raids into Fannin County in the spring and summer of 1864 led to a crisis that mountain Rebels responded to with increasing violence, leading to the massacre of several Tories in separate incidents.

After the war, mountaineers tried to resume their peacetime lives. But political and social rivalries persisted between Tories and Confederates. In Fannin, where more people were disaffected throughout the county, the Republican Party took hold during Reconstruction, offering a counter to Democratic dominance in Lumpkin. In the courtrooms and communities, Tories and Rebels continued to battle over their differing visions of the past and of the future.

The history of the Civil War in north Georgia leads scholars to several conclusions. First, the evidence gives additional support to those historians who criticize the myth of mountain Unionism. While widespread dissent undoubtedly existed in north Georgia, most of the region's Tories were not ideologically committed to the Union in the same way as soldiers from New York or Pennsylvania were. Highlanders were committed to defending their communities first and foremost, and this drove their actions. A related conclusion is that localism was a pervasive force in the mountains, underlying most of the choices north Georgians made. Even Confederates, who possessed a degree of regional solidarity and Southern nationalism, never strayed far from the local roots of their loyalty. When their local and national goals conflicted, Rebels usually sided with the local, even though they continued to consider themselves Confederate nationalists.

Finally, the evidence supports the growing scholarly critique of the violent stereotype in Appalachian society. Unquestionably, north Georgians participated in extralegal violence and bloody massacres during the Civil War. But their behavior stemmed not from cultural retardation or innate savagery but from a series of identifiable events that gradually turned highlanders against each other in the most violent ways. The brutality of the mountain war resulted from dramatic social disruption, as would the later Hatfield-McCoy feud and the Whitecapping campaigns.

Scholars of the Civil War and the Appalachians have much to learn from studying north Georgia. Hopefully, this and other forthcoming scholarship will expand our knowledge of the period and the region, and give us a truly complete picture of the variety and depth of our nation's past.

NOTES

Abbreviations

Anthony Collection	Madeline Anthony Collection. Lumpkin County Public Library, Dahlonega, Georgia.
Barker Papers	Robert B. Barker Papers, C. M. McClung Historical Collection, East Tennessee Historical Center, Knox County Public Library, Knoxville.
Boyd Papers	Weir Boyd Papers; Rare Book, Manuscript, and Special Collections Library; Duke University.
Boyd-Sitton Letters	Boyd-Sitton Letters, Georgia Department of Archives and History, Atlanta.
CMSRUS	Compiled Military Service Records of Volunteer Union Soldiers Who Served during the Civil War, National Archives, Microfilm, Washington DC.
Cobb Papers	Howell Cobb Papers—Correspondence. Hargrett Rare Book and Manuscript Library, University of Georgia.
CSASW	*Letters Received by the Confederate Secretary of War.* Record Group 109, M437, National Archives, Washington, DC.
Cuyler Collection	Telamon Cuyler Collection, Hargrett Rare Book and Manuscript Library, University of Georgia.
DOJ Letters	*Letters Received by the Department of Justice from the State of Georgia.* Microfilm Publication M996, Record Group 60, National Archives, Washington, DC.

EDC	Executive Department Correspondence, Georgia Department of Archives and History.
Fain Letters	Huldah Anne Fain Briant Papers, Rare Book, Manuscript, and Special Collections Library, Duke University.
GAGCM	*Georgia Adjutant General Courts Martial.* Record Group 22, Georgia Department of Archives and History, Atlanta.
GAGIC	*Georgia Adjutant General's Incoming Correspondence.* Record Group 22, Georgia Department of Archives and History, Atlanta.
GDAH	Georgia Department of Archives and History
GGAR	Journals of the Annual Encampments of the Grand Army of the Republic, Department of Georgia Letters, Washington, DC.
OR	*The War of the Rebellion: A Compilation of the Official Records of the Union and Confederate Armies.* Government Printing Office, Washington, DC, 1880–1901.
Reese Collection	A. J. Reese Letters, Georgia Department of Archives and History, Atlanta.
RG Dun	R. G. Dun and Co. Collection, Baker Library, Harvard Business School.
RG105 Complaints	*Records of the Field Offices of the Bureau of Refugees, Freedman, and Abandoned Lands, Register of Complaints, Dahlonega Field Office.* Record Group 105. National Archives, Washington, DC.
RG105 Field Offices	*Records of the Subordinate Field Offices for the State of Georgia, Bureau of Refugees, Freedmen, and Abandoned Lands, Dahlonega Field Office,* Record Group 105, National Archives, Washington, DC.
RG105 Letters	*Records of the Assistant Commissioner for the State of Georgia, Bureau of Refugees, Freedmen, and Abandoned Lands. Letters Received.* Record Group 105. National Archives, Washington, DC.
RG105 Superintendent	*Records of the United States Bureau of Refugees, Freedmen, and Abandoned Lands, Records of the Superintendent of Education for the State of Georgia, 1865–1870,* Record Group 105, National Archives, Washington, DC.
SCCA	*United States Commissioner of Claims, Southern Claims Commission, Barred and Disallowed Claims, Georgia.* National Archives, Microfilm, Washington, DC, 1990.

SCCBD   United States Commissioner of Claims, *Southern
                         Claims Commission Allowed Claims: 1871–1880.
                         Georgia.* National Archives, Microfilm, Washing-
                         ton, DC, 1990.
"Slave Narratives"   Federal Writers Project, "Slave Narratives: A Folk
                         History of Slavery in the United States from Inter-
                         views with Former Slaves." Typewritten Records,
                         1941. National Archives, Washington, DC.
USPM   Records of the U.S. Provost Marshal, *Spies, Scouts,
                         Guides and Detectives.* Record Group 110, National
                         Archives, Washington, DC.
Wilkins Papers   John D. Wilkins Papers; Rare Book, Manuscript, and
                         Special Collections Library; Duke University.

Introduction

1. McPherson, *For Cause and Comrades.*

2. Escott, *After Secession;* Faust, "Altars of Sacrifice"; Thomas, *Confederate Nation;* Beringer, Hattaway, Jones, and Still, *Why the South Lost.*

3. Durrill, *War of Another Kind;* Fellman, *Inside War;* McCaslin, *Tainted Breeze;* Daniel Sutherland, *Seasons of War;* Kenzer, *Kinship and Neighborhood;* Whites, *Civil War.*

4. Johnson, *Toward a Patriarchal Republic;* Hahn, *Roots of Southern Populism;* D. Williams, T. Williams, and Carlson, *Plain Folk.*

5. Crawford, *Ashe County's Civil War;* Groce, *Mountain Rebels;* McKenzie, *One South or Many?* Noe and S. Wilson, eds., *Civil War in Appalachia;* O'Brien, *Mountain Partisans;* Inscoe and McKinney, *Heart of Confederate Appalachia;* Mann, "Family Group, Family Migration"; J. A. Williams, *Appalachia,* 157–85.

1. Mountain Neighbors

1. *Milledgeville (GA) Journal,* August 1, 1829, quoted in D. Williams, *Georgia Gold Rush,* 24.

2. D. Williams, *Georgia Gold Rush,* 37–45; Young, "Southern Gold Rush," 373–92; Perdue, *Slavery and Cherokee Society.*

3. *Auraria Western Herald,* April 9, 1833; Coulter, *Auraria,* 6–7; Cain, *History of Lumpkin County,* 43–44, 394; Paschal, *Ninety-four Years,* 236.

4. *Dahlonega Nugget,* January 29, 1897.

5. Andrews, *Reminiscences,* 93; D. Williams, *Georgia Gold Rush,* 89–90; Paschal, *Ninety-four Years,* 241; Cain, *History of Lumpkin County,* 47; *Dahlonega*

Nugget, January 29, 1897. For more on the frontier culture of north Georgia miners, see Bolton and Culclasure, *Confessions of Edward Isham.*

6. Paschal, *Ninety-four Years,* 243; Coulter, *Auraria,* 17; D. Williams, *Georgia Gold Rush,* 97; Bolton and Culclasure, *Confessions of Edward Isham,* 85–100; *Dahlonega Mountain Signal,* April 6 and May 4, 1894; Andrews, *Reminiscences,* 73. For more on gender in the South and in Appalachia, see Bynum, *Unruly Women,* and John Inscoe, "Moving through Deserter Country," in Noe and Wilson, *Civil War in Appalachia,* 171–76.

7. Cain, *History of Lumpkin County,* 34.

8. D. Williams, *Georgia Gold Rush,* 26–27, 88–89, 98; Gilmer, *Georgians,* 265; *Dahlonega Mountain Signal,* April 6, 13, 20, and May 11, 1894; *Auraria Western Herald,* May 28, 1833; Bolton and Culclasure, *Confessions of Edward Isham,* 1–18.

9. Perdue, *Slavery and Cherokee Society; Auraria Western Herald,* May 1833, July 30 and November 16, 1833. For more on ethnic mixing in Appalachia, see Dunaway, *Slavery in the American Mountain South* 201–5.

10. Green, *Georgia's Forgotten Industry,* 105; *Cherokee Phoenix* (Cherokee Nation), May 27, 1829; D. Williams, *Georgia Gold Rush,* 113; Lumpkin County Grand Jury Presentments, March 1838, GDAH.

11. For a summary of Appalachian historiography, see Pudup, Billings, and Waller, *Appalachian in the Making,* 1–24.

12. Paschal, *Ninety-four Years,* 239–46; Cain, *History of Lumpkin County,* 207–40; *Dahlonega Signal,* January 21, 1887.

13. Cain, *History of Lumpkin County,* 75–76, 134, 336–38; D. Williams, *Georgia Gold Rush,* 95–96; RG Dun, Georgia, vol. 19.

14. Cain, *History of Lumpkin County,* 58–59, 336, 355; J. F. Smith, *Cherokee Land Lottery;* D. Williams, *Georgia Gold Rush,* 47–57; U.S. Bureau of the Census, Agricultural Schedules, 1860, Lumpkin County, Georgia.

15. *Dahlonega Mountain Signal,* January 30, 1874.

16. D. Williams, *Georgia Gold Rush,* 78; Cain, *History of Lumpkin County,* 98–99; Amory Dexter Diary, 1861, GDAH; Young, "Southern Gold Rush," 384–89; D. Davis, *Where There Are Mountains,* 156.

17. Cain, *History of Lumpkin County,* 54–55; D. Williams, *Georgia Gold Rush,* 90–96; *Auraria Western Herald,* April 9 and October 26, 1833; RG Dun, Georgia, vol. 19; Coulter, *Auraria,* 19; *Dahlonega Mountain Signal,* April 23, 1853, and January 21, 1887; Crawford, "Mountain Farmers," 430–50; D. Davis, *Where There Are Mountains,* 123–60.

18. Cain, *History of Lumpkin County,* 52, 413; *Auraria Western Herald,* November 23, 1833; *Dahlonega Signal,* January 21, 1887.

19. Kephart, *Our Southern Highlanders,* 16–17; *Auraria Western Herald,* July 9, 1833; *Dahlonega Mountain Signal,* April 23 and May 7, 1853.

20. Sion Darnell, "North Georgia in the Late Civil War," *Journal of the 13th*

Annual Encampment, GGAR, 41–47; John Inscoe, "Appalachian Otherness," in Georgia Humanities Council, *New Georgia Guide,* 103–7.

21. D. Williams, *Georgia Gold Rush,* 84–87; Cain, *History of Lumpkin County,* 51–53; Dunaway, *Slavery in the American Mountain South,* 123.

22. *Dahlonega Mountain Signal,* May 21, 1853; *Auraria Western Herald,* September 28 and October 26, 1833; *Dahlonega Nugget,* March 3, 1905; Amory Dexter Diary, GDAH; U.S. Bureau of the Census, Slave Schedules, 1850 and 1860, Lumpkin County, Georgia; Andrews, *Reminiscences,* 74; David Williams, "Georgia's Forgotten Miners: African Americans and the Georgia Gold Rush of 1829," in Inscoe, *Appalachians and Race,* 45. For more on nature of slavery in nonfarming work, see Dew, *Bond of Iron,* and also John E. Steally III, "Slavery in the Kanawha Salt Industry," in Inscoe, *Appalachians and Race,* 50–73.

23. Wilma A. Dunaway has done a masterful job of organizing and cataloging all of the WPA slave narratives from Appalachia. See her *Slavery in the American Mountain South* and its accompanying Web site, "Slavery and Emancipation in the Mountain South," http://scholar.lib.vt.edu/faculty_archives/mountain_slavery/ (accessed August 28, 2005).

24. "Slave Narratives," Jordan Smith, vol. 16, pt. 4, 36; "Slave Narratives," Tom Singleton, vol. 4, pt. 3, 265; "Slave Narratives," Anderson Furr, vol. 4, pt. 1, 350.

25. "Slave Narratives," John F. Van Hook, vol. 4, pt. 4, 73; "Slave Narratives," Anderson Furr, vol. 4, pt. 1, 350; "Slave Narratives," Jordan Smith, vol. 16, pt. 4, 36–37; Morris Hillyer, 13:138; Abner Griffin, narrative, in Rawick, *American Slave,* vol. 4, pt. 2; Dunaway, *Slavery in the American Mountain South,* 57–60.

26. "Slave Narratives," Tom Singleton, vol. 4, pt. 3, 268; Abner Griffin; Dunaway, *Slavery in the American Mountain South,* 113–38; D. Williams, "Georgia's Forgotten Miners," in Inscoe, *Appalachians and Race,* 42–44.

27. "Slave Narratives," Anderson Furr, vol. 4, pt. 1, 349; "Slave Narratives," Steve Connally, vol. 16, pt. 1, 249; "Slave Narratives," Morris Hillyer, Oklahoma Narratives, 13:138; Burke, *Pleasure and Pain,* 77; Lumpkin County Grand Jury Presentments, August 1835, GDAH; *Auraria Western Herald,* April 30, 1833; Bolton and Culclasure, *Confessions of Edward Isham,* 2; Coulter, *Auraria,* 7.

28. "Slave Narratives," Anderson Furr, vol. 1, pt. 1, 348; "Slave Narratives," Jordan Smith, vol. 16, pt. 4, 37–38; "Slave Narratives," John F. Van Hook, vol. 4, pt. 4, 77; Dunaway, *Slavery in the American Mountain South,* 166–68.

29. "Slave Narratives," Tom Singleton, vol. 4, pt. 3, 268–69; "Slave Narratives," Jordan Smith, vol. 16, pt. 4, 37–38; "Slave Narratives," Morris Hillyer, 13:141.

30. "Slave Narratives," Morris Hillyer, 13:139–40; "Slave Narratives," John F. Van Hook, vol. 4, pt. 4, 79–80; "Slave Narratives," Jordan Smith, vol. 16, pt. 4, 36–37; Dunaway, *Slavery in the American Mountain South,* 171–240.

31. "Slave Narratives," John F. Van Hook, vol. 4, pt. 4, 79 –80; "Slave Narratives," Jordan Smith, vol. 16, pt. 4, 38; "Slave Narratives," Morris Hillyer, 13 : 141.

32. "Slave Narratives," Tom Singelton, vol. 4, pt. 3, 266; "Slave Narratives," Anderson Furr, vol. 1, pt. 1, 346; "Slave Narratives," Morris Hillyer, 140; Dunaway, *Slavery in the American Mountain South,* 206 –40.

33. *Dahlonega Signal,* August 6, 1886; Cain, *History of Lumpkin County,* 210 –12; Burke, *Pleasure and Pain,* 77; U.S. Bureau of the Census, Slave Schedule, 1860, Lumpkin County, Georgia; Lanman, *Letters from the Alleghany Mountains,* 154; Dunaway, "Diaspora, Death, and Sexual Exploitation," 128 –49; John Inscoe, "Race and Racism in Southern Appalachia," in Pudup, Billings, and Waller, *Appalachia in the Making,* 103 –31.

34. Olmsted, *Journey in the Back Country,* 247 –81; Lanman, *Letters from the Alleghany Mountains,* 155; Andrews, *Reminiscences,* 75; Inscoe, "Olmsted in Appalachia," 171 –82.

35. U.S. Bureau of the Census, 1860, Slave Schedule, Lumpkin County; RG Dun, Georgia, vol. 19.

36. Carey, *Parties, Slavery, and the Union,* 19 –53; *Auraria Western Herald,* April 10, May 7and 23, 1833.

37. *Auraria Western Herald,* April 23, 1833; Carey, *Parties, Slavery, and the Union,* 23; see also Carey's " 'E Pluribus Unum,' " 810 –41; Thornton, "Ethic of Subsistence," 108 –36; *Milledgeville Federal Union,* October 27 1840, October 17, 1843, November 26, 1844, November 14, 1848, November 9, 1852, November 11, 1856.

38. Brashear, "Market Revolution and Party Preference"; *Auraria Western Herald,* August 24, 1833; Paschal, *Ninety-four Years,* 238; Cain, *History of Lumpkin County,* 44 –46.

39. Shryock, *Georgia and the Union,* 258; *Athens Southern Banner,* May 16, 1850.

40. *Auraria Western Herald,* September 28, 1833; Ira Scott to Abner Feimster, November 11, 1850, Abner Feimster Papers, Duke University.

41. Inscoe, "Appalachian Otherness," in Georgia Humanities Council, *New Georgia Guide,* 165 –203.

42. *Auraria Western Herald,* July 9, 1833.

43. M. H. Gathwright, undated letter to "The Times," 1841, Gathwright / Matthews Papers, GDAH; *Atlanta Christian Index,* December 3, 1833; *Auraria Western Herald,* December 14, 1833.

44. *Athens Southern Watchman,* September 17, 1857; *Milledgeville Federal Union,* September 20, 1853; Carey, "Too Southern to Be Americans," 1 –24.

45. Burke, *Pleasure and Pain,* 76 –78; G. White, *Historical Collections of Georgia,* 663 –65; Lanman, *Letters from the Alleghany Mountains,* 154.

46. Cain, *History of Lumpkin County,* 209 –11; G. White, *Historical Collections of Georgia,* 658 –60. For an exploration of James Dickey and his portrayal

of north Georgia, see Inscoe, "Appalachian Otherness," in Georgia Humanities Council, *New Georgia Guide*, 167.

47. Jane Powers Weldon, "Touring Northwest Georgia," in Georgia Humanities Council, *New Georgia Guide*, 136–58.

48. Jones, *Facets of Fannin*, 11–32; J. F. Smith, *Cherokee Land Lottery*, 23–128; U.S. Bureau of the Census, Compendium of the Sixth U.S. Census, 1840.

49. Thompson, *Touching Home*, 75–78; Barclay, *Ducktown Back in Raht's Time*, 17; U.S. Bureau of the Census, Population and Slave Schedules, 1860, Fannin County, Georgia.

50. U.S. Bureau of the Census, Population Schedules, 1850, Gilmer County and Union County, Georgia; *Acts and Resolutions*, 1853–54, 298–300; Barclay, *Ducktown Back in Raht's Time*, 16–18.

51. RG Dun, vol. 15; *Athens Southern Watchman*, January 1, 1862; Barclay, *Ducktown Back in Raht's Time*, 25–76; U.S. Bureau of the Census, U.S. Bureau of the Census, Manufactures of the United States in 1860, Eighth Census, 66–81; Bolton and Culclasure, *Confessions of Edward Isham*, 13–15; Dunaway, *Slavery in the American Mountain South*, 133–35.

52. D. Davis, *Where There Are Mountains*, 158–59; Meredith, *Girl Captives of the Cheyennes*, 3–4; Billings, Blee, and Swanson, "Culture, Family, and Community," 154–70.

53. U.S. Bureau of the Census, Population Schedule, 1860, Fannin County, Georgia; D. Davis, *Where There Are Mountains*, 139.

54. U.S. Bureau of the Census, Agricultural Schedule, 1860, Fannin County, Georgia; U.S. Bureau of the Census, Population Schedules, 1860, Fannin County, Georgia; McKenzie, "Wealth and Income" 260–79, 267.

55. Ward, *Annals of Upper Georgia*, 207–10; U.S. Bureau of the Census, Population and Agricultural Schedules, 1850, Gilmer County, Georgia.

56. U.S. Bureau of the Census, Population and Agricultural Schedules, 1850, Gilmer County, Georgia; Jones, *Facets of Fannin*, 236–37; *Acts and Resolutions*, 1853–54, 298.

57. G. White, *Historical Collection of Georgia*, 658–60; U.S. Bureau of the Census, Population and Agricultural Schedules, Fannin County and Lumpkin County, Georgia; U.S. Bureau of the Census, *Statistics of the U.S. Census*, 1860; RG Dun, Georgia, vols. 12, 15, 19; D. Davis, *Where There Are Mountains*, 139.

58. Barclay, *Ducktown Back in Raht's Time*, 74–76; U.S. Bureau of the Census, *Statistics of the U.S. Census*, 1860.

59. U.S. Bureau of the Census, Population Schedules, 1869, Fannin County and Lumpkin County, Georgia.

60. For more on the recent rededication of the Dickey cemetery, see Patricia Mays's article in *Salon.com*, "James Dickey's Relative Restoring Cemetery," June 1, 1999, http://www.salon.com/people/feature/1999/06/01/dickey (accessed August 28, 2005). Jones, *Facets of Fannin*; U.S. Bureau of the Census,

Slave Schedules, 1850, Lumpkin County, Georgia; U.S. Bureau of the Census, Slave Schedules, 1860, Fannin County and Lumpkin County, Georgia; U.S. Bureau of the Census, *Statistics of the U.S. Census,* 1860.

61. Hettle, "Ambiguous Democrat," 577–92; *Milledgeville Federal Union,* October 11, 1859.

62. Hettle, "Ambiguous Democrat," 577–92.

63. *Dahlonega Mountain Signal,* April 6, 20, and May 11, 1894; U.S. Bureau of the Census, Population Schedules, 1860, Lumpkin County, Georgia.

2. *"This Unpatriotic Imputation"*

1. Johnson, *Toward a Patriarchal Republic.*

2. Barney, *Secessionist Impulse;* Escott, *After Secession;* Horton, "Submitting to the 'Shadow of Slavery,'" 111–36; Thomas, *Confederate Nation;* Thornton, *Politics and Power;* Ford, *Origins of Southern Radicalism;* Crofts, *Reluctant Confederates;* McCurry, *Masters of Small Worlds.*

3. Johnson, *Toward a Patriarchal Republic;* Hahn, *Roots of Southern Populism;* Carey, *Parties, Slavery and the Union.*

4. Degler, *Other South,* 168–70. For examples of the Unionist myth, see J. Campbell, *Southern Highlander,* 94–96; Hume, *Loyal Mountaineers of Tennessee;* Frost, "Our Contemporary Ancestors," 311–19; Kellogg, *Capture and Escape,* 165; Temple, *East Tennessee.* Those recent scholars debunking the myth of Appalachian Unionism include the following: Inscoe, *Mountain Masters;* Inscoe and McKinney, *Heart of Confederate Appalachia;* Noe, "Toward the Myth of Unionist Appalachia," 73–79; Noe and S. Wilson, eds., *Civil War in Appalachia;* Waller, *Feud,* 17–52.

5. *Milledgeville Federal Union,* November 20, 1860.

6. *Albany Patriot,* December 13, 1860; *Milledgeville Federal Union,* December 11, 1860; Howell Cobb to his wife, December 29, 1860, Cobb Papers; Johnson, *Toward a Patriarchal Republic,* 48–51; Hettle, "Ambiguous Democrat"; Thornton, "Ethic of Subsistence."

7. Ira W. Scott to Abner Feimster, November 9, 1851, Abner Feimster Papers, Rare Book, Manuscript, and Special Collections Library, Duke University.

8. "The Union and States Rights Parties of Georgia: Speech of the Honorable E. W. Chastain of Georgia in the House of Representatives, March 5, 1852," *Congressional Globe,* 32nd Cong., 1st sess., 1852, 255–58; "Nebraska and Kansas: Speech of the Honorable EW Chastain, May 20, 1854," *Congressional Globe,* 33rd Cong., 1st sess., 1854, 716–20.

9. *Milledgeville Federal Union,* April 30, 1861; U.S. Bureau of the Census, Population, Agricultural, and Slave Schedules, 1860, Fannin County, Georgia;

W. A. Campbell to Governor Joseph E. Brown, July 12, 1862, and May 27, 1863, Executive Department Correspondence, EDC.

10. *Milledgeville Federal Union,* April 30, 1861; Johnson, "New Look at the Popular Vote."

11. Andrew Young to Howell Cobb, January 4, 1861, Cobb Papers; *Journal of the Public and Secret Proceedings,* 27–35.

12. *Athens Southern Watchman,* December 25, 1860; *Milledgeville Southern Recorder,* November 27, 1860.

13. *Athens Southern Watchman,* January 30, 1861.

14. *Journal of the Public and Secret Proceedings,* 27–46; *Milledgeville Southern Recorder,* January 22, 1861.

15. Johnson, *Toward a Patriarchal Republic,* 123–24; *Journal of the Public and Secret Proceedings,* 51.

16. Crofts, *Reluctant Confederates;* Inscoe and McKinney, *Heart of Confederate Appalachia,* 30–58; Groce, *Mountain Rebels,* 21–45.

17. Cain, *History of Lumpkin County,* 87; Stephen C. Dobbs to Governor Brown, June 11, 1861, EDC; John B. Chastain to Governor Brown, August 1, 1861, EDC.

18. William Martin to Governor Joseph E. Brown, April 13, 1861, Cuyler Collection; Henderson, *Roster of the Confederate Soldiers.*

19. *Dahlonega Mountain Signal,* April 5 and July 6, 1861; Cain, *History of Lumpkin County,* 143–46.

20. *Dahlonega Mountain Signal,* July 6, 1861; McGee, "Home and Friends," 363–88; Inscoe and McKinney, *Heart of Confederate Appalachia,* 71–73.

21. Fannie Boyd to Augustus Boyd, July 21, 1861, Anthony Collection; Cain, *History of Lumpkin County,* 145; Nancy Wimpy to A. J. Reese, August 3, 1861, Anthony Collection.

22. *Dahlonega Mountain Signal,* July 6, 1861; A. J. Reese to Nancy Wimpy, August 8, 1861, Reese Collection; Joan Cashin, "'Since the War Broke Out': The Marriage of Kate and William McLure," in Clinton and Silber, *Divided Houses,* 200–212.

23. Cain, *History of Lumpkin County,* 159, 221–24, 355; Minutes of the Quarterly Conference of the Dahlonega Station of the Methodist Episcopal Church, GDAH; U.S. Bureau of the Census, Population Schedules, 1850, 1860, Lumpkin County, Georgia; Weir Boyd to Governor Brown, January 14, 1862, Cuyler Collection; *Milledgeville Southern Recorder,* December 3, 1861.

24. RG Dun, vol. 19; Crisson, *Report of W. R. Crisson;* U.S. Bureau of the Census, Population and Slave Schedules, 1850, Gilmer County, Georgia; U.S. Bureau of the Census, Population and Slave Schedules, 1870, Hall County, Georgia; James Jefferson Findley to J. H. Worley, April 14, 1863, Anthony Collection.

25. A. J. Reese to Archibald Wimpy, October 15, 1861, Reese Collection.

26. *Journal of the Public and Secret Proceedings,* January 25, 1861, 70.

27. *Milledgeville Federal Union,* April 4, 1850.

28. *Athens Southern Watchman,* July 24 and August 28, 1861.

29. James Miller to Governor Joseph E. Brown, February 15, 1861, Cuyler Collection.

30. John S. Fain to Governor Joseph Brown, April 12, 1861, EDC; Andrew Young to Governor Brown, December 5, 1861, Cuyler Collection; J. A. R. Hanes to Howell Cobb, February 19, 1861, Cobb Papers; James Dobson to Governor Brown, September 19, 1861, EDC.

31. William Martin to Governor Brown, April 12, 1861, EDC.

32. George Kellogg to Governor Brown, January 12 and February 4, 1861, Cuyler Collection; William Martin to Governor Brown, April 12, 1861, EDC.

33. W. A. Campbell to Governor Brown, February 23, 1861, and July 12, 1862, EDC; Darnell, "North Georgia in the Late Civil War"; John B. Chastain to Governor Brown, August 1, 1861, EDC.

34. Nat Mangum to Governor Brown, December 11, 1861, EDC; *Athens Southern Watchman,* August 21 and November 13, 1861; Rome *Weekly Courier,* February 7, 1862.

35. *Athens Southern Watchman,* May 8, 1861; *Rome Weekly Courier,* May 10, 1861; Amory Dexter Diary, GDAH; Cain, *History of Lumpkin County,* 130; J. E. Anderson, "General Harrison W. Riley," 32–41; *Rome Weekly Courier,* November 29, 1860; Amory Dexter Diary, GDAH.

36. Andrew Young to Governor Brown, April 11, 1861, EDC; William Martin to Governor Brown, February 14, 1861, EDC; *Athens Southern Watchman,* September 14, 1861.

37. *Athens Southern Watchman,* May 1, June 19, and August 21, 1861; *Milledgeville Southern Recorder,* December 17, 1861.

38. *Athens Southern Watchman,* May 1, 1861. For a modern perspective on the Celtic propensity for violence and its influence on the Confederacy, see McWhiney and Jamieson, *Attack and Die.*

39. *Dahlonega Mountain Signal,* April 5 and July 14, 1861; Cain, *History of Lumpkin County,* 143–46.

40. Fannie Boyd to Augustus Boyd, July 21, 1861, Anthony Collection; Emily Hughes to Fannie Boyd, July 17, 1861, Anthony Collection.

3. Rebels, Traitors, and Tories

1. *Atlanta Southern Confederacy,* January 29, 1863.

2. Cain, *History of Lumpkin County,* 149–68; Henderson, *Roster of the Confederate Soldiers,* 1:283–90, 400–405, 2:105–13; Coffman, "Vital Unit," 40–45.

3. Henderson, *Roster of the Confederate Soldiers,* 1:283–90, 400–405, 2:105–13; Coffman, "Vital Unit," 40–45; Thompson, *Touching Home,* 97–105; Kinsland, "Band of Brothers," 9–27; U.S. Bureau of the Census, Population Schedules, 1860, Fannin County and Lumpkin County, Georgia; Henderson, *Roster of Confederate Soldiers,* 1:400–405, 2:105–13, 5:462–85, 507–13, 6:585–97, 628–37.

4. Darnell, "North Georgia in the Late Civil War," 42.

5. Thomas, *Confederate Nation,* 152–55; *Athens Southern Watchman,* October 1 and November 5, 1862; A. J. Reese to Nancy Wimpy, April 20 and March 9, 1862, Reese Collection; M. C. Briant to Huldah Fain, September 1, 1863, Fain Letters; Augustus Boyd to Fannie, January 1, 1863, Boyd-Sitton Letters.

6. Petition from Fannin County Residents, June 1863, Governor's Petitions, GDAH; Petition from Fannin County, September 1, 1862, and Petition from Lumpkin County, November 30, 1863, CSASW; Court Martial Proceedings of William Lyle, Co. D., 1st Regiment, Georgia State Line, March 31, 1864, GAGCM; Nancy Oliver to Curtis Oliver, March 28, 1863, Curtis Oliver Papers, GDAH; Escott, "Joseph E. Brown," 59–71.

7. Weir Boyd to Governor Brown, April 28, 1863, EDC; W. C. Cole to Governor Brown, September 9, 1862, EDC; H. W. Bake to Governor Brown, May 6, 1863, EDC; *Athens Southern Watchman,* December 2, 1863; J. F. Morton to Governor Brown, December 24, 1863, EDC; Thomas Wakefield to Office of the Confederate Secretary of War, 1862, CSASW; R. R. Hunt to Governor Brown, February 2, 1862, EDC; Weir Boyd to Augustus Boyd, December 31, 1862, Anthony Collection; Escott, "Joseph E. Brown," 62–63; D. Williams, *Rich Man's War.*

8. Thomas, *Confederate Nation;* Gallagher, *Confederate War;* Beringer, Hattaway, Jones, and Still, *Why the South Lost;* Faust, "Altars of Sacrifice," in Clinton and Silber, *Divided Houses;* A. J. Reese to Archibald Wimpy, December 12, 1863, Reese Letters; Deposition of John Walden, October 1, 1904, Box 38, Old Court Records, Lumpkin County, Dahlonega, Georgia; Oliver Strickland to Mother, December 18, 1863, Oliver V. Strickland Papers, Duke University.

9. Lonn, *Desertion during the Civil War;* Tatum, *Disloyalty in the Confederacy;* Bearman, "Desertion as Localism," 321–42; Sarris, "Anatomy of an Atrocity," 691; Henderson, *Roster of the Confederate Soldiers;* Augustus Boyd to Weir Boyd, May 12, 1863, Boyd-Sitton Letters; John Withers to Governor Brown, October 1863, Cuyler Collection.

10. *Athens Southern Confederacy,* February 4, April 22, and December 30, 1863.

11. U.S. Bureau of the Census, Population Schedules, 1860, Fannin and Lumpkin Counties, Georgia; Henderson, *Roster of Confederate Soldiers;* A. J. Reese to Archibald Wimpy, February 23, 1862, Reese Letters; Deposition of Barney Painter, December 6, 1887, U.S. Army Pension File of Abraham Picklesimer

(W.C. 621004), National Archives; Deposition of William M. Brown, October 1902, U.S. Army Pension File of Ennos Brown (W.C. 568500), National Archives; Case File of Emazire Wilson, Barker Papers; *State v. Rickels Standly,* Fannin County Superior Court Minutes, May 1866, GDAH; Deposition of Robert Woody, May 20, 1896, U.S. Army Pension File of Robert Woody (W.C. 840352), National Archives; Huldah Fain to M. C. Briant, April 14, 1863, Fain Letters.

12. U.S. Bureau of the Census, Population and Agriculture Schedules, 1850, Gilmer County, and 1860, Fannin County, Georgia; Deposition of Levi Wilson, February 13, 1877, and Report of Special Agent John G. Wager, March 8, 1877, U.S. Army Pension File of Solomon Stansbury (W.C. 131753), National Archives; Jones, *Facets of Fannin,* 31; Solomon Stansbury to Ebenezer Fain, April 4, 1863, Fain Letters; J. E. Raht to J. A. Seddon, August 11, 1863, CSASW; Deposition of Joseph Witherow, August 28, 1872, Fannin County, Georgia, Case File of Joseph M. Witherow, SCCBD; Horton, "Submitting to the 'Shadow of Slavery.'"

13. Huldah Fain to M. C. Briant, August 12, 1863, Fain Letters; Darnell, "North Georgia in the Late Civil War," 43; Depositions of David Twiggs and T. C. Corbin, January 5, 1863, Box 24, Old Court Records, Dahlonega; Deposition of George Ledbetter, August 29, 1877, SCCBD, Case File of Martha Ledbetter; Barker Papers, Case File of Emazire Wilson; Hallock, "Role of the Community," 123–34.

14. Thomas, *Confederate Nation,* 196–97; SCCA, Case File of George Campire, Pickens County, Georgia; Escott, "Joseph E. Brown," 66–67.

15. Darnell, "North Georgia in the Late Civil War," 43; SCCA, Case File of Austin Mason, Union County, Georgia; SCCA, Case File of William N. Thomas, Walker County, Georgia; SCCA, Case File of Gerusha Griffin, Walker County, Georgia; SCCA, Case File of James Teasley, Murray County, Georgia; SCCA, Case File of Rickles Stanley, Fannin County, Georgia; SCCA, Case File of John Hawkins, Walker County, Georgia; James G. Brown to General Thomas, June 15, 1864, USPM; John W. Cain to Governor Brown, September 28, 1863, EDC.

16. SCCA, Case File of Royal Brooks; SCCBD, Case File of Martha Ledbetter, Dawson County, Georgia.

17. SCCA, Case File of Mason Austin, Union County, Georgia; John Bryson to Governor Brown, October 5, 1862, EDC; W. A. Campbell to Governor, July 12, 1862, EDC.

18. Undated petition of Floyd County Citizens to General Braxton Bragg, Fouche Papers, Southern Historical Collection, Chapel Hill, North Carolina.

19. Darnell, "North Georgia in the Late Civil War," 43; R. Davis, "Memoirs of a Partisan War," 93–116.

20. SCCBD, Case File of Hosea Hopkins, Pickens County, Georgia; SCCBD, Case File of James Bowers, Union County, Georgia; SCCA, Case

File of Mason Austin, Union County, Georgia; SCCA, Case File of Pinckney
Howell, Murray County, Georgia.

21. SCCBD, Case File of Martha Ledbetter, Dawson County, Georgia;
SCCBD, Case File of Benjamin Holland, Whitfield County, Georgia; SCCBD,
Case File of Moses Simpson, Hall County, Georgia.

22. Darnell, "North Georgia in the Late Civil War," 42; SCCBD, Case File
of Martha Ledbetter; SCCBD, Case File of Susan Davis, Lumpkin County,
Georgia; SCCBD, Case File of John C. Baily, Murray County, Georgia.

23. SCCBD, Case File of Susan Davis, Lumpkin County, Georgia; SCCBD,
Case File of Moses Simpson, Hall County, Georgia; SCCA, Case File of Anna
Bradley, Pickens County, Georgia.

24. McPherson, *For Cause and Comrades.*

25. A. J. Reese to Mrs. Nancy Wimpy, April 20, 1862, Reese Collection; J. M.
Fain to Huldah Fain, May 14, 1862, Fain Letters.

26. A. J. Reese to Nancy Wimpy, October 9, 1862, Reese Letters.

27. A. J. Reese to Mrs. Nancy Wimpy, October 9, 1862. Reese Letters; Weir
Boyd to Augustus Boyd, February 1, 1862, Boyd-Sitton Letters; Augustus Boyd
to Fannie Boyd, August 14, 1862, and January 21, 1863, Boyd-Sitton Letters.

28. Augustus Boyd to A. J. Reese, April 29, 1862, Reese Letters; Benjamin
Sitton to Weir Boyd, November 11, 1861, Boyd-Sitton Letters; Fannie Boyd to
Weir Boyd, November 20, 1862, Boyd-Sitton Letters; Weir Boyd to Augustus
Boyd, January 7, 1862, Anthony Collection, Dahlonega; Weir Boyd to wife,
April 15, 1862, Boyd-Sitton Letters; G. W. Anderson to Weir Boyd, September 15, 1862, Boyd Papers; Augustus Boyd to Fannie Boyd, January 21, 1863,
Boyd-Sitton Letters.

29. Nancy Wimpy to A. J. Reese, May 8, 1863, Reese Letters; Fannie Boyd
to Augustus Boyd, April 5, 1863, May 25 and December 25, 1862, Boyd-Sitton
Letters.

30. Fannie Boyd to Augustus Boyd, April 5, 1863, Boyd-Sitton Letters;
Fannie Boyd to Augustus Boyd, May 10, 1863, Anthony Collection; Nancy
Wimpy to A. J. Reese, July 11, 1862, Reese Letters; Fannie Boyd to Weir Boyd,
May 21, 1862, Boyd Papers.

31. Thomas Hughes to Governor Brown, January 25, 1863, EDC; A. F. Underwood to Weir Boyd, April 2, 1862, Boyd Letters; Spencer Prewitt to Governor Brown, February 26, 1863, EDC; Elijah Chastain to Confederate Secretary
of War, March 6, 1862, CSASW; Mrs. Hyatte to Governor Brown, January 22,
1862, EDC.

32. Henderson, *Roster of Confederate Soldiers,* 1:307, 400, 2:105, 5:475;
Adjutant General Henry Wayne to Colonel J. J. Findley, August 24, 1864,
James J. Findley Papers, Duke University.

33. "Slave Narratives," Mary Emily Eaton Tate, Hamilton County, Tennes-

see, in Rawick, *American Slave,* Indiana Narratives, 5:214; "Slave Narratives,"
Steve Connelly, in Rawick, *American Slave,* Indiana Narratives, vol. 16, pt. 1,
50; "Slave Narratives," John F. Van Hook, vol. 4, pt. 4, 89–90; Mohr, *Threshold
of Freedom,* 99–234; Inscoe and McKinney, *Heart of Confederate Appalachia,*
208–33; Dunaway, *Slavery in the American Mountain South,* 184.

34. Fannie Boyd to Weir Boyd, November 11, 1862, Boyd-Sitton Letters;
H. C. Hirelong to Confederate Secretary of War, November 6, 1862, CSASW;
"Slave Narratives," Tom Singleton, vol. 4, pt. 3, 272; Nancy Wimpy to A. J.
Reese, October 5, 1863, Anthony Collection; A. J. Reese to Nancy Wimpy,
February 2, 1864, Anthony Collection; U.S. Army Pension File of Isaac Rucker,
1st U.S. Colored Heavy Artillery, National Archives; J. E. Anderson, "Isaac
Rucker," 49–52.

35. *Athens Southern Confederacy,* February 4, 1863.

36. Josiah Woody to Governor Brown, September 6, 1862, EDC; W. W.
Findley to Governor Brown, July 26, 1862, EDC; Elijah Chastain to Governor,
August 5, 1863, EDC.

37. Petition from Blairsville Citizens, August 7, 1863, Governor's Petitions,
GDAH; John Bryson to Governor Brown, October 5, 1862, EDC; Josiah Woody
to Governor, September 6, 1862, EDC.

38. James J. Findley to Governor Brown, December 23, 1863, EDC; Huldah
Fain to M. C. Briant, April 14, 1863, Fain Letters.

39. Andrew Young to Governor Brown, December 5, 1861, Cuyler Collection; James Dobson to Governor, September 9, 1861, Cuyler Collection; *Athens
Southern Watchman,* May 8, 1861; William A. Campbell to Governor, February
23, 1861, EDC; Josiah Woody to Governor Brown, September 6, 1862, EDC.

40. Petitions from the Lumpkin County Committee of Public Safety to
Governor Brown, January 3 and 15, 1863, Governor's Petitions, GDAH; *Athens
Southern Watchman,* November 12, 1862; *State v. Henry Anderson,* March 10,
1862, Old Court Records, Box 38, Dahlonega; Kinsland, "Civil War Comes to
Lumpkin County," 22–23.

41. W. A. Campbell to Governor Brown, July 12, 1862, EDC; *Milledgeville
Federal Union,* December 9, 1862.

42. Case File of Lewis Fricks, Barker Papers; Case File of Lemuel Chambers,
Barker Papers; Petition of Lumpkin County Committee of Public Safety, January 3, 1863, Governor's Petitions, GDAH.

43. "A Proclamation by Governor Joseph E. Brown of Georgia," quoted in
Bragg, *Joe Brown's Army,* 20; Adjutant and Inspector General of Georgia to
Lt. J. M. Cowan, April 11, 1864. GAGIC.

44. W. M. Wills to Mrs. Louisa Jane Wills, January 22, 1863, E. Merton
Coulter Papers, Civil War Correspondence, Box 9, Folder 3, Hargrett Library;
Milledgeville Federal Union, February 10, 1863; *Atlanta Southern Confederacy,*
January 29, 1863; George W. Lee to Governor Brown, January 27 and Febru-

ary 3, 1863, EDC; G. W. Lee to Governor, February 9, 1863, Cuyler Collection; *Atlanta Southern Confederacy,* February 1, 1863.

45. J. H. Worley to Governor Brown, March 4, 1863, EDC; *Payne v. John C. Early, et al.,* January 10, 1866, Box 24, Old Court Records, Dahlonega; Court Martial Proceedings of William A. Lyle, Co. D, 1st Regiment, Georgia State Line, April 14, 1864, GAGCM; W. A. Campbell to Governor Brown, February 26, 27, and 28, 1863, EDC.

46. Kelly to Governor Brown, February 3, 1863, EDC; Petition of Lumpkin County Residents, February 4, 1863, Cuyler Collection.

47. Lumpkin County Superior Court, Grand Jury Presentments, February Term, 1863, GDAH.

48. *Athens Southern Watchman,* February 10, February 18, and March 18, 1863.

49. *The State v. James P. Payne,* January 1863, Box 38, Old Court Records, Dahlonega; Deposition of T. C. Corbin before Justice of the Peace William R. Crisson, January 5, 1863, Box 24, Old Court Records, Dahlonega; *The State vs. John Woody,* November 19, 1863, Box 38, Old Court Records, Dahlonega.

50. *The State v. John Woody,* November 19, 1863, Box 38, Old Court Records, Dahlonega.

51. *Athens Southern Watchman,* June 17, 1863; Robert Woody to Captain E. J. Starr, June 10, 1863, CSASW.

52. Elijah Chastain to Governor Brown, August 5 and 11, 1863, EDC; G. W. Lee to Governor Brown, June 12, 1863, EDC; G. W. Lee to Governor Brown, October 9, 1863, Cuyler Collection; Bryan, *Confederate Georgia,* 146.

53. E. W. Chastain, P. D. Claiborne, and James H. Morris to Colonel Chas. A. Harris, June 5, 1863, CSASW.

54. Captain E. J. Starr to Major John P. Anderson, June 13, 1863, CSASW; W. A. Campbell to Governor Brown, May 27, 1863, EDC.

55. George W. Lee to Governor Brown, October 9, 1863, Cuyler Collection; *Athens Southern Watchman,* October 21, 1863; Elijah Chastain to Governor, October 8, 1863, Cuyler Collection.

56. Pension File of John W. Woody, National Archives; U.S. Bureau of the Census, Population Schedule, 1870, Lumpkin County, Georgia. The Woody Family Genealogy contains many of these oral histories. It is available at the "Woody Gap" Web page, http://homepages.rootsweb.com/~woodygap/ (accessed August 28, 2005).

4. Hellish Deeds in a Christian Land

1. Kellogg, *Capture and Escape,* 165–68; Inscoe, "'Moving through Deserter Country'" in Noe and Wilson, *Civil War in Appalachia,* 158–86.

2. Court Martial Proceedings of Francis E. Tumlin, Company D, 1st Regiment, Georgia State Line, March 31, 1864, GAGCM; Elbert Searcy to William Beboarket, January 22, 1864, Cuyler Collection; S. C. Dobbs to General Henry Wayne, January 22, 1864, GAGIC; Darnell, "North Georgia in the Late Civil War," 44–45; E. Fain to M. C. Briant, April 26, 1864, Fain Letters; Ash, "Poor Whites in the Occupied South," 39–62; Barclay, *Ducktown Back in Raht's Time*, 1–20, 122.

3. J. E. Anderson, "Isaac Rucker," 49–52; U.S. Army Pension File of Scipio Henry, Fannin County, Georgia, National Archives; Service Records of James Cowan, Isaac Rucker, Julius Rucker, and Robert Rucker, 1st U.S. Colored Heavy Artillery, CMSRUS; *Unwritten History of Slavery*, in Rawick, *American Slave*, 18:104–9.

4. R. Davis, "White and Black in Blue," 347–74; U.S. Army Pension File of William Lillard, National Archives; U.S. Army Pension File of William A. Twiggs, National Archives; Muster Rolls of the 3rd, 4th, 5th, and 7th Tennessee Mounted Infantry Regiments, the 9th, 10th, 11th, and 12th Tennessee Cavalry Regiments, and the 1st Georgia Battalion State Troops, CMSRUS; "Slave Narratives," Mary Emily Eaton Tate, Hamilton County, Tennessee, in Rawick, *American Slave*, Indiana Narratives, 5:213; *Unwritten History of Slavery*, 18:105; Mohr, *Threshold of Freedom*, 86–96.

5. S. C. Dobbs to General Wayne, January 22, 1864, GAGIC; Thomas Hughes to Governor Brown, January 25, 1863, EDC; General William Wofford to Governor Brown, February 8, 1865, Cuyler Collection; Deposition of James Withrow, July 20, 1916, Pension File of William Collins, Barker Papers; Pension File of John Shelton, Barker Papers; Deposition of Nancy O'Kelly, March 3, 1877, Pension File of Edward O'Kelly, National Archives; SCCA, Case File of Andrew Harris, Murray County, Georgia; Ash, *When the Yankees Came*.

6. Deposition of Nathaniel Parris, April 17, 1885, Pension File of William Lillard, National Archives; Deposition of James Withrow, July 20, 1916, Pension File of William Collins, Barker Papers; Sarris, "Anatomy of an Atrocity," 693–94; Mann, "Family Group, Family Migration," 374–91; Joan E. Cashin, "Into the Trackless Wilderness," in E. Campbell, *Woman's War*, 29–53.

7. Kellogg, *Capture and Escape*, 168; Service Records of James and Alfred Parris, 5th Tennessee Mounted Infantry, CMSRUS; Deposition of S. A. Farrell, March 4, 1889, U.S. Army Pension File of Jacob White, National Archives.

8. Court Martial Proceedings of Private Edward Tumlin, Company D, 1st Regiment, Georgia State Line, GAGCM; U.S. Army Pension Files of William A. Twiggs, James Parris, Peter Parris, Robert Woody, Jacob White, and Lemuel Chambers, National Archives; SCCA Allowed Claim of George Campire, Pickens County, Georgia.

9. Deposition of Louisa Collins, June 9, 1916, U.S. Army Pension of

William W. Collins, National Archives; U.S. Army Pension File of Solomon Stansbury, National Archives; Kinsland, "Murder or Execution," 15.

10. W. A. Campbell to Henry C. Wayne, July 6, 1863, GAGIC; Pension File of William G. Long, Barker Papers.

11. Pension File of William Fox, Barker Papers; Deposition of Jacob White, March 5, 1890, U.S. Army Pension File of Jacob White, National Archives; James G. Brown to General Steedman, July 18, 1864, Brown File, USPM; Deposition of Robert P. Woody, U.S. Army Pension File of Robert Woody, National Archives.

12. Pension File of William Lillard, Barker Papers; SCCA claim of Georgia Campire, Pickens County, Georgia; James G. Brown to General George Thomas, June 15, 1864, Brown File, USPM.

13. Sarris, "Database of Union and Confederate Soldiers"; Henderson, *Roster of the Confederate Soldiers of Georgia;* Muster Rolls of the 3rd, 4th, 5th, and 7th Tennessee Mounted Infantry, the 9th, 10th, 11th, and 12th Tennessee Cavalry, and the 1st Georgia State Troops Battalion, Anthony Collection; Bates, "Southern Unionists," 226–39.

14. U.S. Bureau of the Census, Population and Slave Schedules, 1860, Fannin County, Georgia; U.S. Army Pension File of William C. Fain, National Archives; Ibid., U.S. Army Pension File of Solomon Stansbury, National Archives.

15. Sarris, "Database of Union and Confederate Soldiers."

16. James Taylor Pension File, Barker Papers; Deposition of William Sutton, November 2, 1886, U.S. Army Pension File of Isaac Montgomery, National Archives.

17. Darnell, "North Georgia in the Late Civil War"; James G. Brown to General Steedman, November 29, 1864, USPM.

18. Court Martial Proceedings of Edward Tumlin, Francis Tumlin, and William Lyle, March 1864, GAGCM.

19. SCCA, Case File of Anna Bradley, Pickens County, Georgia; Margaret Espy to Joseph Espy, November 11, 1864, Espy Papers; S. C. Dobbs to General Henry Wayne, January 22, 1864, GAGIC (emphasis added); E. Fain to M. C. Briant, April 26, 1864, Fain Letters.

20. E. Fain to M. C. Briant, April 26, 1864, Fain Letters; Martha Williams to M. C. Briant, October 2, 1864, Fain Letters; Huldah Fain to M. C. Briant, April 5, 1864, Fain Letters; Petition of Fannin County residents to Colonel B. J. Hill, April 18, 1864, Cuyler Collection.

21. Mohr, *Threshold of Freedom,* 91; "Slave Narratives," vol. 4, pt. 2, "Uncle Jake, Ex-Slave," 312–14.

22. Weir Boyd to Augustus Boyd, December 27, 1862, Anthony Collection; E. Fain to M. C. Briant, April 26, 1864, Fain Letters; N. H. Gass to Governor Brown, May 20, 1864, Cuyler Collection; Sarah Hudlow to Governor, May 22,

1864, Cuyler Collection; Alfred Harris to Governor, April 4, 1864, Cuyler Collection; Lumpkin County Inferior Court Minutes, January 9, 1864, GDAH.

23. Maxwell Chastain to Governor Brown, July 1, 1864, Cuyler Collection.

24. *Acts of the General Assembly of Georgia, March 1864,* 123; Petition of Emma Roberts, May 14, 1864, Box 29, Old Court Records, Dahlonega; Petition of Jane Duckett, February, 1865, Box 14, Old Court Records, Dahlonega; U.S. Army Pension File of Robert F. Woody, Barker Papers.

25. Deposition of Jane Duckett, February 1865, Box 14, Old Court Records, Dahlonega.

26. *Message of Joseph E. Brown to the Legislature, March 10, 1864.*

27. Andrew Young to Governor Brown, August 29, 1863, EDC.

28. M. C. Briant to Huldah Fain, April 10 and September 21, 1864, Fain Letters; A. J. Reese to Archibald Wimpy, January 9, 1863, Reese Letters; SCCA, Case File of Wiley Tipton, Fannin County, Georgia; Kenneth W. Noe, "Exterminating Savages: The Union Army and Mountain Guerillas in Southern West Virginia, 1861–1862," in Noe and Wilson, *Civil War in Appalachia,* 104–30.

29. Huldah Fain to Brother, April 20, 1864, Fain Letters; N. Briant and Jane to M. C. Briant, April 15, 1864, Fain Letters; Nancy Wimpy to A. J. Reese, August 27 and July 6, 1863, Anthony Collection. See Samuel Hargis to Margaret Espy, May 3, 1864, Espy Papers.

30. Faust, *Mothers of Invention,* 238–40, and also her important article "Altars of Sacrifice"; Huldah Fain Briant to M. C. Briant, March 1, 1865, Fain Letters.

31. *Athens Southern Watchman,* October 14, November 11, and November 25, 1863.

32. U.S. Army Pension File of William C. Fain, National Archives.

33. Huldah Fain to Brother, April 20, 1864, Fain Letters; *Rome Tri-Weekly Courier,* April 14 and 28, 1864; *Athens Southern Watchman,* March 23, 1864; S. C. Dobbs to General Henry Wayne, March 8, 1864, GAGIC; Ebenezer Fain to M. C. Briant, April 26, 1864, Fain Letters.

34. Dobbs to Wayne, March 8, 1864, AGIC, GDAH; Ebenezer Fain to M. C. Briant, April 26, 1864, Fain Letters.

35. *Athens Southern Watchman,* March 23, 1864; *Rome Tri-Weekly Courier,* April 14 and 28, 1864; Stephen Dobbs to General Wayne, March 8, 1864, GAGIC; E. Fain to M, C. Briant, April 26, 1864, Fain Letters.

36. Bragg, *Joe Brown's Army,* 115; Deposition of Margaret S. Fain, August 21, 1885, U.S. Army Pension File of William C. Fain, National Archives; Deposition of William Postell, November 24, 1885, U.S. Army Pension File of William C. Fain, National Archives; Pension File of Jehu Reed, Barker Papers; Ebenezar Fain to M. C. Briant, April 26, 1864, Fain Letters.

37. Bragg, *Joe Brown's Army,* 115–17; Captain F. M. Cowan to Colonel Gault, May 5, 1864, GACIC.

38. SCCA, Case Files of Issacc Casey (Murray County, Georgia), Joseph Pressley (Pickens County, Georgia), Hugh Rutherford (Walker County, Georgia), Gerusha Griffin, (Walker County, Georgia), Hosea Hopkins (Pickens County, Georgia), and Mason Austin (Union County, Georgia); Memoir of Horatio Hennion, December 14, 1892, transcribed and donated to the author by Keith Bohannon, Pennsylvania State University.

39. P. M. West to Colonel E. M. Gault, April 16, 1864, Cuyler Collection; SCCA, Case Files of Hugh Rutherford, Pinckney Howell, Hosea Hopkins, and Jesse Griggs.

40. SCCA, Case File of Stanley Rickels, Fannin County, Georgia; E. Fain to M. C. Briant, April 26, 1864, Fain Letters; Huldah Fain to Brother, April 20, 1864, Fain Letters; N. Briant and Jane to M. C. Briant, April 15, 1864, Fain Letters.

41. Captain F. M. Cowan to General Henry Wayne, April 24, 1864, GAGIC.

42. SCCA, Case File of Anna Bradley, Pickens County, Georgia; M. C. Briant to Huldah Fain, September 21, 1864, Fain Letters; Nancy Wimpy to A. J. Reese, March 12, 1864, Anthony Collection.

43. U.S. Army Pension File of William Lillard, National Archives; E. Fain to M. C. Briant, April 26, 1864, Fain Letters.

44. Report of Special Examiner A. B. Parkey, June 18, 1895, U.S. Army Pension File of Peter Parris, National Archives; Deposition of Nathaniel and James Parris, April 16, 1885, U.S. Army Pension File of William Lillard, National Archives.

45. U.S. Army Pension File of William A. Twiggs, National Archives.

46. U.S. Army Pension File of Iley T. Stuart, National Archives.

47. Pension Files of Solomon Stansbury, Iley Stuart, and Peter Parris, National Archives; SCCBD, Susan Davis, Lumpkin County, Georgia, National Archives; Bates, "Southern Unionists," 236.

48. Deposition of John Merrel, February 10, 1877, U.S. Army Pension File of Iley Stuart, National Archives; Deposition of Margaret Stuart, February 9, 1877, U.S. Army Pension File of Iley Stuart, National Archives; Report of Pension Bureau Agent John Wager, March 9, 1877, U.S. Army Pension File of Iley Stuart, National Archives.

49. Report of Special Agent John G. Wager, February 28, 1877, U.S. Pension File of Solomon Stansbury, National Archives; Deposition of Monroe A. Defoor, September 20, 1867, and Joseph E. Eldred, September 23, 1867, RG105 Letters, Roll 17, National Archives; Fellman, *Inside War,* 186–89.

50. John S. Fain to Governor Brown, September 26, 1864, EDC; Elijah Chastain to Governor, November 1, 1864, EDC.

51. James Findley to Governor Brown, January 18, 1864, EDC; Findley to General Henry Wayne, February 10, 1864, GAGIC; Nancy Wimpy to A. J. Reese, March 12, 1864, Reese Letters.

52. Superior Court Minutes of Lumpkin County, August and October terms, 1864, GDAH; Lumpkin Grand Jury Presentments, May 1864, GDAH; Weir Boyd to Governor Brown, December 19, 1864, Anthony Collection.

53. *Atlanta Southern Confederacy,* February 10, 1863; *Dahlonega Mountain Signal,* quoted in the *Rome Tri-Weekly Courier,* April 14, 1864; Weir Boyd to Governor Brown, December 19, 1864, EDC.

54. Deposition of Francis Marion Williams, February 28, 1877, U.S. Army Pension File of Iley Stuart, National Archives.

55. U.S. Army Pension Files of Solomon Stansbury and Iley Stuart, National Archives; Kinsland, "Civil War Comes to Lumpkin County," 22; Jones, *Facets of Fannin,* 533.

56. *Athens Southern Watchman,* November 30, 1864; R. Davis, "Forgotten Guerrillas," 33; Weld, *War Diary,* 387–88.

57. Brown, *Strain of Violence,* 91–133; Culberson, *Vigilantism;* Holmes "Moonshining and Collective Violence"; Wyatt-Brown, *Southern Honor;* Waller, *Feud.*

58. Huldah Fain to M. C. Briant, November 16, 1864, Fain Letters.

59. Paludan, *Victims,* 99–116; Williamson, *Crucible of Race,* 180–220; Brundage, *Lynching in the New South.*

60. Minutes of the Superior Court of Lumpkin County, Georgia, September term, 1867, Testimony in the Case of *The State of Georgia v. James Jackson,* GDAH; Kellogg, *Capture and Escape,* 167–73; Report of Colonel J. B. Hill, April 26, 1864, Cuyler Collection.

61. Sarris, "Anatomy of an Atrocity," 697; Barclay, *Ducktown Back in Raht's Time,* 100; Hurlburt, *History of the Rebellion,* Appendix A, 6–7; *Cincinnati Commercial,* June 30, 1873.

62. *Cincinnati Commercial,* June 30, 1873; OR, Series 1, vol. 39, pt. 1, 617; *Macon Telegraph,* November 10, 1864, and March 16, 1865; *Augusta Daily Constitutionalist,* February 11, 1865; Statement of Robert S. Gordon to the Union Provost Marshall, Chattanooga, February 15, 1865, USPM; Bierce, *Collected Works of Ambrose Bierce,* 1:310.

63. Statement of George M. Southworth, December 21, 1864, USPM; Statement of Robert S. Gordon, February 15, 1865, USPM; Statement of Jesse Tucker, October 28, 1864, Daniel Webster Whittle Papers, Library of Congress; *Cincinnati Commercial,* June 30, 1873.

64. Sarris, "Anatomy of an Atrocity," 683.

65. Ibid., 684; Deposition of Peter Parris, January 5, 1903, U.S. Army Pension File of Peter Parris, National Archives; U.S. Army Pension Files of Thomas Bell, Harvey Brewster, James T. Hughes, James B. Nelson, Elijah Robinson, Wyatt Parton, and Samuel Lovell, National Archives; OR, series 1, vol. 45, pt. 1, 1193; Hurlburt, *History of the Rebellion,* Appendix A, 8–10.

66. John S. Fain to Governor Brown, September 26, 1864, EDC; D. M. West to Colonel E. M. Gault, April 16, 1864, Cuyler Collection.

67. Weir Boyd to Governor Brown, December 19, 1864, EDC.

68. *Chattanooga Gazette,* November 18, 1864.

69. Carter, *History of the First Regiment of Tennessee,* 111; Captain J. R. Willard to James G. Brown, June 20, 1864, James G. Brown File, USPM; Horace Boughton to A. H. Ford, December 20, 1864, Barker Papers.

70. Memo from Union Scout "Letty," July 28, 1864, USPM; General H. M. Judah to J. J. Wildes, June 3, 1865, *Letters Received, District of the Etowah,* RG 393, pt. 2, series 2655; Statement of Larson Blanc, June 2, 1865, *Letters Received, District of the Etowah,* RG 393, pt. 2, series 2655; General H. M. Judah to Colonel S. B. Boyd, May 22, 1865, *Letters Received, District of the Etowah,* RG 393, pt. 2, series 2655.

71. OR, series 1, vol. 39, pt. 1, 720; OR, series 1, vol. 49, pt. 2, 606; R. Davis, "Forgotten Union Guerrilla Fighters," 33.

72. M. C. Briant to Ebenezer Fain, February 22, 1865, Fain Letters; E. W. Chastain to Governor Brown, November 1, 1864, EDC.

73. James J. Findley to Governor Brown, January 11 and 26, 1865, EDC; G. M. Martins to Col. J. J. Findley, February 7, 1865, James J. Findley Papers; W. T. Wofford to Col. J. J. Findley, March 18, 1865, James J. Findley Papers.

74. OR, series 1, vol. 49, pt. 2, 605; Sarris, "Anatomy of an Atrocity," 710.

75. Huldah Fain Briant to M. C. Briant, March 1, 1865, Fain Letters; M. C. Briant to Huldah Fain Briant, March 21 and February 21, 1865, Fain Letters.

5. The War They Knew

1. RG 105 *Complaints,* 1867; John Darragh Wilkins to "my dear wife," January 27 and February 3, 1867, Wilkins Papers; Cain, *History of Lumpkin County,* 178–79; Report of June 1867, U.S. Military Post Returns, Dahlonega, Georgia, National Archives.

2. RG Dun, vol. 19 (Lumpkin County, Georgia); McKenzie, "Civil War and Socioeconomic Change," 170–84.

3. Cimbala, *Under the Guardianship,* 90–104; G. W. Selvidge to O. O. Howard, November 13, 1866, RG105 Letters, Roll 16; D. J. Curtis to C. C. Sibley, May 18, 1867, RG105 Letters, Roll 14; C. B. Blacker to J. R. Lewis, November 16, 1867, RG105 Letters, Roll 17; Samuel Crawford to Davis Tillson, February 4, 1867, RG105 Letters, Roll 30; A. A. Buck, Statement of Provisions for the Counties of Dawson and Lumpkin, July 1867, RG105 Letters, Roll 17; F. M. Withorn, "Statement of Provisions Provided, Transferred, and Disbursed under Joint Resolution of Congress Approved March 30, 1867—'To prevent starvation,'"

July 1867, RG105 Letters, Roll 19; A. A. Buck to Eugene Pickett, May 24, 1867, RG105 Letters, Roll 14; A. A. Buck to C. C. Sibley, July 22, 1867, RG105 Letters, Roll 17; C. A. de la Mesa to C. C. Sibley, May 21, 1867, RG105 Letters, Roll 14.

4. C. A. de la Mesa to C. C. Sibley, May 2, 1867, RG105 Letters, Roll 14; A. A. Buck to E. Pickett, May 24, 1867, RG105 Letters, Roll 14; S. Crawford to General D. Tillson, February 4, 1867, RG105 Letters, Roll 30; A. A. Buck to C. C. Sibley, July 22, 1867, RG105 Letters, Roll 17; Cimbala, *Under the Guardianship,* 80 –104.

5. J. H. Caldwell to Attorney General Akerman, August 7 and 14, 1871, DOJ Letters; M. R. Archer to C. C. Sibley, April 15, 1868, RG105 Letters; A. A. Buck to C. A. de la Mesa, June 25, 1867, RG105 Field Offices; John A. Wimpy to Col. Archer, February 18, 1868, RG105 Field Offices; A. A. Buck to C. A. de la Mesa, June 25, 1867, RG105 Field Offices; RG105 Complaints, 1867–68; James G. Brown to Headquarters, Freedman's Bureau, March 10, 1866, RG105 Letters; J. W. Siler to G. H. Thomas, February 26, 1867, RG105 Letters, Roll 16; C. B. Blacker to J. B. Lewis, November 11, 1867, RG105 Letters, Roll 30.

6. Complaints of Rufus Bedford, Joseph Brown, Simon Brooks, George Davis, Paul Duncan, Isaac Franklin, Andy Irvins, "Jenny," Berry Knox, Wylie Moss, Reuben Norman, Anna Quillian, Charity Ramsey, and Thomas Riley, RG105 Complaints; C. B. Blacker to J. B. Lewis, November 16, 1867, RG105 Letters, Roll 17; C. A. de la Mesa to J. B. Lewis, October 16, 1868, RG105 Letters, Roll 23; Zipf, "Reconstructing 'Free Woman,'" 8–31.

7. C. A. de la Mesa to J. B. Lewis, October 26, 1868, RG105 Letters, Roll 23; C. A. de la Mesa to C. C. Sibley, May 2, 1867, RG105 Letters, Roll 14; C. B. Blacker to J. B. Lewis, November 16, 1867, RG105 Letters, Roll 17; District Superintendent's Monthly School Report, Dahlonega, Georgia, November 1868, RG105 Superintendent; Cain, *History of Lumpkin County,* 212 –13; Jennifer Lund Smith, "Negotiating the Terms of Freedom: The Quest for Education in an African American Community in Reconstruction North Georgia," in Inscoe, *Appalachians and Race,* 220 –34.

8. *Dahlonega Nugget,* March 21, 1890, and May 4, 1894; Georgia Executive Department, Returns of Qualified Voters under the Reconstruction Act of 1867—Lumpkin County, GDAH; James C. Cobb, "Georgia Odyssey," in Georgia Humanities Council, *New Georgia Guide,* 21–23; Conway, *Reconstruction of Georgia,* 140 –60; Roberts, *Joseph E. Brown,* 54.

9. McKinney, *Southern Mountain Republicans; Athens Southern Watchman,* October 2, 1867; *Milledgeville Federal Union,* November 24, 1867, and November 21, 1876; *Milledgeville Union and Recorder,* June 26, 1877; *Atlanta Constitution,* November 7 and 15, 1872; *Dahlonega Mountain Signal,* October 3 and 10, 1874, November 14 and 21, 1874; William Smyth to Attorney General Williams, March 4, 1875, DOJ Letters; J. J. Findley to Edwards Pierrpont, February 18,

1876, DOJ Letters; Cain, *History of Lumpkin County,* 181–83; *Milledgeville Union and Recorder,* June 26, 1877.

10. *Dahlonega Mountain Signal,* October 3 and 10, 1874, November 14 and 21, 1874, May 11, 1877, September 7, 1877; Bartley, *Creation of Modern Georgia,* 79.

11. *Athens Southern Watchman,* October 2, 1867; *Milledgeville Federal Union,* November 24, 1868, and November 21, 1876; *Milledgeville Union and Recorder,* June 26, 1877; *Atlanta Constitution,* November 7 and 15, 1872; *Journal of the House of Representatives of the State of Georgia,* 601–2; McKinney, *Southern Mountain Republicans,* 39–41.

12. Bartley, *Creation of Modern Georgia,* 45–74; McKinney, *Southern Mountain Republicans,* 211–13; Fischer, *War at Every Door,* 154–71; Hyman, *Anti-Redeemers,* 208–11; P. [S]hweatt to J. R. Lewis, March 16, 1867, RG105 Letters, Roll 16.

13. June 1867, "Purport," U.S. Military Post Returns—Dahlonega, Georgia, 1867–69, GDAH.

14. Fisher, *War at Every Door,* 154–71; Daniel Crawford to Davis Tillson, February 4, 1867, RG105 Letters, Roll 30; A. A. Buck to C. C. Sibley, July 22, 1867, RG105 Letters, Roll 17; J. W. Siler to G. H. Thomas, February 26, 1867, RG105 Letters, Roll 16; Nancy W. Bowman to Major General Pope, May 2, 1867, RG105 Letters, Roll 14.

15. Nancy Bowman to Major General Pope, May 2, 1867, RG105 Letters, Roll 14; Deposition of John T. Compton before C. A. de la Mesa, May 13, 1867, RG105 Letters, Roll 14; L. P. Gudger to C. A. de la Mesa, April 30, 1867, RG105 Letters, Roll 14.

16. Lumpkin County Superior Court, *Samuel Lovingood v. John C. Clack and Martin Burns*—Motion for New Trial, September 1, 1869, Old Court Records, Box 10, Lumpkin County Courthouse, Dahlonega; Petition of Elisha Hunt against James J. Findley and M. Whelchel (undated), Old Court Records, Box 14, Lumpkin County Courthouse, Dahlonega; Petition of James P. Payne, January 10, 1866, Old Court Records, Box 24, Lumpkin County Courthouse, Dahlonega.

17. *Samuel Lovingood vs. Clark and Burns,* September 1, 1869, Old Court Records, Box 10, Lumpkin County Courthouse, Dahlonega; *The State v. James Jackson,* Lumpkin County Superior Court Minutes, September term, 1867, GDAH; Deposition of Monroe A. DeFoor before M. R. Archer, September 26, 1867, RG105 Letters, Roll 17.

18. *Dahlonega Mountain Signal,* March 20, 1873; *State v. William Crisson, et al.,* and *State vs. Hardy Forrest,* Lumpkin County Superior Court Minutes, Grand Jury Presentments, February and August terms, 1866, GDAH.

19. Deposition of W. B. Phillips, July 10, 1892, U.S. Army Pension File of

William A. Twiggs, National Archives; R. Davis, "North Georgia Moonshine War," 41–46; John C. Inscoe, "Appalachian Otherness," in Georgia Humanities Council, *New Georgia Guide,* 180–83.

20. Miller, *Revenuers and Moonshiners,* 40–61; Darnell, "North Georgia in the Late Civil War," 42; Sion Darnell to Charles Deaver, July 29, 1880, DOJ Letters; *Atlanta Constitution,* May 13, 1880, and October 9, 1890.

21. Miller, *Revenuers and Moonshiners,* 43; Aaron Woody to U.S. Attorney General Benjamin H. Brewster, November 11, 1883, DOJ Letters.

22. *Atlanta Constitution,* May 11 and 13, 1880; *Dahlonega Mountain Signal,* March 3, 1876; *Dahlonega Nugget,* January 8, 1897; Miller, *Revenuers and Moonshiners,* 40–60.

23. *Dahlonega Mountain Signal,* February 23, 1877; *Ellijay Courier,* March 1, 1888; J. C. Norris to Attorney General George H. Williams, March 12, 1874, DOJ Letters; John A. Stuart to D. L. Boyanton, April 12, 1880; Pension File of Robert P. Woody, Barker Papers; James L. Stanton to the Attorney General of the United States, March 8, 1884, Barker Papers; John A. Stuart to B. H. Brewster, August 31, 1882, DOJ Letters.

24. Deposition of Lewis C. Allen, May 11, 1887, U.S. Army Pension File of Robert P. Woody, National Archives; R. P. Woody to "Attorney General for USA," September 28, 1883, DOJ Letters.

25. Blight, *Race and Reunion.*

26. *Annual Report of the United Daughters of the Confederacy, Gus Boyd Chapter No. 912, Dahlonega, Georgia, 1905,* included in LaCevera, *History of the Georgia Division,* 222–24; Andrew, "Martial Spirit, Christian Virtue," 486–505.

27. *Dahlonega Mountain Signal,* April 30, 1886, and May 2, 1890; Cain, *History of Lumpkin County,* 180; LaCavera, *History of the Georgia Division,* 223.

28. *Dahlonega Mountain Signal,* April 24, 1885, and July 10, 1888; *Dahlonega Nugget,* August 21, 1896.

29. Andrew, "Martial Spirit, Christian Virtue," 497; *Dahlonega Mountain Signal,* May 29, 1873, May 7, 1874, September 7, 1877, April 25, 1890, December 3, 1886, and May 2, 1890; Starnes, "Stirring Strains of Dixie," 254–55.

30. *Dahlonega Mountain Signal,* May 29, 1873, and September 7, 1877; LaCavera, *History of the Georgia Division,* 223; Starnes, "Stirring Strains of Dixie," 256.

31. *Dahlonega Mountain Signal,* July 10, 1885, and March 9, 1888.

32. *Ellijay Courier,* 1876–92.

33. Blight, *Race and Reunion,* 64–97; GAR, *Eighth Department* 15–17; GGAR, *Twelfth Encampment,* 16–19; Darnell, "North Georgia in the Late Civil War," 46.

34. GGAR, *First Encampment,* 6–16; GGAR, *Third Encampment,* 20; GGAR, *Fourth Encampment,* 36; GGAR, *First Encampment,* 6.

35. GGAR, *First Encampment,* 7; GGAR, *Tenth Encampment,* 28; GGAR,

Fifth Encampment, 20; GGAR, *Ninth Encampment,* 1; GGAR, *Fourth Encampment,* 10 and 37; GGAR, *Fourteenth Encampment,* 12.

36. CMSRUS, Muster Roll of the 5th Tennessee Mounted Infantry Regiment; Darnell, "North Georgia in the Late Civil War," 40 – 47; H. P. Farrow to U.S. Attorney, Atlanta, December 30, 1878, DOJ Letters; *Dahlonega Mountain Signal,* September 19, 1890; *Atlanta Constitution,* October 23 and November 5, 1890; GGAR, *Twelfth Encampment,* 1.

37. Darnell, "North Georgia in the Late Civil War," 40 – 41.

38. GGAR, *Eleventh Encampment,* 44; Darnell, "North Georgia in the Late Civil War," 43 – 45.

39. I owe a debt of gratitude to Dr. Victoria E. Bynum of Texas State University for sharing her findings on Unionist naming patterns in Mississippi. Analyzing children's names for evidence of a family's wartime Unionism is admittedly inexact work. It is not always evident what parents intended to signify by choosing certain names for their offspring. The names Abraham or Ulysses were not entirely uncommon in the nineteenth century, and they do not necessarily connote wartime allegiance to the Union. However, given the context of north Georgia history, it is reasonable to read a degree of significance into the names that appear on the census schedules. The specific examples listed above are among the most explicit examples of war-related naming patterns, but it is safe to assume that many other children were named for Union or heroes, even if names such as "William T. S. [Tecumseh Sherman?] Baily" or "John U. S. Olivet" could have been entirely innocuous. Pension File of John Pack, Barker Papers; U.S. Bureau of the Census, Population Schedules, 1870 and 1880, Lumpkin County and Fannin County, Georgia.

40. U.S. Army Pension File of Peter Parris, National Archives; Confederate Pension Applications of Wiley Tipton and Nathan Parris, GDAH.

41. U.S. Army Pension Files of Solomon Stansbury, Peter Parris, Robert Woody, John Woody, William Lillard, Edward P. Chastain, and William C. Fain, National Archives.

42. GGAR, *Eighth Encampment,* 11; *Dahlonega Mountain Signal,* May 8 and September 11, 1885, August 12, 1887, and May 1, 1891. For more on sectional reconciliation, see Blight, *Race and Reunion,* and Silber, *Romance of Reunion.*

43. *Dahlonega Mountain Signal,* May 15, 1885, and February 25, 1886.

44. Ibid., July 1, 1887.

45. Ibid., July 1 and 15, 1887.

46. Ibid., August 5 and 26, 1887.

47. U.S. Congress, *Congressional Record,* 49th Cong., 1st sess., 1886, vol. 17.

48. *Dahlonega Mountain Signal,* February 12, 19, and 25, 1886, March 19, 1886, and May 11, 1888.

49. Ibid., March 12, 1886, and May 11, 1888.

50. Ibid., February 12, 1886, May 11, 1888, and March 12, 1886.

51. Ibid., May 11, 1888; *Atlanta Constitution,* May 1, 1888.

52. *Atlanta Constitution,* February 12, 1886; Darnell, "North Georgia in the Late Civil War," 46.

53. *Dahlonega Mountain Signal,* April 6, 13, 27, and May 18, 1894.

Epilogue

1. Frazier, *Cold Mountain,* 345–46.

BIBLIOGRAPHY

Primary Sources

Archival and Manuscript Sources

Madeline Anthony Collection. Lumpkin County Public Library, Dahlonega, GA.

Robert B. Barker Papers. C. M. McClung Historical Collection, East Tennessee Historical Center, Knox County Public Library, Knoxville, TN. Microfilm Copy at the University of Georgia.

Boyd-Sitton Letters. Georgia Department of Archives and History, Atlanta.

Weir Boyd Papers. Rare Book, Manuscript, and Special Collections Library, Duke University.

Howell Cobb Papers. Hargrett Library, University of Georgia.

E. Merton Coulter Manuscript Collection. Hargrett Library, University of Georgia.

Telamon Cuyler Collection. Hargrett Library, University of Georgia.

Amory Dexter Diary. Georgia Department of Archives and History, Atlanta.

R. G. Dun & Company Collection. Baker Library, Harvard Business School.

Joseph Espy Papers. Southern Historical Collection, Wilson Library, University of North Carolina at Chapel Hill.

Federal Writers Project. "Slave Narratives: A Folk History of Slavery in the United States from Interviews with Former Slaves." Typewritten Records, 1941, National Archives, Washington, DC.

Abner Feimster Papers. Rare Book, Manuscript, and Special Collections Library, Duke University.

James J. Findley Papers. Rare Book, Manuscript, and Special Collections Library, Duke University.

Gathwright/Matthews Papers. Georgia Department of Archives and History, Atlanta.

Huldah Anne Fain Briant Papers. Rare Book, Manuscript, and Special Collections Library, Duke University.

Horatio Hennion, Account Taken in Parsippany, N.J., December 1892. Transcribed and donated to the author by Keith Bohannon, Pennsylvania State University.

Curtis Oliver Papers. Georgia Department of Archives and History, Atlanta.

Perkins Family Papers. Southern Historical Collection, Wilson Library, University of North Carolina at Chapel Hill.

A. J. Reese Letters. Georgia Department of Archives and History, Atlanta.

John D. Wilkins Papers. Rare Book, Manuscript, and Special Collections Library, Duke University.

Government Documents

Acts and Resolutions of the General Assembly of the State of Georgia, 1853–1854. Savannah: Samuel Chapman, State Printer, 1854.

Acts of the General Assembly of the State of Georgia, Passed in Milledgeville at the Called Session in March 1864. Milledgeville, GA: Boughton Nisbet, Barnes & Moore, State Printers, 1864.

Executive Department Incoming Correspondence—Governor Joseph E. Brown. Georgia Department of Archives and History, Atlanta.

Georgia Adjutant General Courts Martial. Record Group 22, Georgia Department of Archives and History, Atlanta.

Georgia Adjutant General's Incoming Correspondence. Record Group 22, Georgia Department of Archives and History, Atlanta.

Georgia, Office of the Governor. *Returns of Qualified Voters under the Reconstruction Act of 1867.* Georgia Department of Archives and History, Atlanta.

Georgia, State Division of Confederate Pensions and Records. *Applications and Supporting Documents, 1879–1960.* Georgia Department of Archives and History, Atlanta.

Governor's Petitions. Joseph E. Brown, 1861–1865, Georgia Department of Archives and History, Atlanta.

Journal of the House of Representatives of the State of Georgia. 1861–70. Hargrett Library, University of Georgia.

Journal of the Public and Secret Proceedings of the Convention of the People of Georgia Held in Milledgeville and Savannah in 1861. Milledgeville, GA: Boughton, Nisbet, and Barnes, 1861.

Journal of the Senate of the State of Georgia, 1861–1870. Hargrett Library, University of Georgia.

Letters Received by the Confederate Secretary of War. Record Group 109, M437, National Archives, Washington, DC.

Letters Received by the Department of Justice from the State of Georgia. Microfilm Publication M996, Record Group 60, National Archives, Washington, DC.

Letters Sent and Received, Federal District of the Etowah. Record Group 393, part 2, series 2655, National Archives, Washington, DC.

Message of His Excellency Joseph E. Brown to the Extra Session of the Legislature, Convened March 10, 1864. Milledgeville, Georgia: Boughton, Nisbet, and Barnes and Moore, State Printer, 1864.

Old Court Records. Boxes 14-38, Lumpkin County Courthouse, Dahlonega, GA.

Records of the Assistant Commissioner for the State of Georgia, Bureau of Refugees, Freedmen, and Abandoned Lands, Letters Received. Record Group 105. National Archives, Washington, DC.

Records of the Field Offices of the Bureau of Refugees, Freedmen, and Abandoned Lands, Register of Complaints, Dahlonega Field Office. Record Group 105, National Archives, Washington, DC.

Records of the Subordinate Field Offices for the State of Georgia, Bureau of Refugees, Freedmen, and Abandoned Lands, Dahlonega Field Office. Record Group 105, National Archives, Washington, DC.

Records of the United States Bureau of Refugees, Freedmen, and Abandoned Lands, Records of the Superintendent of Education for the State of Georgia, 1865–1870. Record Group 105, National Archives, Washington, DC.

Records of the U.S. Provost Marshal, Spies, Scouts, Guides and Detectives. Record Group 110, National Archives, Washington, DC.

Records of the United States Department of War, Bureau of Pensions. National Archives, Washington, DC.

Superior and Inferior Court Minutes, Lumpkin County and Fannin County. Georgia Department of Archives and History, Atlanta.

Records of Volunteer Union Soldiers Who Served during the Civil War—Compiled Service Records of Union Soldiers Who Served in Organizations from the State of Georgia. National Archives Microfilm M403, Washington, DC.

Records of Volunteer Union Soldiers Who Served during the Civil War—Compiled Service Records of Union Soldiers Who Served in Organizations from the State of Tennessee. National Archives Microfilm M395, Washington, DC.

Records of Volunteer Union Soldiers Who Served during the Civil War—Compiled Service Records of Union Soldiers Who Served with the United States Colored Troops. National Archives Microfilm, Washington, DC.

Returns from United States Military Posts, 1800–1916. National Archives, Micofilm M617, Washington, DC.

U.S. Bureau of the Census. Agricultural Schedules. Georgia. 1850, 1860, 1870, 1880. National Archives Microfilm, Washington, DC.

U.S. Bureau of the Census. Manufactures of the United States in 1860, Eighth Census. National Archives Microfilm, Washington, DC.

U.S. Bureau of the Census. Population Schedules. Georgia. 1850, 1860, 1870, 1880. National Archives Microfilm, Washington, DC.

U.S. Bureau of the Census. Slave Schedules. Georgia. 1850, 1860. Georgia Department of Archives and History, Atlanta.

U.S. Bureau of the Census. *Statistics of the United States (including mortality, property, &c.) in 1860: Compiled from the Original Returns and Being the Final Exhibit of the Eighth Census, Under the Direction of the Secretary of the Interior.* Washington, DC: Government Printing Office, 1866.

U.S. Commissioner of Claims. *Southern Claims Commission Allowed Claims: 1871–1880, Georgia.* National Archives Microfilm, 1990.

U.S. Commissioner of Claims. *Southern Claims Commission Barred and Disallowed Claims.* National Archives, Washington, DC.

U.S. Congress. *Congressional Globe.* 32nd Cong., 2nd sess., 1853, and 33rd Cong., 1st sess., 1854.

U.S. Congress. *Congressional Record.* 49th Cong., 1st sess. and special sess. of Senate, vol. 17 Washington: Government Printing Office, 1886.

U.S. Department of War. *The War of the Rebellion: A Compilation of the Official Records of the Union and Confederate Armies.* Washington, DC: Government Printing Office, 1880–1901.

Newspapers

Albany (GA) Patriot
Athens (GA) Southern Banner
Athens (GA) Southern Watchman
Atlanta Christian Index
Atlanta Constitution
Atlanta Southern Confederacy
Augusta (GA) Daily Constitutionalist
Auraria (GA) Western Herald
Chattanooga Gazette
Cherokee Phoenix
Cincinnati Commercial
Dahlonega (GA) Mountain Signal, Dahlonega Signal
Dahlonega (GA) Nugget
Ellijay (GA) Courier
Macon (GA) Telegraph
Milledgeville (GA) Confederate Union, Milledgeville Federal Union
Milledgeville (GA) Southern Recorder
Rome (GA) Tri-Weekly Courier, Rome Weekly Courier

Books and Bound Volumes

Andrews, Garrett. *Reminiscences of an Old Georgia Lawyer.* Atlanta: Franklin Steam, Print House, 1870.

Bergeron, Paul H., ed. *The Papers of Andrew Johnson.* Vols. 8–15. Knoxville: University of Tennessee Press, 1989–1998.

Bierce, Ambrose. *The Collected Works of Ambrose Bierce.* Vol. 1. New York: Neale, 1909.

Browne, Junius Henri. *Four Years in Secessia: Adventures within and beyond the Union Lines: Embracing a Great Variety of Facts, Incidents, and Romance of the War.* Hartford, CT: O. D. Case, 1865.

Brownlow, William Gannaway. *Sketches of the Rise, Progress, and Decline of Secession: With a Narrative of Personal Adventures among the Rebels.* Philadelphia: George W. Childs, 1862.

Burke, Emily. *Pleasure and Pain: Reminiscences of Georgia in the 1840s.* Savannah: Beehive Press, 1978.

Crisson, W. R. *Report of W. R. Crisson on the Mineral Resources around Dahlonega.* Dahlonega, GA: Mountain Signal Print, 1875.

Ellis, Daniel. *The Thrilling Adventures of Daniel Ellis, the Great Union Guide of East Tennessee for a Period of Nearly Four Years during the Great Southern Rebellion.* New York: Harper and Brothers, 1867.

Henderson, Lillian. *Roster of the Confederate Soldiers of Georgia, 1861–1865.* 6 vols. Hopeville, GA: Logino and Porter, 1959–1964.

Hume, Thomas. *The Loyal Mountaineers of Tennessee.* Knoxville: Ogden Brothers, 1888.

Hurlburt, John S. *History of the Rebellion in Bradley County, East Tennessee.* Indianapolis, 1866.

Journal of the Eighth Annual Session of the Department Encampment of Georgia and South Carolina, Grand Army of the Republic, Held at Atlanta, Ga., March 28th, 1896. Atlanta: C. P. Byrd, 1896.

Journal of the Fifth Annual Session of the Department of Georgia, Grand Army of the Republic, Held at Savannah, Georgia, February 27, 1893. Savannah, GA: Braid & Hutton, 1893.

Journal of the First Encampment of the Provisional Department of Georgia for the Organization of the Permanent Department of Georgia, Grand Army of the Republic, Held at Atlanta, Georgia, January 25, 1889. Atlanta: Atlanta Constitution, 1889.

Journal of the Fourth Annual Session of the Department Encampment of Georgia, Grand Army of the Republic, Held at Augusta, Georgia, January 27, 1892. Savannah, GA: Braid & Hutton, 1892.

Journal of the Ninth Annual Encampment of the Department of Georgia (States of Georgia and South Carolina), Grand Army of the Republic, at Fitzgerald, Ga., March 13, 1897. Atlanta: C. P. Byrd, 1897.

Journal of the Proceedings of the Eleventh Annual Encampment of the Department of Georgia (States of Georgia and South Carolina), Grand Army of the Republic, at Atlanta, Georgia, April 28, 1899. Atlanta: C. P. Byrd, 1899.

Journal of the Proceedings of the Twelfth Annual Encampment of the Department of Georgia, Grand Army of the Republic, at Atlanta, Georgia, March 8, 1900. Atlanta, 1900.

Journal of the Proceedings of the Thirteenth Annual Encampment of the Department of Georgia (States of Georgia and South Carolina), Grand Army of the Potomac at Fitzgerald, Georgia, April 20, 1901.

Journal of the Proceedings of the Fourteenth Annual Encampment of the Department of Georgia (States of Georgia and South Carolina) Grand Army of the Republic, at Atlanta, Georgia April 15, 1902. Atlanta, 1902.

Journal of the Public and Secret Meetings of the Convention of the People of Georgia Held in Savannah in 1861. Milledgeville, GA: Boughton, Nisbet, and Barnes, 1861.

Journal of the Tenth Annual Encampment of the Department of Georgia (States of Georgia and South Carolina), Grand Army of the Republic, at Atlanta, Ga., March 2d, 1898. Atlanta: Atlanta Constitution, 1898.

Journal of the Third Annual Session of the Department Encampment of Georgia, Grand Army of the Republic, Held at Savannah, Georgia, January 22, 1890. Savannah, GA: Times, 1891.

Kellogg, John Azor. *Capture and Escape: A Narrative of Army and Prison Life.* Madison: Wisconsin History Commission, 1908.

LaCevera, Tommie Phillips. *The History of the Georgia Division of the United Daughters of the Confederacy, 1895–1995,* Vol. 1. Atlanta: Georgia Division, 1995.

Lanman, Charles. *Letters from the Alleghany Mountains.* New York: George Putnam, 1849.

Olmstead, Frederick Law. *A Journey in the Back Country in the Winter of 1853–4.* New York: G. P. Putnam's Sons, 1860.

Paschal, George. *Ninety-Four Years: Agnes Paschal.* Washington, DC: M'Gill & Withrow, 1871.

Sarris, Jonathan D. "Database of Union and Confederate Soldiers from Fannin and Lumpkin Counties in Georgia—Compiled from Statistics Available in the 1860 U.S. Census, Population and Slave Schedules; The Roster of Confederate Soldiers from Georgia; Muster Rolls of the U.S. Third, Fourth, Fifth, and Seventh Tennessee Mounted Infantry; Muster Rolls of the U.S. Ninth, Tenth, Eleventh, and Twelfth Tennessee Cavalry; Muster Roll of the U.S. First Georgia State Troops; Madeline Anthony Collection."

Temple, Oliver P. *East Tennessee and the Civil War.* Freeport, NY: Books for Libraries Press, 1971. (Originally published 1899)

Thompson, K., ed. *Touching Home: A Collection of History and Folklore from the Copper Basin, Fannin County Area.* Blue Ridge, GA: Thompson, 1976.

Weld, Stephen Minot. *War Diary and Letters of Stephen Minot Weld, 1861–1865.* Boston: Massachusetts Historical Society, 1979.

White, George. *Historical Collections of Georgia: Containing the Most Interesting Facts, Traditions, Biographical Sketches, Anecdotes, etc., Relating to Its History and Antiquities, From Its First Settlement to the Present Time.* New York: Pudney and Russell, 1855.

Secondary Sources

Books

Anderson, William L., ed., *Cherokee Removal: Before and After.* Athens: University of Georgia Press, 1991.

Barclay, Robert. *Ducktown Back in Raht's Time.* Chapel Hill: University of North Carolina Press, 1946.

Barney, William L. *The Secessionist Impulse: Alabama and Mississippi in 1860.* Princeton, N.J.: Princeton University Press, 1974.

Bartley, Numan. *The Creation of Modern Georgia.* Athens: University of Georgia Press, 1983.

Batteau, Allen. *The Invention of Appalachia.* Tucson: University of Arizona Press, 1990.

Beringer, Richard E., Herman Hattaway, Archer Jones, and William N. Still Jr. *Why the South Lost the Civil War.* Athens: University of Georgia Press, 1986.

Blee, Kathleen B., and Dwight B. Billings. *The Road to Poverty: The Making of Wealth and Hardship in Appalachia.* New York: Cambridge University Press, 2000.

Blight, David W. *Race and Reunion: The Civil War in American Memory.* Cambridge, MA: Harvard University Press, 2001.

Bode, Frederick, and Donald Ginter. *Farm Tenancy and the Census in Antebellum Georgia.* Athens: University of Georgia Press, 1986.

Bolton, Charles E., and Scott P. Culclasure. *The Confessions of Edward Isham: A Poor White Life of the Old South.* Athens: University of Georgia Press, 1998.

Bragg, William Harris. *Joe Brown's Army: The Georgia State Line, 1862–1865.* Macon, GA: Mercer University Press, 1987.

Brown, Richard Maxwell. *Strain of Violence: Historical Studies of American Violence and Vigilantism.* New York: Oxford University Press, 1975.

Brundage, Fitzhugh. *Lynching in the New South: Georgia and Virginia, 1880–1930.* Urbana: University of Illinois Press, 1993.

Bryan, T. Conn. *Confederate Georgia*. Athens: University of Georgia Press, 1953.

Buck, Paul H. *The Road to Reunion, 1865–1900*. New York: Alfred A. Knopf, 1937.

Bynum, Victoria. *The Free State of Jones: Mississippi's Longest Civil War*. Chapel Hill: University of North Carolina Press, 2001.

———. *Unruly Women: The Politics of Social and Sexual Control in the Old South*. Chapel Hill: University of North Carolina Press, 1992

Cain, Andrew. *The History of Lumpkin County for the First Hundred Years, 1832–1932*. Atlanta: Stearn, 1932.

Campbell, Edward D. C., Jr. *A Woman's War: Southern Women, Civil War, and the Confederate Legacy*. Charlottesville: University Press of Virginia, 1996.

Campbell, John C. *The Southern Highlander and His Homeland*. New York: Russell Sage Foundation, 1921.

Carey, Anthony. *Parties, Slavery, and the Union in Antebellum Georgia*. Athens: University of Georgia Press, 1997.

Carter, William R. *History of the First Regiment of Tennessee Volunteer Cavalry in the Great War of the Rebellion*. Johnson City, TN: Overmountain Press, 1992.

Cimbala, Paul A. *Under the Guardianship of the Nation: The Freedman's Bureau and the Reconstruction of Georgia, 1865–1870*. Athens: University of Georgia Press, 1997.

Civil War Centennial Commission. *Tennesseans in the Civil War*. Nashville, TN: Civil War Centennial Commission Press, 1964.

Clinton, Catherine, and Nina Silber, eds. *Divided Houses: Gender and the Civil War*. New York: Oxford University Press, 1992.

Connelly, Thomas L., and Barbara L. Bellows. *God and General Longstreet: The Lost Cause and the Southern Mind*. Baton Rouge: Louisiana State University Press, 1982.

Conway, Alan. *The Reconstruction of Georgia*. Minneapolis: University of Minnesota Press, 1966.

Coulter, E. Merton, *Auraria: The Story of a Georgia Gold Mining Town*. Athens: University of Georgia Press, 1956.

Crawford, Martin. *Ashe County's Civil War: Community and Society in the Appalachian South*. Charlottesville: University Press of Virginia, 2001.

Crofts, Daniel. *Reluctant Confederates: Upper South Unionists in the Secession Crisis*. Chapel Hill: University of North Carolina Press, 1989.

Culberson, William C. *Vigilantism: Political History of Private Power in America*. New York: Greenwood Press, 1990.

Current, Richard N. *Lincoln's Loyalists: Union Soldiers from the Confederacy*. Boston: Northeastern University Press, 1992.

Davis, Donald Edward, *Where There Are Mountains: An Environmental History of the Southern Appalachians*. Athens: University of Georgia Press, 2000.

Degler, Carl. *The Other South: Southern Dissenters in the Nineteenth Century.* New York: Harper and Row, 1974.

Dew, Charles B. *Bond of Iron: Master and Slave at Buffalo Forge.* New York: W. W. Norton, 1994.

Dunaway, Wilma. *The First American Frontier: The Transition to Capitalism in Southern Appalachia, 1700–1860.* Chapel Hill: University of North Carolina Press, 1996.

———. *Slavery in the American Mountain South.* New York: Cambridge University Press, 2003.

Duncan, Russell, *Entrepreneur for Equality: Governor Rufus Bullock, Commerce, and Race in Post-Civil War Georgia.* Athens: University of Georgia Press, 1994.

Dunn, Durwood. *Cades Cove: The Life and Death of a Southern Appalachian Community, 1818–1937.* Knoxville: University of Tennessee Press, 1988.

Durrill, Wayne. *War of Another Kind: A Southern Community in the Great Rebellion.* New York: Oxford University Press, 1990.

Dyer, Thomas, *Secret Yankees: The Union Circle in Confederate Atlanta.* Baltimore: Johns Hopkins University Press, 1999.

Edwards, Laura F. *Scarlett Doesn't Live Here Anymore: Southern Women in the Civil War Era.* Urbana: University of Illinois Press, 2000.

Escott, Paul. *After Secession: Jefferson Davis and the Failure of Confederate Nationalism.* Baton Rouge: Louisiana State University Press, 1975.

———. *Many Excellent People: Power and Privilege in North Carolina, 1850–1900.* Chapel Hill: University of North Carolina Press, 1985.

Faust, Drew Gilpin. *The Creation of Confederate Nationalism: Ideology and Identity in the Civil War South.* Baton Rouge: Louisiana State University Press, 1988.

———. *Mothers of Invention: Women of the Slaveholding South in the American Civil War.* Chapel Hill: University of North Carolina Press, 1996.

Fellman, Michael. *Inside War: The Guerrilla Conflict in Missouri during the American Civil War.* New York: Oxford University Press, 1989.

Finger, John R., *The Eastern Band of Cherokees, 1819–1900.* Knoxville: University of Tennessee Press, 1984.

Fischer, Noel C., *War at Every Door: Guerrilla Violence in East Tennessee, 1860–1869.* Chapel Hill: University of North Carolina Press, 1997.

Foner, Eric. *Reconstruction: America's Unfinished Revolution.* New York: Harper and Row, 1988.

Ford, Lacy K. *The Origins of Southern Radicalism: The South Carolina Upcountry, 1800–1860.* New York: Oxford University Press, 1988.

Foster, Gaines M. *Ghosts of the Confederacy: Defeat, the Lost Cause, and the Emergence of the New South, 1865–1913.* New York: Oxford University Press, 1987.

Franklin, John Hope. *The Militant South, 1800–1861.* Cambridge, MA: Harvard University Press, 1956.

Frazier, Charles. *Cold Mountain.* New York: Atlantic Monthly Press, 1997.

Freehling, William W. *The South vs. The South: How Anti-Confederate Southerners Shaped the Course of the Civil War.* Oxford: Oxford University Press, 2001.

Gallagher, Gary W. *The Confederate War.* Cambridge, MA: Harvard University Press, 1997.

Gallagher, Gary W., and Alan T. Nolan, eds. *The Myth of the Lost Cause and Civil War History.* Bloomington: Indiana University Press, 2000.

Georgia Humanities Council. *The New Georgia Guide.* Athens: University of Georgia Press, 1996.

Gilmer, George R. *Georgians: Sketches of Some of the First Settlers of Upper Georgia, of the Cherokees, and the Author.* Danielsville, GA: Heritage Papers, 1989.

Green, Fletcher M. *Georgia's Forgotten Industry: Gold Mining.* Savannah: Georgia Historical Society, 1935.

Groce, W. Todd. *Mountain Rebels: East Tennessee Confederates and the Civil War.* Knoxville: University of Tennessee Press, 1999.

Hahn, Steven. *The Roots of Southern Populism: Yeoman Farmers and the Transformation of the Georgia Upcountry.* New York: Oxford University Press, 1983.

Hale, William T. *The History of Dekalb County, Tennessee.* McMinnville, TN: Ben Lamond Press, 1915.

Hill, Louise B. *Joseph E. Brown and the Confederacy.* Chapel Hill: University of North Carolina Press, 1939.

Hsiung, David. *Two Worlds in the Tennessee Mountains: Exploring the Origins of Appalachian Stereotypes.* Lexington: University of Kentucky Press, 1997.

Hyman, Michael R. *The Anti-Redeemers: Hill Country Political Dissenters in the Lower South from Redemption to Populism.* Baton Rouge: Louisiana State University Press, 1990.

Inscoe, John C., ed. *Appalachians and Race: The Mountain South from Slavery to Segregation.* Lexington: University of Kentucky Press, 2001.

———. *Mountain Masters: Slavery and the Secession Crisis in Western North Carolina.* Knoxville: University of Tennessee Press, 1989.

Inscoe, John C., and Robert C. Kenzer, eds. *Enemies of the Country: New Perspectives on Unionists in the Civil War South.* Athens: University of Georgia Press, 2001.

Inscoe, John C. and Gordon B. McKinney. *The Heart of Confederate Appalachia: Western North Carolina in the Civil War.* Chapel Hill: University of North Carolina Press, 2000.

Johnson, Michael P. *Toward a Patriarchal Republic: The Secession of Georgia.* Baton Rouge: Louisiana State University Press, 1977.

Jones, Ethelene Dyer. *Facets of Fannin: A History of Fannin County, Georgia.* Dallas: Curtis Media, 1989.

Kenzer, Robert. *Kinship and Neighborhood in a Southern Community: Orange County, North Carolina, 1849–1881.* Knoxville: University of Tennessee Press, 1987.

Kephart, Horace. *Our Southern Highlanders: A Narrative of Adventures in the Southern Appalachians and a Study of Life among the Mountaineers.* New York: Macmillan, 1936.

Kruman, Marc W. *Parties and Politics in North Carolina, 1836–1865.* Baton Rouge: Louisiana State University Press, 1983.

Lane, Mills, ed. *Times That Prove People's Principles: The Civil War in Georgia; A Documentary History.* Savannah, GA: Beehive Press, 1993.

Lillard, Roy G. *Bradley County, Tennessee.* Memphis, TN: Memphis State University Press, 1980.

Linderman, Gerald. *Embattled Courage: The Experience of Combat in the American Civil War.* New York: Oxford University Press, 1987.

Lonn, Ella. *Desertion during the Civil War.* Gloucester, MA: Peter Smith, 1966.

McCaslin, Richard. *Tainted Breeze: The Great Hanging at Gainesville, Texas, 1862.* Baton Rouge: Louisiana State University Press, 1994.

McCurry, Stephanie. *Masters of Small Worlds: Yeoman Households, Gender Relations, and the Political Culture of the Antebellum South Carolina Low Country.* New York: Oxford University Press, 1995.

McKenzie, Robert Tracy. *One South or Many? Plantation Belt and Upcountry in Civil War Era Tennessee.* New York: Cambridge University Press, 1994.

McKinney, Gordon. *Southern Mountain Republicans, 1865–1900: Politics and the Appalachian Community.* Chapel Hill: University of North Carolina Press, 1978.

McLoughlin, William G., *Cherokees and Missionaries, 1789–1839.* Norman: University of Oklahoma Press, 1995.

McPherson, James B. *For Cause and Comrades: Why Men Fought in the Civil War.* New York: Oxford University Press, 1997.

————. *What They Fought For.* Baton Rouge: Louisiana State University Press, 1994.

McWhiney, Grady, and Perry Jamison. *Attack and Die: Civil War Military Tactics and the Southern Heritage.* Birmingham: University of Alabama Press, 1982.

Meredith, Grace E., ed. *Girl Captives of the Cheyennes: A True Story of the Capture and Rescue of Four Pioneer Girls, 1874.* Los Angeles: Gem, 1927.

Miller, Wilbur R. *Revenuers and Moonshiners: Enforcing the Federal Liquor Law in the Mountain South, 1865–1900.* Chapel Hill: University of North Carolina Press, 1991.

Mitchell, Robert D., ed., *Appalachian Frontiers: Settlement, Society and Development in the Preindustrial Era.* Lexington: University of Kentucky Press, 1990.

Mohr, Clarence L. *On the Threshold of Freedom: Masters and Slaves in Civil War Georgia.* Athens: University of Georgia Press, 1986.

Montell, William Lynwood. *Killings: Folk Justice in the Upper South.* Lexington: University of Kentucky Press, 1986.

Nagel, Paul C. *One Nation Indivisible: The Union in American Thought.* New York: Oxford University Press, 1964.

Noe, Kenneth. *Southwest Virginia's Railroad: Modernization and the Sectional Crisis.* Urbana: University of Illinois Press, 1994.

Noe, Kenneth, and Shannon Wilson, eds. *The Civil War in Appalachia: Collected Essays.* Knoxville: University of Tennessee Press, 1997.

O'Brien, Sean Michael. *Mountain Partisans: Guerrilla Warfare in the Southern Appalachians, 1861–1865.* Westport, CT: Praeger, 1999.

Otto, James Solomon, *The Southern Frontiers, 1607–1860.* Westport, CT: Greenwood Press, 1982.

Paludan, Phillip. *Victims: A True Story of the Civil War.* Knoxville: University of Tennessee Press, 1981.

Perdue, Theda. *Slavery and the Evolution of Cherokee Society, 1540–1866.* Knoxville: University of Tennessee Press, 1979.

Pudup, Mary Beth, Dwight Billings, and Altina Waller, eds. *Appalachia in the Making: The Mountain South in the Nineteenth Century.* Chapel Hill: University of North Carolina Press, 1995.

Rable, George, *Civil Wars: Women and the Crisis of Southern Nationalism.* Urbana: University of Illinois Press, 1988.

Rawick, George P., ed. *The American Slave: A Composite Autobiography.* Supplement, Series 1. Vol. 4, pt. 2, and vol. 5. Westport, CT: Greenwood Press, 1977.

Reston, James. *Sherman's March and Vietnam.* New York: Macmillan, 1984.

Roberts, Derrell C. *Joseph E. Brown and the Politics of Reconstruction.* University: University of Alabama Press, 1973.

Royster, Charles. *The Destructive War: William Tecumseh Sherman, Stonewall Jackson, and the Americans.* New York: Alfred A. Knopf, 1991.

Sartain, James A. *A History of Walker County, Georgia.* Dalton, GA: Showalter, 1932.

Sensing, Thurman. *Champ Ferguson: Confederate Guerrilla.* Nashville, TN: Vanderbilt University Press, 1942.

Shadgett, Olive Hall. *The Republican Party in Georgia: From Reconstruction through 1900.* Athens: University of Georgia Press, 1964.

Shapiro, Henry D. *Appalachia on Our Mind: The Southern Mountains and Mountaineers in American Consciousness, 1870–1920.* Chapel Hill: University of North Carolina Press, 1978.

Shryock, Richard H. *Georgia and the Union in 1850*. Reprint, New York: AMS Press, 1968.

Silber, Nina. *The Romance of Reunion: Northerners and the South, 1865–1900*. Chapel Hill: University of North Carolina Press, 1993.

Smith, James F. *The Cherokee Land Lottery: Containing a Numerical List of the Names of the Fortunate Drawers in Said Lottery, with an Engraved Map of Each District*. New York: Harper and Brothers, 1838.

Stealy, John E., III. *The Antebellum Kanawha Salt Business and Western Markets*. Lexington: University of Kentucky Press, 1993.

Sutherland, Daniel E. *Seasons of War: The Ordeal of a Southern Community, 1861–1865*. New York: Free Press, 1995.

Tate, Luke E. *History of Pickens County, Georgia*. Atlanta: Walter Brown, 1978.

Tatum, Georgia. *Disloyalty in the Confederacy*. Chapel Hill: University of North Carolina Press, 1934.

Thomas, Emory M. *The Confederacy as a Revolutionary Experience*. Columbia: University of South Carolina Press, 1991.

———. *The Confederate Nation, 1861–1865*. New York: Harper and Row, 1979.

Thornton, J. Mills. *Politics and Power in a Slave Society: Alabama, 1800–1860*. Baton Rouge: Louisiana State University Press, 1978.

Vinovskis, Maris. *Toward a Social History of the Civil War: Exploratory Essays*. New York: Cambridge University Press, 1990.

Wallenstein, Peter. *From Slave South to New South: Public Policy in Nineteenth-Century Georgia*. Chapel Hill: University of North Carolina Press, 1987.

Waller, Altina. *Feud: Hatfields, McCoys, and Social Change in Appalachia, 1860–1900*. Chapel Hill: University of North Carolina Press, 1988.

Ward, George G. *The Annals of Upper Georgia, Centered in Gilmer County*. Carrollton, GA: Thomasson, 1965.

Whites, LeeAnn. *The Civil War as a Crisis in Gender: Augusta, Georgia, 1860–1890*. Athens: University of Georgia Press, 1995.

Williams, David. *The Georgia Gold Rush: Twenty-Niners, Cherokees, and Gold Fever*. Columbia: University of South Carolina Press, 1993.

———. *Rich Man's War: Class, Caste, and Confederate Defeat in the Lower Chattahoochee Valley*. Athens: University of Georgia Press, 1998.

Williams, David, Teresa Crisp Williams, and David Carlson. *Plain Folk in a Rich Man's War: Class and Dissent in Confederate Georgia*. Gainesville: University Press of Florida, 2002.

Williams, John Alexander. *Appalachia: A History*. Chapel Hill: University of North Carolina Press, 2002.

Williamson, Joel. *The Crucible of Race: Black-White Relations in the South Since Reconstruction*. New York: Oxford University Press, 1984.

Wilson, Charles Reagan. *Baptized in Blood: The Religion of the Lost Cause, 1865–1920*. Athens: University of Georgia Press, 1980.

Wyatt-Brown, Bertram. *Southern Honor: Ethics and Behavior in the Old South.* New York: Oxford University Press, 1982.

Articles

Anderson, Jimmy E. "General Harrison W. Riley—His Rough Life," *North Georgia Journal* 2, no. 1 (Spring 1985): 32–41.

———. "Isaac Rucker: Slave, Soldier, Citizen." *North Georgia Journal,* Winter 1989–90, 49–52.

Andrew, Rod. "Martial Spirit, Christian Virtue, and the Lost Cause: Military Education at North Georgia College, 1871–1915." *Georgia Historical Quarterly* 80 (Fall 1996): 486–505.

———. "Soldiers, Christians, and Patriots: The 'Lost Cause' and Southern Military Schools, 1865–1915." *Journal of Southern History* 64 (November 1998): 677–710.

Ash, Stephen V. "Poor Whites in the Occupied South, 1861–1865." *Journal of Southern History* 58 (February 1991): 39–62.

Barney, William L. "Resisting the Republicans: Georgia's Secession Debate." *Georgia Historical Quarterly* 77 (Spring 1993): 70–85.

Bates, Walter Lynn. "Southern Unionists: A Socio-Economic Examination of the Third East Tennessee Volunteers Infantry Regiment, U.S.A." *Tennessee Historical Quarterly* 50 (Winter 1991): 226–39.

Bearman, Peter. "Desertion as Localism: Army Unit Solidarity and Group Norms in the U.S. Civil War." *Social Forces* 70 (December 1991): 321–42.

Billings, Dwight, Kathleen Blee, and Louis Swanson. "Culture, Family, and Community in Preindustrial Appalachia." *Appalachian Journal* 13 (Winter 1986): 154–70.

Brashear, C. Craig. "The Market Revolution and Party Preference in East Tennessee: Spatial Patterns of Partisanship in the 1840 Presidential Election." *Appalachian Journal* 25, no. 1 (Fall 1997): 8–29.

Carey, Anthony Gene. "'E Pluribus Unum': Georgia Politics and the Dynamics of the Jacksonian Party System, 1840–1844." *Georgia Historical Quarterly* 79 (Winter 1995): 810–41.

———. "Too Southern to Be Americans: Proslavery Politics and the Failure of the Know-Nothing Party in Georgia, 1854–1856." *Civil War History* 41 (March 1995): 22–40.

Carlson, David. "'The Distemper of the Time': Conscription, the Courts, and Planter Privilege in Civil War South Georgia." *Journal of Southwest Georgia History* 45 (May 1998): 1–24.

Coffman, Richard M. "A Vital Unit: Being a Brief and True History of 10,000 Volunteers, Phillips' Legion." *Civil War Times Illustrated* 20 (January 1982): 40–45.

Collins, Bruce W. "Governor Joseph E. Brown, Economic Issues, and Georgia's Road to Secession, 1857–1859." *Georgia Historical Quarterly* 71 (Summer 1987): 189–225.

Crawford, Martin. "Confederate Volunteering and Enlistment in Ashe County, North Carolina, 1861–1862." *Civil War History* 38 (March 1991): 29–50.

———. "Mountain Farmers and the Market Economy: Ashe County during the 1850s." *North Carolina Historical Review* 71 (October 1994): 430–50.

———. "Political Society in a Southern Mountain Community: Ashe County, North Carolina, 1850–1861." *Journal of Southern History* 55 (August 1989): 373–90.

Davis, Robert S. "Forgotten Union Guerrillas from the North Georgia Mountains." *North Georgia Journal,* Summer 1988, 30–49.

———. "Memoirs of a Partisan War: Sion Darnell Remembers North Georgia, 1861–1865." *Georgia Historical Quarterly* 80 (Spring 1996): 93–116.

———. "The North Georgia Moonshine War of 1876–77." *North Georgia Journal,* Autumn 1989, 41–46.

———. "White and Black in Blue: The Recruitment of Federal Units in Civil War North Georgia." *Georgia Historical Quarterly* 85 (Fall 2001): 347–74.

Doyon, Roy R. R., and Thomas W. Hodler. "Secessionist Sentiment and Slavery: A Geographic Analysis," *Georgia Historical Quarterly* 72 (Summer 1989): 323–47.

Dunaway, Wilma. "Diaspora, Death, and Sexual Exploitation: Slave Families at Risk in the Mountain South." *Appalachian Journal* 26 (Winter 1999): 128–49.

Escott, Paul D. "The Context of Freedom: Georgia's Slaves during the Civil War." *Georgia Historical Quarterly* 58 (Spring 1974): 79–104.

———. "Joseph E. Brown, Jefferson Davis, and the Problem of Poverty in the Confederacy." *Georgia Historical Quarterly* 61 (Spring 1977): 59–71.

Faust, Drew Gilpin. "Altars of Sacrifice: Confederate Women and the Narratives of War." In *Divided Houses: Gender and the American Civil War,* ed. Catherine Clinton and Nina Silber. New York: Oxford University Press, 1992.

Frost, William Goodell. "Our Contemporary Ancestors in the Southern Mountains." *Atlantic Monthly* 83 (March 1899): 311–19.

Gildrie, Richard P. "Guerrilla Warfare in the Lower Cumberland River Valley, 1862–1865." *Tennessee Historical Quarterly* 49 (Fall 1990): 161–76.

Hallock, Judith L. "The Role of the Community in Civil War Desertion." *Civil War History* 29 (June 1983): 123–34.

Harris, J. William. "The Organization of Work on a Yeoman Slaveholder's Farm." *Agricultural History* 64 (Winter 1990): 39–52.

Harris, William C. "The Southern Unionist Critique of the Civil War." *Civil War History* 31 (March 1985): 39–56.

Hettle, Wallace. "An Ambiguous Democrat: Joseph E. Brown and Georgia's Road to Secession." *Georgia Historical Quarterly* 81 (Fall 1987): 577–92.

Holmes, William F. "Moonshining and Collective Violence in North Georgia, 1889–1895." *Journal of American History* 67 (December 1980): 589–611.

Horton, Paul. "Submitting to the 'Shadow of Slavery': The Secession Crisis and Civil War in Alabama's Lawrence County." *Civil War History* 44 (June 1998): 111–36.

Inscoe, John. "Olmsted in Appalachia: A Connecticut Yankee Encounters Slavery and Racism in the Southern Highlands." *Slavery and Abolition* 9 (September 1988): 171–82.

Kinsland, William S. "A Band of Brothers: The Men and the Legend of the 52nd Georgia Regiment." Parts 1 and 2. *North Georgia Journal,* Summer 1985, 9–27, and Fall 1985, 18–39.

———. "The Civil War Comes to Lumpkin County." *North Georgia Journal,* 1 (Summer 1984): 20–29.

———. "Murder or Execution? A Tale of Two Counties." *North Georgia Journal,* 2 (Fall 1984): 13–27.

Komlos, John, and Peter Coclanis. "On the Puzzling Cycle in the Biological Standard of Living: The Case of Antebellum Georgia." *Explorations in Economic History* 34 (October 1997): 433–59.

Johnson, Michael. "A New Look at the Popular Vote for Delegates to the Georgia Secession Convention." *Georgia Historical Quarterly* 56, no. 2 (Summer 1972): 259–75.

Mann, Ralph. "Family Group, Family Migration, and the Civil War in the Sandy Basin of Virginia." *Appalachian Journal* 19 (Summer 1992): 374–91.

———. "Guerrilla Warfare and Gender Roles: Sandy Basin, Virginia, as a Test Case." *Journal of the Appalachian Studies Association* 5 (1993): 59–66.

———. "Mountains, Land, and Kin Networks: Burkes Garden, Virginia in the 1840s and 1850s." *Journal of Southern History* 58 (August 1992): 411–32.

Matthews, Don. "Wealth and Its Distribution in the Antebellum South: Where Do We Stand and Why Does It Matter?" *Essays in Economic and Business History* 15 (1997): 109–20.

McGee, David H. "Home and Friends: Kinship, Community, and Elite Women in Caldwell County, North Carolina during the Civil War." *North Carolina Historical Review* 74 (October 1997): 363–88.

McKenzie, Robert Tracy. "Civil War and Socioeconomic Change in the Upper South: The Survival of Local Agricultural Elites in Tennessee, 1850–1870." *Tennessee Historical Quarterly* 52 (Fall 1993): 170–84.

———. "Wealth and Income: The Preindustrial Structure of East Tennessee in 1860." *Appalachian Journal* 21 (Spring 1994): 260–79.

McKinney, Gordon. "Women's Roles in Civil War Western North Carolina." *North Carolina Historical Review* 69 (January 1992): 37–56.

Mering, John V. "The Slave-State Constitutional Unionists and the Politics of Consensus." *Journal of Southern History* 53 (August 1977): 395–410.

Moore, John Hammond. "Sherman's Fifth Column: A Guide to Unionist Activities in Georgia." *Georgia Historical Quarterly* 68 (Fall 1984): 383–409.

Noe, Kenneth. "Red String Scare: Civil War Southwest Virginia and the Heroes of America." *North Carolina Historical Review* 69 (July 1992): 301–22.

———. "Toward the Myth of a Unionist Appalachia." *Journal of the Appalachian Studies Association* 6 (1994): 73–79.

Pace, Robert F. "Abandoning Self-Sufficiency: Corn in the Lower South, 1849–1879." *Southern Studies* 4 (Fall 1993): 271–93.

Sarris, Jonathan D. "Anatomy of an Atrocity: The Madden Branch Massacre and Guerrilla Warfare in North Georgia, 1861–1865." *Georgia Historical Quarterly* 78 (Winter 1993): 677–92.

Scott, Carole E. "Coping with Inflation: Atlanta, 1860–1865." *Georgia Historical Quarterly* 69 (Winter 1985): 536–56.

Starnes, Richard D. "The Stirring Strains of Dixie: The Civil War and Southern Identity in Haywood County, North Carolina." *North Carolina Historical Review* 79 (July 1997): 237–59.

Thornton, J. Mills, III. "The Ethic of Subsistence and the Origins of Southern Secession." *Tennessee Historical Quarterly* 48 (Summer 1989): 108–36.

Vinovskis, Maris. "Have Social Historians Lost the Civil War?" *Journal of American History* 76 (June 1989): 34–58.

Wallenstein, Peter. "Rich Man's War, Rich Man's Fight: Civil War and the Transformation of Public Finance in Georgia." *Journal of Southern History* 50 (February 1984): 15–42.

Weiman, David F. "Farmers and the Market Economy in Antebellum America: A View from Georgia's Upcountry." *Journal of Economic History,* 47 (September 1987): 627–47.

Young, Otis. "The Southern Gold Rush, 1828–1836." *Journal of Southern History* 48 (August 1982): 373–92.

Zipf, Karin L. "Reconstructing 'Free Woman': African-American Women, Apprenticeship, and Custody Rights during Reconstruction." *Journal of Women's History* 12, no. 1 (Spring 2000): 8–31.

INDEX

A Nation Divided

NEW STUDIES IN CIVIL WAR HISTORY

Neither Ballots nor Bullets: Women Abolitionists and the Civil War
Wendy Hamand Venet

Black Confederates and Afro-Yankees in Civil War Virginia
Ervin L. Jordan Jr.

Longstreet's Aide: The Civil War Letters of Major Thomas J. Goree
Thomas W. Cutrer

Lee's Young Artillerist: William R. J. Pegram
Peter S. Carmichael

Yankee Correspondence: Civil War Letters between New England Soldiers and the Homefront
Nina Silber and Mary Beth Sievens, editors

Southern Rights: Political Prisoners and the Myth of Confederate Constitutionalism
Mark E. Neely Jr.

Apostles of Disunion: Southern Secession Commissioners and the Causes of the Civil War
Charles B. Dew

Exile in Richmond: The Confederate Journal of Henri Garidel
Michael Bedout Chesson and Leslie Jean Roberts, editors

Ashe County's Civil War: Community and Society in the Appalachian South
Martin Crawford

The War Hits Home: The Civil War in Southeastern Virginia
Brian Steel Wills

Lincoln's Tragic Admiral: The Life of Samuel Francis Du Pont
Kevin John Weddle

A Separate Civil War: Communities in Conflict in the Mountain South
Jonathan Dean Sarris